JAPAN AND THE EUROPEAN PERIPHERY

Japan and the European Periphery

Edited by

James Darby
Senior Research Fellow
Institute of European Studies
The Queen's University, Belfast

First published in Great Britain 1996 by
MACMILLAN PRESS LTD
Houndmills, Basingstoke, Hampshire RG21 6XS
and London
Companies and representatives
throughout the world

A catalogue record for this book is available
from the British Library.

ISBN 0–333–66967–3

First published in the United States of America 1996 by
ST. MARTIN'S PRESS, INC.,
Scholarly and Reference Division,
175 Fifth Avenue,
New York, N.Y. 10010

ISBN 0–312–16161–1

Library of Congress Cataloging-in-Publication Data
Japan and the European periphery / edited by James Darby.
p.   cm.
Includes bibliographical references and index.
ISBN 0–312–16161–1
1. Corporations, Japanese—Europe—Congresses.   2. Investments,
Japanese—Europe—Congresses.   3. Industries—Europe—Congresses.
4. Europe—Manufactures—Employees—Congresses.   5. Europe—Economic
conditions—1945–   —Regional disparities—Congresses.   I. Darby,
James, 1952–   .
HD2844.J36   1996
338.8'895204—dc20

96–15980
CIP

10   9   8   7   6   5   4   3   2   1
05   04   03   02   01   00   99   98   97   96

Printed and bound in Great Britain by
Antony Rowe Ltd, Chippenham, Wiltshire

HD
2844
.J36
1996

Contents

List of Tables

List of Figures

List of Contributors

Andy Adcroft	University of East London, Dagenham
Claes Alvstam	University of Gothenburg
Bernadette Andréosso	University of Limerick
Gábor Bakos	Chukyo University, Nagoya
Judit Berényi	Kopint Datorg, Budapest
James Darby	Queen's University, Belfast
Bert Edström	University of Stockholm
Colin Haslam	Royal Holloway College, Egham
Inge Ivarsson	University of Gothenburg
Sukhdev Johal	University of East London, Dagenham
Yui Kimura	Tsukuba University (Japan)
Corrado Molteni	Bocconi University, Milan
Jonathan Morris	University of Glamorgan
Max Munday	Cardiff Business School
Montserrat Pallares-Barbera	Autonomous University, Barcelona
Paloma Peláez	Autonomous University, Madrid
Javier de Quinto	Autonomous University, Madrid
Paolo Ramazzotti	University of Macerata (Italy)
Santos Ruesga	Autonomous University, Madrid
Jean-Marc Thiran	Catholic University, Louvain
Kazuei Tokado	Kanda University, Tokyo
Barry Wilkinson	Cardiff Business School
John Williams	University of Manchester
Karel Williams	University of Manchester
Hideki Yamawaki	Catholic University, Louvain

Acknowledgements

I would like to acknowledge the generous support of the Japan Foundation for the conference *Japan and the Peripheral Regions of Europe*, which took place in March 1995 in Belfast. Most of the papers included in this volume are a selection of the contributions to that conference. I would also like to thank Zoltan Berényi, Scott Dixon and Keith Wilson for their advice on the word-processing involved in preparing this edited collection.

1 Introduction: Japan and the European Periphery

James Darby

Europe's peripheral regions offer a wide variety of manufacturing environments to the foreign investor. In the case of investment by Japanese firms, which began cautiously at the end of the 1960s, this has been reflected in the uneven distribution of subsidiaries. Some countries and regions have been disproportionately successful in encouraging Japanese manufacturers to establish assembly and manufacturing plants. Others, particularly those areas which have made little effort to promote themselves, have received few if any Japanese projects.

This volume will describe the pattern of establishment of Japanese manufacturing subsidiaries in the disparate areas which form the economic and geographic periphery of Europe, and begin to explain the very uneven and fragmented distribution of these plants. It will be noted that an overwhelming majority of projects are located in Western Europe, with only around 1 per cent of the total in Central or Eastern Europe, while Northern Europe, for its part, has four times as much employment in Japanese-owned plants as Southern Europe. Examination of the distribution of Japanese manufacturing investment in Europe in a core–periphery perspective fails to reveal the same type of simple imbalance, but it will be seen that both national and European notions of peripherality have typically influenced locational choice in the case of the more important and larger-scale investments.

A comparison of levels of income, employment and outmigration reveals that some regions of Europe clearly belong to the economic core, while others belong to the economic periphery. Both core and periphery are discontinuous, and some regions can be more properly described as semi-peripheral or belonging to the outer core. Some countries can also be assigned in their entirety to the core or periphery, while a third category, which is of particular importance to this study, includes important European economies which contain within their national territory both core and peripheral regions.

In the UK, the peripheral and semi-peripheral areas of Europe largely correspond to the areas that were eligible for regional assistance before 1979: Scotland, Wales, Northern Ireland, most of the three northern regions of England and parts of the Midlands and South-West. In the rest of the country, as in the greater part of northern and central Italy, the two great urban agglomerations in Spain and most of France apart from the extreme south and west, the national economic core also forms part of the European economic core. These countries are, therefore, greatly preoccupied with regional imbalance within the domestic economy and offer generous subsidies to deflect investment to assisted areas. Not all these countries have shown equal determination to attract mobile inward investment projects however, with the UK making far greater efforts than Spain and Italy to promote (successfully) the establishment of Japanese manufacturing plants.

Foreign investors see advantages in investing in core regions in so far as they tend to be closer to markets, offer better productive environments in terms of supply linkages and infrastructure, and contain existing operations which are most attractive as potential acquisitions or partnerships. Many of these advantages may also be substantially accessible from peripheral locations, where production costs are lower and problems of access to other parts of the national and European markets may be of declining importance. For some of the most peripheral areas this may be less valid, but the assisted areas in countries which are partly within the European core are clearly favoured territory for Japanese investors seeking to reduce operating and establishment costs. This is also further underlined when firms are encouraged to invest by host governments, regional development agencies and the prospect of material incentives.

Firms may choose to invest in a region according to the cost and availability of labour, as well as the quality of the local transport and supply linkages. These factors are inseparable from the tax rates and support for inward investors administered nationally by host authorities, which may include not only material inducements but also support in market access negotiations conducted at the European level. Taken together, these national and regional features go a long way towards explaining which regions are the most popular with inward investors. Providing some indication of this, regions which have received proportionately more investment by Japanese manufacturing firms can be identified by comparing regional shares of European employment with corresponding figures for employment in Japanese subsidiaries, as shown in Table 1.1.

The presence of Brussels at the top of the list can be explained by the Asahi Glass Company's Glaverbel project, which is a major employer in the city region. The presence of Bavaria, Bremen, Luxembourg

Table 1.1 EC-12 regions with highest shares of employment in Japanese-owned subsidiaries as a proportion of total employment in Europe, 1993

Region	Country	% Japanese-owned Employment in EC-12	% Total EC-12 Employment	% Japanese-owned / % Total Employment
Brussels	Belgium	2.9	0.2	14.50
Wales	UK	6.1	0.9	6.78
North	UK	4.4	0.9	4.89
Bremen	Germany	0.8	0.2	4.00
Luxembourg	Luxembourg	0.4	0.1	4.00
West Midlands	UK	6.0	1.7	3.53
Madrid	Spain	4.0	1.2	3.34
Este	Spain	7.0	2.6	2.69
Ireland	Ireland	1.9	0.8	2.37
Bavaria	Germany	8.8	4.0	2.20
South-West	UK	3.3	1.5	2.20
Île-de-France	France	7.4	3.4	2.18

Source: Adapted from Toyo Keizai (1994) and Eurostat (1994) statistics[1] presented in Table 3.2 (see below).

and Île-de-France also demonstrates that leading regions and leading sectors are attractive to inward investors as they seek to gain access to national competitive advantages. Perhaps the most salient feature of Table 1.1, however, is the prominence of those regions in the UK and Spain, which may be described as *semi-peripheral* in a purely European context, having attracted a large proportion of Japanese projects for both cost minimisation and market access reasons. Ireland, despite its sophisticated and consistent incentive strategy, is too peripheral and lacking in high-performance equipment producers to equal the appeal of the most favoured British regions. In Italy, Japanese inward investment has not had a major impact, with most successful projects being established in the highly developed northern regions. Of these, the north-west region has the largest cluster, with 2.3 per cent of total Japanese manufacturing employment and 1.7 per cent of total employment in the EC-12 in 1993.

While external factors may influence the volume of inward investment entering Europe, individual regions or countries can become increasingly or decreasingly popular as a location for individual projects. Since 1985 the UK, Ireland and Italy have received a greater proportion of Japanese projects in a variety of sectors, while the Netherlands has witnessed the establishment of a Mitsubishi Motors joint venture, employing almost 4000. Less favoured countries, Spain in particular, as well as France and Belgium, have seen a decline in the number of new projects or jobs created and preserved in the same period, following periods of fairly rapid growth for France in the mid-1980s and in Spain and Belgium during the 1970s. Some peripheral regions which had received little or no Japanese manufacturing investment before 1985 have also begun to witness the emergence of local Japanese manufacturing operations, reflecting their deeper involvement in the processes of European economic integration.

Central Europe has traditionally had very little contact with Japan, but in recent years various economic links have developed. Direct investment in manufacturing has emerged in a number of projects, and the most important of these have appeared in Hungary, with the $US160 million Magyar Suzuki joint venture of paramount importance. In the paper by Gabor Bakos, the origins and establishment of this car assembly project are outlined, and the crucial significance of the project as an example of Japanese industry *testing the waters* in Central Europe is explained and clarified. Touching upon this theme also, the context within which Japanese firms have cautiously begun to develop economic links with the former Soviet bloc and the singular position of Hungary as a possible bridgehead for further involvement in this part of Europe are more closely analysed in the paper by Judit Berényi. An unwillingness to confront European and American multinationals in Central and Eastern Europe, lack of deep or lasting knowledge of the area and a possible greater preoccupation with the resource-rich republics of Central Asia are mentioned to explain the cautiousness of Japan's approach.

The Nordic countries and Scandinavia have also been a low-priority area for trade and investment links with Japan, with a change of attitudes and practice only emerging tentatively in the last few years. Like the countries of Central Europe, but for dissimilar reasons, inward foreign direct investment (FDI) in the Nordic countries has been relatively scarce, partly through the prospect of low returns and partly through a lack of effort to persuade foreign firms to establish local manufacturing operations. Bert Edström's paper underlines the self-preoccupation which allowed Sweden to disregard the possibility of developing stronger economic and political links with Japan until recently, and describes the background to recent initiatives which have further eroded what might in early modern Japan be called a *sakoku* or closed country mentality. The importance of the accession of Sweden and Finland to the European Union at the beginning of 1995 is seen as crucial for the prospects of inward FDI into the region, and in the paper by Claes

Alvstam and Inge Ivarsson the pre-existing pattern of Japanese manufacturing activities in the region is linked closely to local competitive advantages, rather than the European expansion strategies of Japan's leading industrial sectors.

In Spain Japanese manufacturing investment grew rapidly until the early 1980s, and the country has remained important as a destination for inward investment in Europe. A major Nissan investment in Barcelona, discussed in the paper by Montserrat Pallares-Barbera, remains the largest single Japanese project in Europe in terms of employment and an important indicator of Japan's investment strategies for manufacturing in Southern Europe, as well as automobile manufacturing in Europe as a whole. In their analysis of regional patterns of Japanese investment in Spain, Paloma Peláez, Javier de Quinto, Santos Ruesga and Kazuei Tokado demonstrate that the regions which include Barcelona and Madrid are the most favoured destinations for inward investment projects, with investment by Japan's highly competitive carmakers and their suppliers prominent in these two leading urban areas.

Nissan, the most important Japanese manufacturing investor in Europe, had sought to enter the protected markets of Southern Europe by means of a joint venture with Alfa Romeo to produce saloon cars near Naples in the early 1980s. The demise of this project, and the problems encountered by Japanese manufacturers in Italy, particularly in the less industrialised southern regions of the country, are referred to in detail by Corrado Molteni. Lack of co-ordinated policy measures to encourage inward investment and a comparative lack of investment in the key sectors of automobiles and consumer or industrial electronics have meant that there has been a relative scarcity of Japanese investment in Italy, despite a recent increase in new projects. For Paolo Ramazzotti, the overvaluation of the lira after 1980 and its recent weakening have also been key influences upon the timing and scale of Japanese investments in all parts of the country. Italy, nevertheless, is a country which straddles all the dividing lines between the core and peripheral regions of Europe's economy, and like the UK should offer greater scope for inward investment strategies which seek a variety of locational advantages, particularly for multi-site, multi-task and pan-European operations. Clearly, differing host government policies and attitudes in Italy and the UK go a long way towards explaining the differences in patterns of Japanese investment in these two countries.

In the north-west of Europe, in the UK, France and the Republic of Ireland, we can find the most sustained and successful strategies to encourage non-European investors to establish manufacturing operations in the European periphery. Unlike the UK and the Republic of Ireland, France receives most of its foreign investment from within Europe, and has been identified with policies of constraint towards non-European multinational firms.[2] France began to direct promotional efforts towards potential Japanese investors in the mid-1980s, following periods of energetic hostility towards the growth of Japanese imports in the automobile and electronics sectors. This led to a fourfold increase in the number of Japanese plants and their employment totals in France between 1983 and 1987 as a direct result of these complementary strategies,[3] although this period of rapid growth does not appear to have been sustained since 1989. In Bernadette Andréosso's paper the spatial distribution of Japanese manufacturing operations in France is shown to be heavily concentrated in the region around Paris and the city itself, with relatively few projects located in areas furthest from Europe's economic core, to the west and south of the country.

It is clear that competition exists between regions and countries that seek to attract inward investment projects, and that for some parts of Europe the process of encouraging foreign firms to create manufacturing jobs and generate other attendant benefits is a vital part of the strategy of national economic development. The Republic of Ireland is interesting as a country in Europe that is wholly peripheral in economic terms, has devoted a great deal of effort and resources to attracting foreign manufacturing operations, and is subject to numerous external competitive influences which determine the success of its *industrialisation-by-invitation* strategy. The discontinuous pattern of Japanese investment in Ireland, both North and South, is presented and explained in the paper written by James Darby and Max Munday, which also provides an analysis of the costs involved in promoting this type of project.

In the UK many of the regions with the most significant groupings of Japanese-owned plants in Europe can be found. Investment by firms in the most competitive sectors of Japanese industry have taken place uninterruptedly since the late 1970s, becoming more frequent in the three years up to 1992, and few significant closures have occurred. Wales in particular has been well populated with Japanese-owned plants since the pathbreaking Sony and Matsushita investments in the mid-1970s, and they have brought with them a range of benefits for the Welsh economy; these are discussed in Max Munday's paper. Critical attention has nevertheless been focused upon the attendant costs and questionable performance attributes of Japanese manufacturing operations in the UK, and these themes are developed more fully in the paper by Colin Haslam and Karel Williams. It is perhaps ironic that the UK has been most successful in attracting Japanese manufacturing and research and development operations to Europe in recent years, while provoking the greatest scepticism regarding the benefits associated with their establishment.

Japanese manufacturing plants in Europe are now associated with the most competitive sectors of Japanese industry, such as automobiles and electronics, with machine tool and semiconductor projects also evident. Many early investments were, however, involved with chemicals-related projects, following the environmental crisis in Japan in the late 1960s, and the legacy of this earliest wave of Japanese investment is still evident in the remoter corners of Europe: the west of Ireland, Portugal, Italy and Greece. Plastics and synthetic fibre projects have been established in a number of countries, and acquisition of the tyre producers Dunlop in 1983 and Firestone in 1988 has resulted in sizeable Japanese-owned tyre plants in all five of the major EU economies.

Regions with Japanese-owned plants in sectors with the largest average plant size, such as automobile assembly, glassworks and tyre plants, tend to have the largest average plant size, as well as the largest individual projects, and this is evident in the case of regions such as Northern England, Catalonia and West Netherlands, where Japanese auto assembly plants have been established. Yui Kimura, in his introductory chapter, makes the point that Japanese auto investors are investing outside the economic core of Europe to avoid competitive pressures, as indicated by the absence of volume car production in France, Germany or Italy. The automotive components sector, where the highest wages in Europe's Japanese-owned manufacturing subsidiaries are to be found, has investments located in all the car-producing countries of Western Europe, however.

Many Japanese manufacturing projects in Europe, as Jean-Marc Thiran and Hideki Yamawaki point out, are confined to the most competitive sectors of local industry, and seek to gain from the competitive strengths of indigenous firms. Japanese firms have invested in the most competitive sectors of Swedish industry, and in France projects involving the domestically competitive food, telecommunications and rubber industries are prominent. In the sectors which have experienced significant growth in Japanese investment since 1985, such as machinery and instruments and automobile production, differing location patterns are apparent, given that the countries and regions of Europe's main indigenous car producers have been avoided. Machinery and instruments investments have tended, however, to locate in high-income core regions such as Bavaria, Baden-Württemberg, north-west Italy and the UK's South-East, where many of Europe's leading producers are located.

Employment totals in Japanese manufacturing subsidiaries increase as a result of greenfield investments, acquisitions or expansions of existing operations. The method of establishment is important for domestic authorities concerned with job-creation, given that new jobs are more closely identified with greenfield projects, which also have a higher likelihood of employment growth through a subsequent expansion of operations. It is interesting, therefore, as an example of how Japanese firms internalise the objectives of certain host authorities, to note that in some countries projects by Japanese manufacturers are normally greenfield, while this form of establishment is rare in others, such as Italy, or completely absent, as in the case of Sweden.

Although two-thirds of Japanese manufacturing subsidiaries in Europe are estimated to be greenfield in origin, there seems to be less hesitation over the use of the acquisition method in recent years, particularly in the more energetic attempts to acquire European production capacity in the period immediately preceding 1992 and the completion of the single market in Europe. In regions where many Japanese subsidiaries are well established, such as Wales, many jobs have been created in recent expansions, while in Ireland, both North and South, the prominence of acquisitions among projects established since 1989 has meant fewer new jobs have been created, and investment activity has been concentrated in the more industrialised areas.

Japanese manufacturing plants in Europe vary in size, and despite some evidence of spatial ordering according to sector and region, it is apparent that an absence of concentration has meant that the average plant size is small and the overall distribution is fragmented. Integrated production has been obviated in many cases by a lack of scale in planned or existing operations, and this has meant that levels of local content have remained low. Sophisticated components tend to be directly imported to assembly operations in Europe, or supplied by other locally established Japanese manufacturers. Contracts for non-Japanese local supply firms are often low volume with low margins, and contain many individual specifications which are difficult to satisfy, irrespective of quality considerations. It has been suggested nevertheless that there has been a continuing improvement in the integration of Japanese equipment and supplier firms in Europe, leading to higher average local content levels. This has been associated with the appreciation of the yen, rather than the efforts of the European Commission to monitor local content levels, however.

As with levels of local content, labour relations in Japanese manufacturing plants in Europe have their distinctive features. Experience of operational problems with early projects in Spain and Italy has accompanied closures and the erosion of employment levels in some of the larger plants. This was originally linked with the acquisition of large-scale local producers, and was evident also in the early history of Japanese television production in the UK. After difficulties caused by the strength of the pound and labour problems, Hitachi and Toshiba joint ventures in the UK became wholly-owned Japanese subsidiaries at the beginning of the 1980s, with the loss of most existing jobs. The desire for a hand-picked workforce, single union agreement and a declining labour component in total costs have been common features of many examples of the process by which potential Japanese investors choose a preferred site in Europe, and have certainly influenced their distribution among the regions.

The location of Japanese manufacturing plants in Europe is the product of local and national, European and extra-European factors. Expansion plans by Japanese firms, which are only partly dependent upon the success of trade and investment relations between Japan and Europe, and depend more upon the global level of economic activity, determine the scale of resources which firms are able to mobilise for foreign expansion. At the European level, tariff and non-tariff barriers to unrestricted trade can encourage firms, particularly those in sensitive sectors, to expand sales through the medium of local production.[4] Constraints such as anti-dumping campaigns, local content targets and voluntary agreements tend to involve the more competitive sectors of Japanese industry, which are the least likely to choose the most peripheral locations for plants in Europe. National and local factors more clearly determine in which country and region Japanese manufacturing firms choose to establish themselves, and it can be inferred from the fragmented nature of investment patterns that a very wide choice and variety of operating environments are available.

Investment by Japanese firms in the most peripheral regions of Europe tends to be in less competitive sectors or by firms which are less competitive. Projects in chemicals-related, pharmaceutical, synthetic fibre, textile and metals sectors are common in Greece, Portugal, Ireland and the more peripheral regions of Italy and Spain, while all but one of the Japanese manufacturers in Hungary operate in these sectors. Investors in more competitive sectors, which are often identified with well-known international firms from Japan's automobile, electronics and sophisticated machinery sectors, tend to invest closer to the core, being

Table 1.2   National distribution of Japanese R&D facilities in Western Europe and national shares of EC-12 employment, 1993

Country	Japanese Firms with Production Bases (%)		Western Europe Japanese Firms with R&D Bases (%)		Independent Japanese R&D Base (%)		EC-12	
							% Japanese-owned EC-12 Employment	% Total EC-12 Employment
UK	198	(27.8%)	86	(37.1%)	20	(29.9%)	32.6	18.5
Germany	107	(15.0%)	44	(19.0%)	19	(28.4%)	19.5	26.1
France	121	(17.0%)	26	(11.2%)	10	(14.9%)	12.0	15.6
Belgium	39	(5.5%)	18	(7.8%)	5	(7.5%)	5.1	2.6
Spain	63	(8.8%)	17	(7.3%)	2	(3.0%)	12.0	8.9
Netherlands	46	(6.5%)	13	(5.6%)	3	(4.5%)	6.5	4.5
Italy	45	(6.3%)	9	(3.9%)	3	(4.5%)	4.2	15.2
Sweden	9	(1.3%)	5	(2.2%)	1	(1.5%)		
Ireland	30	(4.2%)	4	(1.7%)	1	(1.5%)	1.9	0.8
Switzerland	9	(1.3%)	3	(1.3%)	2	(3.0%)		
Austria	17	(2.4%)	3	(1.3%)	0			
Norway	1	(0.1%)	2	(0.9%)	0			
Denmark	3	(0.4%)	1	(0.4%)	1	(1.5%)	0.0	1.9
Finland	5	(0.7%)	1	(0.4%)	0			
Others	20	(2.7%)	0		0		5.8	6.1
Total	713	(100%)	232	(100%)	67 (100%)		100.0*	100.0*

Note: JETRO surveys of Japanese manufacturing in Europe exclude Central and Eastern Europe, where at least one independent Japanese research facility has been established. (See below, Chapter 15.)
*Aggregated totals may not total 100 per cent exactly.

Source: JETRO (1994); EC-12 figures adapted from Toyo Keizai (1994) and Eurostat (1994) statistics presented in Table 3.1 (see below).[5]

influenced by three factors which determine the region where investment takes place: access to markets, proximity to major competitors and lower costs, including establishment costs. In the central core regions access to leading indigenous manufacturers can be seen to compensate for higher costs and greater local competition, while in the outer core or semi-peripheral regions the largest automobile and many of the largest electronics projects have chosen to locate away from their strongest European competitors, usually in well-subsidised locations.

As an indication of the growing appeal of core regions the relatively recent emergence of Japanese R&D facilities in Europe suggests that more sophisticated investments may gravitate towards higher income areas (Table 1.2). Just as manufacturing investments seek to utilise higher level inputs in core regions, R&D facilities, especially when disestablished from local assembly operations, tend to locate in areas which contain highly qualified labour resources. As this type of project becomes more significant, core economies may appear to gain at the expense of more peripheral regions, and there is some evidence that

Table 1.3 Regional distribution of Japanese-owned research facilities in the UK, 1994

Region	Japanese Plants (%)	Japanese R&D Facilities (%)	Independent R&D Facilities (%)	R&D Facilities in Universities	Share of UK Employment (%)
South-East	51 (23.8%)	41 (37.6%)	12 (52.2%)	6 (54.5%)	31.9
West Midlands	23 (10.7%)	11 (10.1%)	1 (4.3%)	0	9.2
Scotland	24 (11.2%)	10 (9.2%)	2 (8.7%)	2 (18.2%)	8.7
Wales	31 (14.5%)	9 (8.3%)	1 (4.3%)	0	4.8
North	24 (11.2%)	9 (8.3%)	1 (4.3%)	0	4.9
North-West	15 (7.0%)	7 (6.4%)	2 (8.7%)	1 (9.1%)	10.8
South-West	11 (5.1%)	7 (6.4%)	1 (4.3%)	0	8.1
East Anglia	4 (1.9%)	5 (4.6%)	2 (8.7%)	2 (18.2%)	3.8
East Midlands	15 (7.0%)	4 (3.7%)	1 (4.3%)	0	7.0
Yorks/H'side	10 (4.7%)	4 (3.7%)	0	0	8.6
N. Ireland	6 (2.8%)	2 (1.8%)	0	0	2.2
Total	214 (100%)	109 (100%)	23 (100%)	11 (100%)	100.0

Source: IBB (January 1994); JETRO (5 October 1994).[6]

these independent facilities are showing a preference for Europe's core economies, particularly Germany.

At the regional level, the emergence of Japanese R&D facilities suggests that core areas are becoming more favoured, particularly for independent research centres (Table 1.3). In the UK, the South-East has a higher national share of Japanese-owned R&D facilities than Japanese-owned manufacturing operations and a much higher share of independent R&D bases. This is despite the fact that approximately half of the latter are attached to universities, which are widely dispersed throughout the country. Universities in the UK with associated Japanese research facilities are clearly those with a high status however, and all but three are located within 160 km of London.

In terms of arriving at an overall assessment of the emerging spatial distribution of Japanese investments in Europe some trends are discernible, therefore, while others may be detected through monitoring developments in the near future. Attention to the policy environment at both the national and European levels is one essential factor, as is the local operating environment for manufacturing firms. Clearly, lack of a consistent policy of encouraging Japanese manufacturers to establish local operations has meant that some countries and regions have received little or no inward investment from this source. Also, lack of support for a liberal trade régime within Europe can discourage the uninterrupted growth of Japanese plants, which may explain the discontinuous patterns of investment in France, Italy and Spain. It is certain also that the stability of employment in Japanese subsidiaries in Europe seems to be linked to the degree of support shown by host governments for the export-led strategies of Japan's major international firms, as well as the jobs and innovative production methods which are associated with them.

Countries which have both core and peripheral regions of the European economy within their national territory seem best placed, therefore, to benefit from future developments in the growth of Japanese manufacturing in Europe, at least in terms of employment creation and the stimulation of exports. Provided that they are prepared to show the commitment necessary to encourage Japanese firms to establish themselves, these countries are likely to attract the bulk of projects, although the cultivation of skills and technology transfer through the medium of inward investment may increasingly favour core regions and core economies. In this context, therefore, major changes are foreseen in the distribution of benefits across Europe, as the future operation of Japanese subsidiaries becomes more integrated and sophisticated. It is too early to conclude that this will be part of a more general process that will make the peripheral regions of Europe *more peripheral*, but this is clearly a possibility, and continuing research will be necessary before a full appreciation of the problem can be achieved.

NOTES

1. Toyo Keizai ed., *Kaigai Shinshutsu Kigyo Soran* (Tokyo: Toyo Keizai Shimposha, 1994); Eurostat, *Regions Statistical Yearbook* (Luxembourg: 1994).
2. J. Darby, 'A New Environment for Public Policy: Japanese Manufacturing in Europe', *West European Politics*, Vol. 9, No. 2 (April 1986), p. 217.
3. See J. Darby, *The Political Economy of Japanese Manufacturing Investment in France and the UK (1970–86)*, unpublished doctoral thesis (Florence: European University Institute, 1987), p. 320; JETRO, *10th Survey of European Operations of Japanese Companies in the Manufacturing Sector* (Tokyo: Japan External Trade Organisation, October 1994), p. 3.
4. Import substitution is not a realistic objective.
5. See Keizai (1994); Eurostat (1994); Darby (1987); JETRO (1994).
6. Invest in Britain Bureau, *List of Japanese Manufacturing Companies in the UK*, Mimeo (January 1994); JETRO, *Japanese Companies Involved in Research Development and/or Design in the UK*, Mimeo (5 October 1994).

2 Japanese Direct Investment in the Peripheral Regions of Europe: An Overview
Yui Kimura

INTRODUCTION

Japanese foreign direct investment (FDI) has expanded rapidly in the 1980s and early 1990s, with the stock of investment totalling $US387 billion as of 1992. Japanese FDI has been targeted largely towards the US, the core of the European Union and South-East Asian countries. Overall, investment from Japan in the peripheral regions of Europe (PRE) has been limited in size. Of this limited investment directed towards the peripheries of Europe, there are only a few projects which are large-scale. This may well be a natural consequence of very limited economic relationships and the great distances between these countries and Japan. To Japanese firms, the US and, to a lesser extent, Europe have been the largest market in most key industries. Furthermore, for Japanese big business, South-East Asian countries have for some considerable time been important markets and sources of supply for natural resources and labour-intensive manufactures.

However, the fall of communist regimes in Central and Eastern Europe after 1989, and the moves towards a single market in the then European Community by the end of 1992, gave rise to increased awareness by Japanese interests of direct investment opportunities in the peripheral countries and regions of Europe. Expectations of an expansion of local economies and their increasing linkages with the core of the European Union (EU) have prompted this interest on the part of Japanese firms.

The purpose of this paper is to examine Japanese FDI activities in the PRE countries, and this raises a number of immediate questions. What, for example, are the target countries and industries for Japanese direct investment among the PRE countries? What patterns do we find in Japanese direct investment into these regions? What motivates Japanese firms to invest in these areas, and what are their strategies? What influence is the investment likely to have upon the economies and industries

13

of host countries, and, finally, what are the implications for investment and trade relationships between these countries and Japan? It is perhaps due to the limited scale of Japanese FDI in PRE countries and their geographic remoteness from Japan that researchers have so far failed to ask these questions. This paper will thus attempt to rescue these issues from comparative neglect and address them explicitly by giving an overview of Japanese direct investment in the peripheral areas of Europe.

This paper is organised as follows. The second section will look at patterns of distribution of Japanese FDI across PRE countries and industries. It will be confirmed that Japanese FDI in the PRE countries is still very limited and small-scale. A concentration of this limited Japanese FDI in a relatively small number of PRE countries and a narrow range of industries will also be identified. Some explanation for these concentrations of Japanese FDI will then be presented. The third section will examine the incentives available to Japanese firms to undertake FDI in a given region and the strategies of these firms. The fourth section will consider the impact of Japanese direct investment upon local industries and economies and will examine the government policies of host countries to encourage Japanese FDI to establish itself in a local peripheral region. Finally, the last section will outline the results of the analysis, and the paper will end with a discussion of the implications for both host government policy and the strategies of multinational investors.

PATTERNS OF JAPANESE INVESTMENT IN THE EUROPEAN PERIPHERY

We begin with a very broad picture of Japanese FDI and consider investment in the PRE in a global perspective. We will then focus upon investment in the regions and examine its pattern of locational and sectoral distribution.

First, we need to clarify what is meant by the *peripheral regions of Europe* (PRE). One definition may be that the peripheral regions of Europe include areas west of Russia and north of the Mediterranean but exclude the member-states of the European Union. A looser definition may also include, in addition to those areas identified above, some EU member countries and regions that are geographically and economically located on the periphery of the Union. For our analytical purpose, we adopt the latter, looser definition. On occasion, we will also refer to

Table 2.1 Cumulative value of Japanese global FDI by region, 1992

Region	Cumulative Value ($US millions)
North America	169 580
Central/South America	46 547
Asia	59 880
Middle East	4 231
Europe	75 697
Africa	6 813
Oceania	23 782
Total	386 530

Source: *Kaigai Shinshutsu Kigyo Soran* (Toyo Keizai, 1994).

Japanese FDI in other countries, such as Turkey. Whether member-states or not, these countries are economically linked with the core of the EU, and Japanese FDI located there has some relevance to our analysis.

We may well ask how Japanese direct investment in these countries compares with investment in other parts of the world. Furthermore, it is pertinent to inquire how extensively and intensively Japan has invested in the European periphery in manufacturing projects, and how this investment is distributed geographically, and across industries. Table 2.1 shows the significance of Europe as a whole as a recipient of Japanese FDI. It lists the cumulative value of Japanese foreign direct investment in all regions of the world, indicating that the global stock of Japanese FDI totalled $US387 billion by March 1992. Before then, the growth of direct investment by Japanese firms was most rapid in the second half of the 1980s, and peaked in 1989. Significantly, the proportion of investment going into manufacturing has also grown rapidly and accounted for 76 per cent of the total stock of Japanese direct investment in the late 1980s. Of this total stock of global Japanese FDI, investment in the US accounted for 43.9 per cent, Europe 19.6 per cent, Asia 15.5 per cent and Central and South America 12 per cent in 1992. Europe received Japanese FDI totalling a cumulative $US76 billion by March 1992, and therefore ranks a distant second as a global recipient of Japanese FDI.

It will be useful to determine how much of this $US76 billion of Japanese FDI into Europe has gone to the peripheral regions, and how significant Japanese FDI is in the PRE relative to investment in European core regions. Based on the sales data of foreign affiliates of Japanese firms, Table 2.2 compares Japanese FDI in the EU with that in the rest of Europe with regard to total sales made by Japanese affiliates

Table 2.2   Sales of Japanese affiliates in Europe by sector, 1993

Industry	Europe ¥ million	EU ¥ million	% EU Europe	Other Europe ¥m	% Other E. Europe
Food	33 699	32 657	96.91	1 042	3.09
Textile products	44 885	25 553	56.93	19 332	43.07
Clothes, other fabrics	16 259	16 259	100.00	0	0.00
Lumber products	0	0	0.00	0	0.00
Furniture,	0	0	0.00	0	0.00
Pulp and paper	0	0	0.00	0	0.00
Publishing	3 660	3 660	100.00	0	0.00
Chemical products	203 669	202 733	99.54	936	0.46
Petroleum products	685 213	685 213	100.00	0	0.00
Rubber products	25 035	11 035	44.08	14 000	55.92
Leather products	1 762	1 762	100.00	0	0.00
Pottery/stone products	13 651	13 651	100.00	0	0.00
Steel	14 564	14 564	100.00	0	0.00
Non-ferrous metals	1 568 079	1 534 557	97.86	33 522	214
Other metals	20 618	1 114	5.40	19 504	94.60
General machinery	956 639	930 598	97.28	26 041	2.72
Electrical machinery	432 139	410 723	95.04	21 416	4.96
Transport equipment	1 826 636	1 734 615	94.96	92 021	5.04
Precision machinery	204 898	190 832	93.14	14 066	6.86
Other products	165 097	161 422	97.77	3 675	2.23
Total	6 182 804	5 938 291	96.05	244 513	3.95

Source: MITI, *Kaigai Tosho Tokei Soran* (1994).

in both areas in 1993. Despite the fact that the category of the rest of Europe, or *other Europe*, does not match exactly that of our working definition of the PRE, the table is none the less quite indicative of the significance of Japanese FDI in the peripheral regions, relative to the European economic core.

We can immediately see from Table 2.2 that there is a significant asymmetry between the PRE and the European core in the total volume of FDI activities by Japanese firms in each area. The value of sales made by Japanese affiliates in the EU and the rest of Europe totalled ¥5938 billion and ¥245 billion respectively, or to put it another way, the value of sales in the EU in 1993 was over 24 times larger than sales in the PRE. The data also indicate that the range of industries in which Japanese firms invested directly is much wider in the EU than that in the PRE. Japanese direct investment in the EU involves many additional sectors, while that in the rest of Europe focuses mainly upon transport equipment, non-ferrous metals and machinery.

These asymmetries seem to reflect the market size of these two areas.

In terms of their combined Gross National Product and the purchasing power of their populations, the core of Europe offers much greater market opportunities than the PRE countries, and this may have attracted Japanese firms to the core. The table may also imply a disparity in the breadth and depth of the industrial infrastructure between the advanced core regions of Europe and the emerging PRE countries and regions. Michael Porter argues that the breadth and depth of the industrial infrastructure of a nation is an important element of national competitive advantage, and such national competitive advantage clearly attracts inward investment by foreign firms.[1] The differing strategies and productive requirements of Japanese investors in these two areas may also underline this disparity.

It is nevertheless apparent from the table that Japanese FDI is focused on a more or less narrow range of industries in both the core of Europe and the PRE. The transport equipment industry has been the largest recipient of Japanese FDI in sectoral terms in both the EU and non-EU regions, accounting for 29.1 and 34.5 per cent of total sales of Japanese affiliates respectively. Other industries where Japanese firms are prominent investors include non-ferrous metals, machinery and electrical machinery.

The analysis, therefore, suggests that the Japanese direct investment presence in the PRE areas is indeed very limited in size, relative to the scale of establishment at locations in the US, Asia and the European core. Furthermore, the sectoral distribution of investing industries is narrower in the European periphery than in other regions of the world. Japanese FDI in these peripheral regions appears to be concentrated in a small range of industries, such as motor vehicles, machinery and electrical machinery.

Geographical Distribution of Japanese FDI in the European Periphery

Table 2.3 summarises the geographical distribution of Japanese FDI in the peripheral countries of Europe. Unlike Table 2.2, it distinguishes and includes peripheral countries *within* the EU. It shows the stock of Japanese FDI in all sectors of industry (natural resources, trade and services included) in the PRE countries, their populations and GNP per capita. The population and GNP per capita are included as a reference, as they may be used to provide some explanation for the presence of Japanese FDI.

Table 2.3 Stock of Japanese FDI in peripheral European countries

Country	Investment ($US millions)	Population (thousands)	GNP per Capita ($US)
Norway	903	4 200	25 800
Sweden	91	8 680	26 780
Denmark	66	5 170	25 930
Republic of Ireland	829	3 550	12 100
Austria	231	7 880	22 110
Switzerland	2 701	6 900	36 230
Portugal	204	9 850	7 450
Spain	2 577	39 080	14 020
Poland	5	38 360	1 960
Romania	9	22 750	1 090
Czech Republic	4	15 580	2 450
Bulgaria	1	8 470	1 330
Hungary	224	10 320	3 010
Greece	102	10 060	7 180
Turkey	370	58 780	1 950

Source: JETRO (1994).

From Table 2.3, it is immediately apparent that Japanese FDI is not distributed evenly among PRE countries. Rather, it is concentrated to a greater or lesser degree in Spain, Switzerland,[2] Portugal, Norway, Ireland and Hungary, and it will be useful to ascertain why Japanese investment seems to favour, or neglect, some peripheral countries.

The large size of the local market is often a strong incentive for foreign firms to undertake FDI in a country, and the population and per capita income may be good proxy indices for market size, as well as a measure of market potential for firms' FDI activities. However, the information in Table 2.3 seems to suggest that population and per capita income may have no direct bearing on the size of the Japanese FDI presence. Japanese FDI is relatively underdeveloped in Sweden and Denmark, despite the high per capita income in these two countries. Yet while the population is marginally greater and per capita income lower in the case of Hungary, the Japanese FDI presence is better established. Thus, the market size and purchasing power of the population may not provide sufficient direct explanation for the scale of Japanese FDI activities in these countries. Other factors which explain the geographic distribution of the Japanese FDI in PRE countries must also be considered.

It is also interesting to note that the cross-country distribution patterns

of Japanese FDI contrast sharply with those of investing firms based
in other parts of Europe. Indeed, European firms have invested in the
same peripheral countries but have gone much more aggressively and
much further into the peripheral regions, particularly in Central European countries. For example, large German firms like Volkswagen and
Siemens have made large-scale investments in motor vehicles and electrical machinery in the Czech Republic. Smaller-sized German firms
have also made significant investments in the same country. Poland is
also a major target for European and US multinational firms, but the
Japanese FDI presence in the country still remains limited. This contrast in FDI behaviour between Japanese and European firms in some
Central European countries is therefore marked and will receive further consideration below.

Industry Distribution of Japanese FDI

Tables 2.4 and 2.5 show the geographic and industry distribution of
Japanese FDI in terms, respectively, of the total number of cases and
total paid-in equity capital. These tables refer only to FDI in manufacturing, excluding investments in natural resources, commerce and services.

In these tables, we can once more observe a concentration of Japanese FDI in a small number of the PRE countries and a narrow range
of industries. Table 2.4 shows the number of cases of direct investment, revealing concentrations in Ireland (21), Switzerland (10), Spain
(49) and Austria (10). All other countries have fewer than 10 cases of
manufacturing investment. These investments are most prevalent in
general machinery, electrical machinery and transport equipment. Table
2.5 shows the value of paid-in equity capital of Japanese affiliates, not
including retained earnings and debt financing from parents. With regard to the value of the equity capital invested, Spain ($1310 million),
Portugal ($435 million), Turkey ($94 million), Iceland ($83 million),
Northern Ireland (UK) ($65 million) and Austria ($64 million) are the
key target countries for Japanese FDI in the periphery of Europe.

Concerning the distribution of Japanese FDI across different industries, we see again concentration in the general machinery, electrical
machinery and transport equipment industries. In terms of the number
of investment cases, the general machinery industry accounts for 24
cases, electrical machinery for 21 cases and transport equipment for
25 cases. The largest sectoral recipients of equity capital invested are
transport equipment ($1479 million), chemicals ($188 million), electrical
machinery ($153 million) and precision machinery ($102 million) in

Table 2.4 Japanese manufacturing FDI in peripheral European countries: Number of cases by industry, 1993

Country	Food	Textiles	Lumber Paper/Pulp	Chemicals	Steel	Metals	General Machinery	Electrical Machinery	Transport Equipment	Precision Machinery	Others	Total
Iceland	0	0	0	1	0	0	0	0	0	0	0	1
Norway	0	0	0	0	0	0	0	0	1	0	0	1
Sweden	0	0	1	0	0	0	1	0	1	0	0	3
Denmark	0	0	0	0	0	0	2	0	1	0	0	3
N. Ireland	0	0	0	4	0	0	0	1	0	0	0	5
Rep. Ireland	0	2	0	4	0	0	2	7	1	3	2	21
Switzerland	0	2	0	2	0	1	2	1	1	1	0	10
Portugal	0	0	0	2	0	1	0	0	3	2	0	8
Spain	0	1	1	9	1	3	10	11	11	0	2	49
Finland	0	0	0	0	0	1	1	0	0	0	2	4
Russia	1	0	3	0	0	1	3	0	0	0	0	8
Austria	0	1	0	0	4	1	2	0	1	0	1	10
Czech Republic	0	0	0	0	0	0	0	0	0	0	1	1
Hungary	0	0	0	1	0	0	0	1	1	0	2	5
Greece	0	0	0	0	0	0	1	0	1	0	0	2
Bulgaria	0	0	0	1	0	0	0	0	0	0	0	1
Turkey	1	0	0	0	0	2	0	0	2	0	0	5
Croatia	0	0	0	0	0	0	0	0	1	0	0	1
Total	2	6	5	24	5	10	24	21	25	6	10	138

Source: Kaigai Shinshutsu Kigyo Soran (Toyo Keizai, 1994).

Table 2.5 Japanese manufacturing FDI in peripheral European countries: Total paid-in capital by industry, 1993 ($US thousands)

Country	Food	Textiles	Lumber Paper/Pulp	Chemicals	Steel	Metals	General Machinery	Electric Machinery	Transport Equipment	Precision Machinery	Others	Total
Iceland	0	0	0	82 846	0	0	0	0	0	0	0	82 846
Norway	0	0	0	0	0	0	0	0	4 002	0	0	4 002
Sweden	0	0	120	0	0	0	961	0	3 243	0	0	4 325
Denmark	0	0	0	0	0	592	20 710	0	0	0	0	21 301
N. Ireland	0	0	0	0	0	2 952	0	62 170	NA	0	369	65 491
Rep. Ireland	0	7 451	0	15 619	0	0	880	14 412	355	6 458	1 919	-47 094
Switzerland	0	0	0	19 581	0	338	574	34	2 026	NA	0	22 552
Portugal	0	40 987	0	9 530	0	1 420	0	0	382 781	0	0	434 717
Spain	0	1 690	0	32 755	2 464	70 173	13 214	75 646	1 007 548	96 036	10 879	1 310 405
Finland	0	0	19 372	0	0	259	0	0	0	0	1 159	20 790
Russia	1	0	1 503	0	0	300	889	0	0	0	0	2 692
Austria	0	32 881	0	0	18 430	4 932	62	0	1 644	0	6 576	64 525
Czech Republic	0	0	0	0	0	0	0	0	0	0	8	8
Hungary	0	0	0	10 437	0	0	0	1 000	973	0	6 741	19 151
Greece	0	0	0	6 690	0	1 124	0	0	0	0	0	7 813
Bulgaria	0	0	0	0	0	0	100	0	0	0	0	100
Turkey	6 259	0	0	10 562	0	0	35	0	76 755	0	0	93 611
Croatia	0	0	0	0	0	0	0	0	NA	0	0	0
Total	6 260	83 009	20 995	188 020	20 894	82 090	37 425	153 262	1 479 327	102 494	27 651	2 201 423

Note: Individual totals have been adjusted to the nearest $1000.

Source: Kaigai Shinshutsu Kigyo Soran (Toyo Keizai, 1994).

that order. From this, we can see that industries such as electrical machinery, in which Japanese FDI is prevalent elsewhere, have only a limited manufacturing presence in the PRE countries. Thus, in terms of both the number of cases of investment and the value of equity capital invested, we confirm the concentration of Japanese FDI in a small range of industries.

Further insights may be gained from examining the average values of capital invested per case by country and industry. Tables 2.6 summarises the average values of equity capital invested. The average asset size per case may be a much better measure, but the data on total assets by each investment case are not available. The average equity capital invested does not measure the size of FDI activities as accurately as average total assets, but it none the less provides some information on the size of FDI activities.

In the table, the transport equipment industry shows the highest per case equity investment. This may suggest that even a relatively small-scale assembly plant in this sector requires significant capital investment. Furthermore, FDI by the Japanese automotive industry is very clearly concentrated in Portugal, Spain and Turkey, with manufacturing plants in these countries tending to be large scale. Japanese FDI in the automotive industry in other PRE countries may, as the smaller investment totals suggest, involve simpler knock-down assembly, possibly including component manufacture. In the case of the textile industry, there are some relatively large investments in Portugal and Austria, whereas in chemicals, investments are, to some extent, of similar size across different countries, and more evenly distributed than in other industries. The size of investment in the electrical machinery sector seems generally very small and concentrated in Spain and Northern Ireland, despite the relatively large numbers of investments in these regions. We also observe a large number of Japanese projects in the same industry in the core regions of the EU, and these investments also seem to be relatively small in size. This may perhaps be due to the fact that the operations involved are largely basic assembly, not requiring major capital investment.

INCENTIVES AND STRATEGIES FOR DIRECT INVESTMENT

To explain the cross-country, cross-industry distribution patterns of Japanese FDI among the PRE countries, and in particular the concentration of FDI in certain industries and countries, we may turn to Dunning's

Table 2.6 Japanese manufacturing FDI in peripheral European countries: Total paid-in capital per case, 1993 ($US thousands)

Country	Food	Textiles	Lumber Paper/Pulp	Chemicals	Steel	Metals	General Machinery	Electrical Machinery	Transport Equipment	Precision Machinery	Others	Country Average
Iceland	0	0	0	82 846	0	0	0	0	0	0	0	82 846
Norway	0	0	0	0	0	0	0	0	4 002	0	0	4 002
Sweden	0	0	120	0	0	0	961	0	3 243	0	0	1 442
Denmark	0	0	0	0	0	592	10 355	0	0	0	0	7 100
N. Ireland	0	0	0	3 905	0	2 952	0	62 170	NA	0	369	13 098
Rep. Ireland	3 726	0	0	4 895	0	338	440	2 059	355	2 153	960	2 243
Switzerland	0	0	0	4 768	0	1 420	287	34	2 026	NA	0	2 255
Portugal	0	20 494	0	0	0	0	0	0	127 594	0	0	54 340
Spain	0	1 690	0	3 639	2 464	35 087	1 321	6 877	91 595	48 018	5 439	26 743
Finland	0	0	19 372	0	0	259	0	0	0	0	579	5 198
Russia	1	0	501	0	0	300	296	0	0	0	0	336
Austria	0	32 881	0	0	4 607	4 932	31	0	1 644	0	6 576	6 453
Czech Republic	0	0	0	0	0	0	0	0	0	0	8	8
Hungary	0	0	0	5 218	0	0	0	1 000	973	0	6 741	3 830
Greece	0	0	0	6 689	0	1 126	0	0	0	0	0	3 907
Bulgaria	0	0	0	0	0	0	100	0	0	0	0	100
Turkey	6 259	0	0	10 562	0	0	35	0	38 377	0	0	18 722
Croatia	0	0	0	0	0	0	0	0	NA	0	0	0
Ind. Average	3 130	13 835	4 199	7 834	4 179	8 209	1 559	7 298	59 173	17 082	2 765	

Note: Individual totals have been adjusted to the nearest $1000.

Source: Kaigai Shinshutsu Kigyo Soran (Toyo Keizai, 1994).

eclectic theory. According to this theory, firm-specific competitive advantage based on internalisable intangible assets, typically technological knowledge and marketing expertise, gives rise to direct investment when the firm sees that it can exploit advantages by coupling them with the locational advantages a specific foreign location offers.[3] The theory's focus on industry- and firm-specific intangible assets, as well as locational factors, is appropriate in a cross-industry and cross-country analysis.

Industry- and Firm-Specific Competitive Advantage

It is well known that Japanese firms have a strong advantage in technology and/or marketing skills in motor vehicles, machinery and electrical machinery, and these are the industries in which Japanese FDI is prevalent throughout the world. Some earlier empirical studies of Japanese FDI have found that technology and the marketing of intangible assets are important determinants of Japanese FDI elsewhere, and that Japanese FDI is particularly prevalent in machinery, electric machinery and motor vehicles.[4] This would naturally lead us to assume the significant presence of Japanese FDI in these industries in the PRE countries as well, other things being equal. Indeed, we find in the data that Japanese FDI is also heavily concentrated in these industries in the PRE. The concentration in these industries in these countries is highly consistent with the intangible asset theory of FDI and the earlier findings for Japanese FDI in other locations.

Locational Factors

According to the eclectic theory, location factors should explain why Japanese manufacturing investment is concentrated in a small group of PRE countries. These location factors affecting FDI include: local market size and market potential, relative cost and quality of input factors, endowment of input factors, industrial infrastructure, market access impediments and government policies.

Japanese FDI in the PRE both inside and outside the EU (i.e. Scotland, Northern Ireland, Spain, Portugal, Ireland and Turkey) can be understood in terms of such locational factors. Japanese firms traditionally served large European markets in those industries through export from their home base in Japan. In the process of consolidation and expansion of the European Community into the European Union, there was always a fear on the part of Japanese firms serving Europe through exports that these exports would be impeded by tariff and non-tariff barriers (NTBs) arising from the creation of a single European market. Their concern with the possible formation of a Fortress Europe triggered a surge of Japanese FDI in Europe from the second half of the 1980s up to 1992.[5] A number of FDI projects undertaken by Japanese in Europe prior to 1992 are thus by nature *tariff-jumping*. Belderbos has documented this type of FDI behaviour by Japanese firms in a number of different electronics industries.[6] According to his study, a number of Japanese electronics firms invested in the core of Europe as well as the PRE in the assembly of CTV, VCR, CD players, printers, car telephones, etc., and the timing of these investments coincided with the timing of the initiation of anti-dumping investigations by the EC. Japanese FDI was motivated to protect the market in Europe that had been developed through export from Japanese sources. Indeed, the fear of Japanese firms of impeded market access became a reality when the EC initiated anti-dumping investigations against Japanese manufacturers and issued directives for local content requirements.

In making location decisions for FDI, Japanese firms were faced with the high cost of both initial establishment and subsequent operation in the core economies of Europe, particularly Germany, and some firms searched for low-cost locations within the Community, either on its periphery or in countries about to accede to Community membership. If they were to locate in a high operating cost country such as Germany, they could have gained market access by locating in the very centre of Europe's economic core, but they would have remained only at par with local firms in terms of operating costs, without the means to undercut them. European-based firms had already initiated relocation of some of their production activities to such PRE locations in order to maintain their cost competitiveness, and Japanese firms needed to meet this potential renewal of cost competitiveness by European firms.

It seems that Japanese firms initially adopted this strategy in the motor vehicle industry and located in Portugal, Spain and later Turkey, and now engage in substantial assembly operations which serve local as well as core EU markets. In contrast, in the electrical machinery industry, particularly in consumer electronics products, many Japanese firms located production activities, despite high operating costs, in the core EC countries.[7]

These contrasting features may suggest that factors other than cost considerations may be influencing firms' locational decisions in the automotive industry. One such factor may well be the presence of strong indigenous firms, and in motor vehicles there are dominant indigenous firms in various core EU countries, such as Volkswagen, Mercedes Benz and BMW in Germany, Peugeot-Citroën and Renault in France, and Fiat in Italy. If attempted, entry into the well-established home markets of these firms may evoke political responses from the domestic authorities, as well as competitive responses from the local firms themselves, particularly in Germany and France. Entry into the core producing areas of this type of industry is highly risky and costly, and the advance of Japanese automotive firms into the core of Europe has thus far taken the form of small-scale joint ventures and contract production with local competitors. This is one factor that has encouraged Japanese automotive firms to prefer location in the geographic and competitive peripheries of the industry.

A qualified exception to this is the UK. Recognising the problems of indigenous producers in the UK, the government has encouraged the entry of multinational firms into this industry, and Japanese investments have followed those of American and French motor manufacturers. By the mid-1990s, Toyota, Nissan, Honda and Isuzu had developed a significant manufacturing presence in the country and now engage in the export of completed motor vehicles to Continental Europe. Also, there are a large number of investments (22 as of 1992) in component manufacturing in the UK by Japanese suppliers, which may partly explain the large sales of Japanese affiliates operating in the EU in this sector, as recorded in Table 2.2.

Compared with their experiences in the motor vehicle industry, Japanese firms have faced no serious competition even in the core EC countries in the consumer electronics industry. The presence of Philips and Siemens and some attempts by the French government to raise the cost of Japanese entry do not seem to have much affected the Japanese firms' decisions to locate manufacturing activities in Germany, France, Belgium, Luxembourg and the Netherlands. As suggested earlier however, the scale of these investments in the core countries is generally relatively small. It seems that Japanese firms in consumer electronics chose to locate production largely in the centre of a market rather than in the peripheries, and serve the market from there. It also seems evident that Japanese firms have avoided high-cost peripheral countries, such as those in Scandinavia, despite the local availability of a high quality labour force and industrial infrastructure.

In any event, in the late 1970s and early 1980s, many Japanese firms chose areas such as Ireland, Wales, Scotland or the North of England, in so far as they were perceived as relatively low-cost locations with market access to the core of Europe. The periphery of the British Isles offered the Japanese firms market access within the EC, and in addition, a low-cost yet highly educated labour force that Japanese managers could communicate with in English, as well as quite liberal government incentives to locate in these regions. Direct investment in semiconductor plants by NEC in Scotland, and by Fujitsu in Newton Aycliffe in the North-East of England, may be seen as excellent case studies of such investment.

NEC established NEC Semiconductors (Ireland) in 1974, and since then has been engaged in the assembly of semiconductor devices in Ireland to serve the EC market. However, the firm later experienced difficulties in securing qualified local manpower, suggesting that the labour market for highly qualified technicians would be relatively limited in Ireland for some time. NEC thus decided to build a more elaborate second plant in another peripheral region when expansion became necessary. The company established NEC Semiconductors (UK) in 1981, and initiated assembly of memory ICs in Scotland in the following year, adding the wafer process to integrate fully the production of memory ICs in 1984. Of all Japanese semiconductor firms that eventually located in Europe, this NEC plant in Livingston, near Edinburgh, was the first to be ready for the planned completion of the single European market at the end of 1992, having already established its foothold on the periphery of the EU. By way of response to the relocation of expansion investment to other locations, exemplified by the disappointing decision of NEC to begin integrated production in Scotland, the Irish government has now attempted to shift from assembly work to more knowledge-intensive aspects of production, such as software development.[8]

NEC gave several reasons for its choice of a location in central Scotland.[9] It accepted that the UK government and Scottish development agencies were serious about the development of the region, and that the industrial infrastructure necessary for its operations was already in place by the time the company made the decision. Other key factors behind NEC's decision included: the presence of supply industries in the local area necessary for the manufacture of integrated circuits, such as electricity, chemicals and various industrial gases; government incentives for financing the capital investment; proximity to an international airport (critical for shipment of completed products by air); the close proximity of five universities; and the availability of a high quality local labour force.[10] Unlike other transplant operations, NEC emphasised the development of operational long-term linkages with local suppliers, particularly in the construction of buildings and also in the supply of chemicals and industrial gases.[11] This emphasis on continuing linkages with local suppliers by NEC was designed to attain lower costs, and the firm provided technical assistance to suppliers so that they might achieve consistently high quality and low cost supplies. In effect, the firm attempted to replicate long-term domestic purchase and supply (*keiretsu*) relationships in Scotland. Such developing linkages between multinationals and local supply firms are critical for effective technology transfer and the integration of offshore production into the local economy, and as such have determined the scale of NEC's positive impact in Scotland.

Fujitsu also chose a location in the UK for IC production, 200 km south of NEC's Scottish plant. Although Fujitsu had operated an assembly plant in Ireland since 1982, it decided in 1983, for reasons similar to those of NEC, to build a fully integrated semiconductor plant in the UK. The location chosen was in Newton Aycliffe, in the North-East of England, and the facility was due to come on-stream in 1991, with planned investment of ¥90 billion in the plant by 1994.[12] The plant was expected to employ about 1500 by the final year of the project, producing state-of-the-art memory and logic ICs. Like NEC, Fujitsu stressed operating linkages with local firms, together with the provision of technical assistance. It was the general judgement of Japanese semiconductor firms in early 1990s that locally available supplies did not meet their requirements and that technical assistance by Japanese assembly firms was therefore necessary to upgrade the quality of locally available supplies. These new semiconductor plants were designed to duplicate the most modern domestic plants in Japan and were established as key sources to service the European market. Indeed, transplants such as those of NEC and Fujitsu in the UK represented an important component of the global strategy of the Japanese semiconductor industry.

A number of Japanese firms also chose to locate in Spain and Portugal in the 1980s, in anticipation of their accession to the EC in 1986, whereby they could service competitively core EC markets from peripheral regions within the Community. Nissan and Suzuki invested in vehicle assembly in Spain, while Toyota established a joint venture in Portugal. As suggested earlier, these two firms came to Spain to avoid head-on competition with major automotive firms from core EU countries and to take advantage of lower production costs. Nissan Motor Ibérica, Nissan's Spanish affiliate, engages in the production of recreational vehicles, trucks, commercial vans, engines, transmissions and parts, and it supplements the production of the UK plant in the firm's European marketing activities. Over time, Nissan's plants in UK and Spain have been integrated into its global strategy.[13] Suzuki-Santana

Motor, Suzuki's joint venture with Land Rover, engages in the assembly of its recreational vehicles in Spain for sale locally as well as in the core EU markets. Furthermore, Japanese firms in related industries have also become active in Spain. For instance, to meet demand for tyres from Japanese firms operating in Spain, as well as indigenous demand, Bridgestone/Firestone invested in production in Spain in 1992.[14] Additionally, there are eight Japanese investments in vehicle component manufacturing in Spain, more than in any other European country, with the exception of the UK.[15]

Yet another important peripheral region is Central Europe. As the Central European countries abandoned centralised economic planning in the late 1980s, they emerged as peripheral to the European core economies, rather than part of a separate economic bloc. As part of this process, they opened their national borders to direct investment from the West, and the opening of these countries has led to a surge of direct investment by firms based in the core of Europe, as well as from North America. In particular, German, US, French, British and Italian firms have been active investors in the region. Some of these firms are aggressively seeking the new market opportunities that the opening of these countries has presented, while others are investing in production activities in these locations to take advantage of lower production costs.

Some EU countries, particularly Germany, are losing international cost-competitiveness as a location for production, as a result of currency appreciation. Following from this, large and small manufacturing firms in Germany have invested directly in the peripheral regions of Europe, and this has given rise to concern over the potential hollowing-out of the German manufacturing economy.[16] It would seem that this process is a mirror image of massive Japanese investment in South-East Asia. Japanese firms have, to a marked extent, lost cost-competitiveness at home, and a large number of manufacturing firms have adopted a strategy of relocating production in low-cost South-East Asian countries. Also, like their Japanese counterparts, many US firms operating in Japan have lost competitiveness, and have begun shifting their production activities out of Japan to these lower-cost countries.[17]

It might appear natural that, like US firms shifting from Japan to South-East Asia, Japanese firms may consider shifting their production activities from the core EU locations to peripheral regions such as the Central European countries. However, it is interesting to note that the Japanese presence is still very limited in these locations, even though

European and US firms are increasing very rapidly their market presence through FDI. For example, many German firms are rushing to Poland, Hungary and the Czech Republic, establishing a strong presence in these countries, whereas Japanese firms seem very slow in increasing their involvement.

There are only a few investments of any significance by Japanese firms in this area. One of these is Suzuki's joint venture with a local state enterprise in Hungary to produce passenger cars on a small scale (15 000 cars a year, to be increased to 50 000 per year by 1995). The affiliate of Suzuki is targeting the domestic market until it develops sufficient domestic supply capacity to support larger-scale production. Some Japanese suppliers have also followed Suzuki to produce automotive components for the company's Hungarian venture. Japanese FDI in manufacturing in this region nevertheless tends to be on a very small scale, and is largely concerned with supplying local domestic markets.

The asymmetry in FDI behaviour between German and Japanese firms may be explained by the fact that Japanese firms are relatively new investors in Europe, and they are too busy in favoured investment locations in Western Europe to establish a foothold in Central Europe. Another explanation may lie in the geographic and, perhaps more important, cultural distance between Japan and Central European countries. Often historical events and cultural proximity have a critical influence on firms' locational decisions regarding foreign direct investment.[18] These countries were and are culturally and historically close to Europe and the US, while they have remained quite distant from Japan in terms of historical links. Thus, until the process of Japanese investment matures, Japanese firms may not seriously rethink their existing location strategies, which until now have precluded major investment in Central Europe.

Having examined the incentives for Japanese firms to undertake FDI, and their investment strategies in the PRE countries, we have seen that Japanese firms have undertaken FDI in the European periphery to extend the use of their competitive advantage based upon *internalisable intangible assets*, most notably technologies and/or marketing know-how, particularly in chemicals, electric machinery, transport equipment and precision machinery. These investments did not seek market opportunities specifically in the markets where they were located. Rather, they targeted core EU markets. Their location decisions thus hinged largely upon access to markets in the core of the EU from productive locations on the peripheries of the EU, and the cost advantages these locations offered to Japanese firms. Another factor that was sometimes influential was the anticipated rivalry of dominant firms based in the EU core.

IMPACT OF JAPANESE DIRECT INVESTMENT

This section will analyse the effects of Japanese FDI upon the industries, economies and societies of the PRE countries. However, it will be highly impractical to attempt a systematic and quantitative evaluation of the effects of Japanese FDI in this paper, and issues relating to the likely impact of Japanese FDI on local industry, economy and society in PRE countries will be discussed instead.

FDI inevitably affects the industry, economy and society of a host country in a number of ways, and these effects of FDI may be classified as follows: resource transfer effects, employment effects, trade and balance of payments effects, and competitive and anti-competitive effects.[19] FDI transfers capital, technology and managerial resources in a package and transplants them to host country locations, where it employs a local workforce to engage in production. The transplant firm may import necessary components from outside the host country, and it may export the finished product, thus affecting its balance of payments. Also, the presence of a foreign affiliate may bring with it additional production capacity, thus increasing domestic competition.

These effects of FDI may be of lesser significance in large countries like the US, Japan or the larger core economies of the EU, and not a source of concern to policy-makers. However, they can be more significant in smaller countries. The PRE countries belong for the most part in this category, and the policy-makers of these countries are generally more concerned with the impact of foreign direct investments. With an expectation of potential benefits, all the PRE countries have sought inward investments, including those by Japanese firms. How these investments have fared relative to host country expectations, and the question of identifying the types of operation, Japanese or otherwise, which tend to generate the most positive impact upon host countries, remain key issues to be examined.

It has been noted that Japanese firms engage in production in PRE countries to gain access to the core EU markets, and seek low-cost locations for production. This pattern of FDI resembles that of footloose offshore transplants, which may produce benefits for a local economy in terms of employment effects and trade and balance of payments effects in the short run, as long as production at the location is cost-competitive. However, due to the very foot-loose nature of these investments, they tend to move away from the location as soon as it loses its cost-competitive advantages. Such foot-loose transplants are often self-contained, with few linkages with local suppliers, and the degree of their integration with the local industry and economy tends to be low. In this sense, host countries cannot seriously expect transfers of resources, particularly technology and managerial resources, to take place through this type of FDI.

There is a danger in making generalisations from a small sample, but the examples cited above may suggest that some Japanese firms have undertaken FDI in the PRE for the long haul. Japanese FDI transfers capital, technology and other managerial resources in a package to the PRE host countries. Because many Japanese investments in these host countries were designed to serve the core EU markets, they export finished products to core EU markets, among others, and contribute to the host countries' balance of payments. Moreover, we may expect transfers of technology and other managerial resources to devolve upon local industries and economies.

Japanese firms may initially rely upon the import of components and parts from the parents or sister subsidiaries, but eventually many find themselves obliged, due in part to the local content requirements of the EU, to integrate their production activities with local suppliers. These firms effectively train not only their own employees but also those of suppliers through the technical assistance that they provide. Such linkages between Japanese affiliates and local suppliers provide a conduit for technology and other managerial resource transfers. And in addition to these direct transfers, there may be demonstration effects of Japanese management practices available to local vendors.

In a number of these PRE countries, FDI may represent the initial establishment of an industry. In effect, direct investment may bring an industry to a country. The semiconductor investments by NEC and Fujitsu in Ireland, and Japanese videorecorder assembly plants in Europe, may be cases in point. The presence of plants in these locations promotes the development of local supply and service industries, expanding and deepening the industrial base of the country over time. These transfers help to upgrade the technological and managerial capabilities of supplier firms and industry, and increase over time their international competitiveness. As Porter argues, upgrading the technological capabilities of supplier industries and building a broad base for supporting industries helps improve the international competitiveness of a nation state.[20]

All this suggests that policy-makers in host countries need to institute a policy that fosters the integration of multinational linkages with local industries. Local content requirements are one such instrument, but the relationships between foreign affiliates and local suppliers and vendors need to go beyond that of buyers and sellers in a spot market. Much closer linkages, such as in design functions, are necessary. Various forms of strategic alliances between foreign firms and local firms may also be possible. These policy considerations are critical to avoid inward investment becoming foot-loose.

To the PRE countries, this may be a very good time to encourage the development of long-term relationships between affiliates and domestic supplier firms, in a form of *keiretsu* relationship. However, these relationships between buyer firms and supplier firms are now in jeopardy due to the high costs of supplies in Japan, and buyer firms have begun to look for alternative supplier sources for both domestic and foreign production.[21] In the PRE locations, there may be scope for local supplier firms and vendors to take the place of Japanese domestic *keiretsu* suppliers.

CONCLUSIONS

This paper has attempted to offer an overview of Japanese FDI in the PRE countries. It has been confirmed that the magnitude of Japanese FDI in these countries, relative to that in the rest of the world and the European Union, is indeed very small. The cross-country, cross-industry distribution patterns of Japanese FDI in PRE countries have revealed that Japanese FDI is concentrated in a small number of these countries and industries, in terms of both the number of cases and the value of the investments. Japanese investment in these countries is concentrated in Spain, Portugal, Ireland, Switzerland, Austria and Turkey, and Japanese investors in these countries have focused upon the chemicals, machinery, electrical machinery and transport equipment sectors.

To explain the factors behind the distribution of Japanese FDI in the PRE countries we may turn to John Dunning's eclectic theory. The intangible asset theory seems to provide a good explanation for the cross-industry distribution of Japanese FDI. From previous empirical studies of Japanese FDI, we know that Japanese firms have competitive advantage based on technology and/or marketing skills in those industries, and this seems to extend to the direct investments in PRE countries.

The theory also suggests that locational advantage provides an explanation for the specific location of these investments. Using this concept as a guide, we found that access to the core EU markets (tariff-jumping) and search for low-cost production sites were the major factors behind the decision of Japanese firms to locate production activities in PRE countries. In particular, we noted the cases of NEC and Fujitsu semiconductor plants in Ireland and UK, and Nissan and Suzuki car plants in Spain.

In contrast to European and US multinationals, Japanese firms have been slow in moving into Central Europe. The observed behaviour of European firms in Central Europe may parallel that of Japanese multinationals in South-East Asia, and geographic, historical and cultural affinities may explain both the behaviour of European firms in Central Europe and that of Japanese firms in East and South-East Asia. Thus the geographic, historical and cultural distance between Central Europe and Japan may be the major factor that is preventing prompt large-scale investment in these countries.

There is neither information nor data sufficient to conclude whether Japanese FDI has had a positive or negative impact overall in PRE host countries. Through FDI, some managerial resources have been transferred to affiliates in these countries. Given the nature of these investments as export platforms for the core EU markets, Japanese investments have tended to generate exports and to contribute positively to the host countries' balance of payments, at least in the countries where assembly takes place.

Aside from these effects, perhaps the most important impact that Japanese FDI has had upon production in Europe may be in its establishment of links with local supplier industries and vendors, whereby operational long-term relationships can provide a conduit for technology and skill transfers. These transfers can upgrade the latter's technological capabilities, while the overall broadening of the industrial base and deepening of technical skills are central to improving the competitive advantage of a nation. Moreover, further extension of such linkages may be envisaged through various forms of strategic alliance between foreign and domestic firms.

One implication of this for policy-makers in PRE countries is that they need to institute a policy that goes beyond the provision of incentives for multinationals, rather facilitating and fostering the development of such linkages between multinational firms and local supplier firms. This will increase the value of the location to foreign or Japanese investors, and would discourage inward investment projects from becoming foot-loose. Also, such linkages clearly require effort on the part of multinationals themselves. They must be willing to share with local firms the knowledge and skills necessary for producing components and supplies which are consistent and high quality. They must develop trust and respect for each other, as well as a sense of co-operation.

The Japanese presence through FDI in the PRE countries is still very small, although it is increasing. As the Japanese presence in Europe as a whole matures and deepens, it is to be expected that Japanese FDI will also increase in the PRE countries. However, this will hinge ultimately on whether these PRE countries can be perceived as increasingly attractive to Japanese firms as investment locations, as well as depending upon the cost-effectiveness of what Japanese investors·might be seen to be offering their European hosts. Clearly, therefore, successful collaboration between Japanese multinationals and the PRE countries requires continued efforts towards mutual understanding and co-operation, not just in terms of the perceived operating environment for foreign firms, but also with respect to the development strategies pursued by both multinationals and host economies in an increasingly unified European market.

NOTES

1. M.E. Porter, *The Competitive Advantage of Nations* (New York: Basic Books, 1990).
2. Japanese direct investment in Switzerland is concentrated in the financial services industry. As the focus of this paper is manufacturing investment, Japanese FDI in this country is somewhat outside the scope of this paper, especially as Switzerland is clearly at the heart of Europe's manufacturing economy, although remaining outside the EU.
3. For example, R.E. Caves, *Multinational Enterprise and Economic Analysis* (Cambridge: Cambridge University Press, 1982); J.H. Dunning, *Multinational Enterprises and the Global Economy* (Wokingham: Addison-Wesley, 1992).
4. For example, B. Kogut and Sea Jin Chang, 'Technological Capabilities and Japanese Direct Investment in the United States', *Review of Economics and Statistics* (1989); T.A. Pugel, E. Kragas and Yui Kimura, 'Further Evidence on Japanese Direct Investment in U.S. Manufacturing', *Review of Economics and Statistics* (forthcoming); and Yui Kimura and T.A. Pugel, 'Keiretsu and Japanese Direct Investment in U.S. Manufacturing', *Japan and the World Economy* (forthcoming).
5. Yui Kimura, 'Host Country and Industry Effects on Multinationals'

Competitiveness: The Case of Foreign Direct Investment in the Semiconductor Industry in Japan', in Schon Beechler and Allan Bird, eds., *Research in International Business and International Relations: Emerging Trends in Japanese Management* (Greenwich, CT: JAI Press, 1994); R. Belderbos, *Strategic Trade Policy and Multinational Enterprises: Essays on Trade and Investment by Japanese Electronics Firms* (Amsterdam: Thesis Publishers, Tinbergen Institute Research Series No. 68, 1994).
6. Belderbos (1994).
7. Ibid.
8. *Hakusho Toshi-hen: Sekai to Nihon no Kaigai Chokusetsu Toshi* (JETRO White Paper on Direct Investment: Direct Investment of Japan and the World) (JETRO: Tokyo, 1994).
9. Y. Shimura, *IC Sangyo no Himitsu* (The Secret of the IC Industry) (Tokyo: Shobunsha, 1981).
10. See ibid.
11. 'DRAM de Soki-Tachiage' (Launching Production Early Using DRAM as a Vehicle), *Nikkei Microdevices* (July 1990).
12. See ibid.
13. T. Fujimoto, T. Nishiguchi and S. Sei, 'The Strategy and Structure of Japanese Automobile Manufacturing in Europe', in Mark Mason and Dennis Encarnation, eds., *Does Ownership Matter? Japanese Multinationals in Europe* (Oxford: Oxford University Press, 1994).
14. JETRO, White Paper (1994).
15. JETRO, *10th Survey of European Operations of Japanese Companies in the Manufacturing Sector* (Tokyo: Japan External Trade Organisation, October 1994).
16. JETRO, White Paper (1994).
17. Kimura (1994).
18. B. Kogut and A. Singh, 'The Effects of National Culture on the Choice of Entry Mode', *Journal of International Business Studies* Vol. 19 (1988).
19. N. Hood and S. Young, *The Economics of Multinational Enterprise* (London: Longman, 1979).
20. Porter (1990).
21. Kimura and Pugel (forthcoming).

3 Patterns of Japanese Manufacturing Employment in the European Regions

Jean-Marc Thiran and
Hideki Yamawaki

INTRODUCTION

From the multinational firm's strategic point of view, the choice of production location abroad is crucial inasmuch as it determines the performance of its foreign operations in that region. For the foreign country which serves as a potential host location for the foreign multinational enterprise (MNE), the MNE's locational decision will also become a potentially important factor as it comes to influence the host country's prospects for regional economic development. Because of the great economic importance attached to the MNE's locational decision an extensive literature[1] has emerged to examine the factors that determine the MNE's locational choice.

The purpose of this paper is to give an overview of the patterns of Japanese direct investment in the European countries, regions and manufacturing industries. The statistical source used in this study is a Toyo Keizai directory,[2] which lists the manufacturing subsidiaries more than 10 per cent controlled by Japanese firms in 15 European countries in 1993. From this list, we selected 432 subsidiaries which were in the European Community (95 per cent of the total), and for which we were able to determine the NUTS-1 region in which they were located, and for which the number of employees was given. This NUTS (Nomenclature des Unités Territoriales Statistiques) classification is the official classification of the Statistical Office of the European Community (EUROSTAT), and can be disaggregated at three levels: NUTS-1 which consists of 71 regions, NUTS-2 (183 regions) and NUTS-3 (1044 regions).

The number of employees in the European manufacturing subsidiaries of Japanese firms was finally aggregated to the two-digit industry level (NACE-2)[3] and to the one-digit region level (NUTS-1) to obtain the number of employees in Japanese subsidiaries in a specific region and industry in 1993. Following from this, all the tables that will be discussed in the following section use the number of employees to measure the extent of Japanese direct investment (JDI). The following section provides a description and discussion of the data, and the main conclusion resulting from this analysis is that Japanese direct investment varies across countries, regions and industries.

DESCRIPTIVE ANALYSIS

Japanese Direct Investment in the Countries of Europe

Previous studies on the locational decisions of MNEs have shown a pattern which varies across different host countries. This pattern is also present for Japanese MNEs that invest in the European Union (EU). Table 3.1 shows the distribution of Japanese manufacturing subsidiaries in the EC, as it then was, in 1993. Among the host countries that are most preferred by Japanese MNEs are the UK, Germany, France and Spain. The UK is by far the most favoured destination (32.6 per cent), with a third of the total employment derived from Japanese investment in the EC-12, followed by Germany with a fifth (19.5 per cent). Indeed, employment in Japanese subsidiaries in the United Kingdom is almost three times larger than the equivalent totals for France (12 per cent) and Spain (12 per cent). In fact, the UK and Germany together account for more than half (52.1 per cent) of the Japanese employment in manufacturing sectors in the EU. Also, several countries each account for approximately 5 per cent of the total, and these include the Netherlands, Portugal, Belgium and Italy. Finally, the smallest countries of the EU (Ireland, Luxembourg, Greece, Denmark) collectively account for a share of less than 3 per cent of the total.

Also included in Table 3.1 is the percentage distribution of total employment[4] in the different EC/EU countries,[5] provided as a means of comparing the country share of Japanese subsidiaries' employment with the country share of total employment in the EC-12. From this comparison, we may distinguish two groups of countries. On the one hand, the UK, Spain, the Benelux countries, Portugal and Ireland are countries where Japanese direct investment is proportionately more concentrated when we compare Japanese and total employment shares, suggesting that JDI in these countries is relatively prominent. On the other hand, in a second group, containing Germany, France, Italy, Greece

Table 3.1 Employment in Japanese firms and total employment in EC-12, 1993

Country	JDI Employment	JDI Employment %	Total Employment %
United Kingdom	43 626	32.6	18.5
Germany	26 113	19.5	26.1
France	16 089	12.0	15.6
Spain	16 028	12.0	8.9
Netherlands	8 695	6.5	4.5
Portugal	7 221	5.4	3.4
Belgium	6 886	5.1	2.6
Italy	5 658	4.2	15.2
Republic of Ireland	2 564	1.9	0.8
Luxembourg	575	0.4	0.1
Greece	166	0.0	2.6
Denmark	131	0.0	1.9
Subtotal UK + Germany	69 739	52.1	44.6
Total	133 752	100*	100*

Note: *Aggregated totals may not total 100 per cent exactly.

Source: Toyo Keizai (1994); Eurostat (1994).

and Denmark, Japanese activity is less visible in comparison to their share of total European (EC-12) employment. To sum up, JDI tends to be concentrated in the UK, with Spain also having a non-negligible share of employment derived from Japanese direct investment.

Japanese Direct Investment in the European Regions

When the EU is divided into regions according to the NUTS-1 level of regional classification and these regions are placed in order according to the number of employees in the subsidiaries of Japanese MNEs (Table 3.2), it is evident that there are huge differences. Some regions are totally neglected by Japanese investors while others have experienced heavy Japanese investment. The latter appear to be Bayern in Germany, the South-East, Wales and the West Midlands in the United Kingdom, Île de France, Este in Spain, and Portugal. In fact, these regions (with a share of more than 5 per cent each) account for almost half of employment in Japanese subsidiaries in the European Union (48 per cent).

Table 3.2 Employment in Japanese firms and total employment in EC-12 regions, 1993

Region	Country	JDI Employment	JDI Employment %	Total Employment %
Bayern	D	11 704	8.8	4.0
South-East	UK	10 204	7.6	5.9
Île de France	F	9 838	7.4	3.4
Este	E	9 333	7.0	2.6
Wales	UK	8 191	6.1	0.9
West Midlands	UK	7 978	6.0	1.7
PORTUGAL	P	7 221	5.4	3.4
North	UK	5 858	4.4	0.9
West-Nederland	NL	5 748	4.3	2.2
Madrid	E	5 392	4.0	1.2
Hessen	D	4 877	3.6	1.9
South-West	UK	4 375	3.3	1.5
Brussels	B	3 813	2.9	0.2
Niedersachsen	D	3 160	2.4	2.3
Nord-ovest	I	3 037	2.3	1.7
Nordrhein-Westfalen	D	2 945	2.2	5.2
Bassin Parisien	F	2 858	2.1	2.8
IRELAND	IRL	2 564	1.9	0.8
North-West	UK	2 394	1.8	2.0
Scotland	UK	2 292	1.7	1.6
Zuid-Nederland	NL	1 893	1.4	1.0
Vlaanderen	B	1 838	1.4	1.6
Ouest	F	1 667	1.2	2.0
Lombardia	I	1 613	1.2	2.7
Baden-Württemberg	D	1 429	1.1	3.4
Yorkshire & Humberside	UK	1 383	1.0	1.6
Wallonie	B	1 235	0.9	0.8
Centre-est	F	1 168	0.9	1.8
Bremen	D	1 099	0.8	0.2
Oost-Holland	NL	1 054	0.8	0.9
Hamburg	D	899	0.7	0.5
East-Midlands	UK	786	0.6	1.3
Noreste	E	628	0.5	1.0
LUXEMBOURG	L	575	0.4	0.1
Est	F	461	0.3	1.4
Noroeste	E	451	0.3	1.1
Centro	I	410	0.3	1.6
Sicilia	I	271	0.2	1.0
Centro	E	181	0.1	1.2
GREECE	GR	166	0.1	2.6

Table 3.2 continued

Region	Country	JDI Employment	JDI Employment %	Total Employment %
Northern Ireland	UK	165	0.1	0.4
Lazio	I	150	0.1	1.4
Nord est	I	143	0.1	1.9
DENMARK	DK	131	0.1	1.9
Sud-ouest	F	84	0.1	1.6
Sur	E	43	0.0	1.6
Sud	I	34	0.0	1.5
Méditerranée	F	13	0.0	1.6
Schleswig-Holstein	D	0	0.0	0.8
Rheinland-Pfalz	D	0	0.0	1.2
Saarland	D	0	0.0	0.3
Nord-Pas-de-Calais	F	0	0.0	0.9
Emilia-Romagna	I	0	0.0	1.2
Campania	I	0	0.0	1.2
Abruzzi-Molise	I	0	0.0	0.4
Noord-Holland	NL	0	0.0	0.4
East Anglia	UK	0	0.0	0.7
Subtotal >5%		64 469	48.2	21.9
Subtotal CORE		65 070	48.6	55.2
Subtotal PERIPHERY		68 682	51.4	44.8
Subtotal NORTH		104 728	78.3	69.0
Subtotal SOUTH		29 024	21.7	31.0
Total		133 752	100.0	100.0

Source: As for Table 3.1.

Two methods can be used to describe and interpret the location of multinational activity in the EU. First, MNEs may be attracted to core regions of the EU to the detriment of peripheral ones. This is due to a number of factors, including the existence of highly developed transport infrastructure networks and highly skilled labour resources in these core regions. In order to test the validity of this explanation, we have classified the European regions into two groups. With regard to levels of GDP per capita, a region was assigned to the core or periphery according to whether it exceeded or fell short of the European GDP per capita average. However, Japanese direct investment seems to be almost evenly distributed between core (48.6 per cent) and peripheral (51.4 per cent) regions, suggesting that the simple view of JDI concentrated in core regions and avoiding the peripheral regions is inadequate.

The locational patterns of foreign investors can also be analysed in terms of their preference for northern or southern regions of Europe.[6] This seems to present a clearer imbalance in terms of the relative popularity of the two areas, with almost 80 per cent of JDI in the north, and only 20 per cent in the south. Hence, while JDI is unevenly distributed among European regions, there is a clearer concentration in the north of Europe, as such, rather than in the economic core.

As in Table 3.1, Table 3.2 also lists the distribution of the share of total employment.[7] The comparison between the patterns of Japanese and total employment reveals that for most of the regions in the upper part of Table 3.2 (i.e. regions which have the largest number of employees of subsidiaries of Japanese MNEs), the Japanese share is higher than the total share. However, for four regions (Este (E), Wales (UK), West Midlands (UK) and Brussels (B)), the share of the former is markedly higher than the latter. By contrast, in two German regions (Nordrhein-Westfalen and Baden-Württemberg), the total employment share is substantially higher than the share of Japanese-derived employment, suggesting that Japanese investors have not identified these areas as favoured regions for their investment.

Another important pattern which also emerges from Table 3.2 is that Japanese subsidiaries are not evenly distributed across regions within a host country. For example, Japanese MNEs in the UK are greatly attracted to the South-East and West Midlands but hardly at all to East Anglia. In Germany, Japanese MNEs invest in Bayern and Hessen but not in Schleswig-Holstein, Rheinland-Pfalz or Saarland. This difference in the presence of Japanese MNEs among the various domestic regions can also be seen to persist even when the regions are adjacent, as in the cases of the West Midlands (7978 employees) and East Midlands (786 employees) in the United Kingdom, and the *Länder* of Hessen (4877) and Rheinland-Pfalz (0) in Germany.

Japanese Direct Investment in European Manufacturing Industries

The sectoral composition of employment in Japanese subsidiaries is presented in Table 3.3.[8] As has been well documented in previous research, Japanese direct investment in the EU is heavily concentrated in two sectors, the electrical and electronic products sector (31.5 per cent) and automobiles (25.2 per cent), which together account for more than half of the total employment in Japanese subsidiaries (56.7 per cent).

Table 3.3 Distribution of JDI in Europe by NACE 2-digit industries, 1993

Industry	JDI Employment	JDI Employment %	Total Employment %
Electrical products	42 114	31.5	14.3
Automobiles	33 820	25.3	10.2
Machinery	12 387	9.3	12.8
Rubber and plastics	12 088	9.0	1.3
Stone, clay, glass	9 992	7.5	5.6
Chemicals	6 036	4.5	9.3
Instruments	5 966	4.5	3.2
Textiles	4 631	3.5	4.2
Ferrous and non-ferrous	3 355	2.5	4.6
Other transport	2 483	1.9	4.1
Food	538	0.4	12.9
Paper	220	0.2	5.9
Metal products	122	0.1	11.6
Subtotal: Electrical+ Automobile	75 934	56.8	24.5
Total	133 752	100.0*	100.0*

Note: *Aggregated total may not sum to 100 per cent exactly.

Source: As for Table 3.1.

In comparison to the sectoral distribution of total manufacturing employment, Japanese multinationals have in 1993 favoured three sectors in their European operations: electrical and electronic products (31.5 per cent versus 14.3 per cent), automobiles (25.3 per cent versus 10.2 per cent), and rubber and plastics (9 per cent versus 1.3 per cent), while they seem to have neglected sectors like food (0.4 per cent versus 12.9 per cent), metal products (0.1 per cent versus 11.6 per cent) and the paper industries (0.2 per cent versus 5.9 per cent). Overall, JDI investors seem to have favoured high-technology industries at the expense of low-technology industries in their choice of sectoral involvement in European manufacturing.

Japanese Direct Investment in Europe's Regions and Manufacturing Industries

Table 3.4 examines cross-industry differences in the choice of region by listing the most preferred regions for Japanese MNEs in each industrial

Table 3.4 Japanese investors' most preferred regions in Europe by sector, 1993

Industry	Regions	CRG 3*
Ferrous and non-ferrous	Madrid (E), Nordrhein-Westfalen (D), Ireland	78
Stone, clay, glass	Bruxelles (B), Île de France (F), West Midlands (UK)	74
Chemicals	Bayern (D), Zuid-Nederland (NL), Bruxelles (B)	54
Machinery	Bayern (D), Niedersachsen (D), Nord-ovest (I)	31
Instruments	South-East (UK), Nord-ovest (I), B.-Württemberg (D)	· 36
Electrical products	Bayern (D), South-East (UK), South-West (UK)	37
Automobiles	Portugal, North (UK), West-Nederland (NL)	46
Other transport	Bassin Parisien (F), Noroeste (E), Este (E)	82
Food	Île de France (F), North-West (UK), B.-Württemberg (D)	92
Textile	South-East (UK), Lombardia (I), Portugal	59
Rubber and plastics	Île de France (F), Hessen (D), West Midlands (UK)	91

Note: *CRG 3 is the geographical concentration ratio of the three most important regions in terms of employment in Japanese subsidiaries.

Source: Toyo Keizai (1994).

sector. The list of regions in Table 3.4 confirms the earlier supposition that the choice of regions varies across industries. For example, in electrical and electronic products and automobiles, the lists of the most favoured regions are completely different. While the Japanese electrical and electronics firms are likely to choose Bayern (D), the South-East (UK) and the South-West (UK) as their manufacturing locations, the car manufacturers tend to be more prominent in Portugal, in the UK's North Region and in West Nederland (NL). This pattern of cross-industry difference in the choice of locations is also present in the other industries in Table 3.4.

Another interesting finding that emerges from Table 3.4 is that the geographic concentration of Japanese investment varies across industries. The right-hand column of Table 3.4 indicates the share of the three largest regions in the total employment of Japanese subsidiaries. Food, rubber and plastics, other transport equipment, ferrous and non-ferrous metals, and stone, clay and glass are the industries where, in each, more than 70 per cent of Japanese employment in Europe is concentrated in three favoured regions. By contrast, in the machinery, electrical and electronic products sector, and the instruments industries, the regional concentration of Japanese investment is relatively low, with approximately 30 per cent of Japanese employment concentrated in the three most popular regional locations. This suggests that Japanese direct investment is highly unevenly distributed among the manufacturing industries of the EU, as it also appears to be with regard to countries and regions.

Japanese Subsidiary Size in European Regions and Manufacturing Industries

The average number of employees for a Japanese manufacturing subsidiary in a given region, as shown in Table 3.5, varies greatly across the EU. Average size of Japanese subsidiaries is largest in the regions of Hessen (D) (1424 employees per subsidiary), Madrid (E) (1187), West Midlands (UK) (906) and Portugal (846). By contrast, in two regions where the Japanese presence is large, Wales (UK) (214) and South-East (UK) (440), the average subsidiary size is substantially smaller.

This apparent discrepancy may be explained by differences in the sectoral composition of Japanese direct investment from region to region. The last row of Table 3.5 gives the average size of a Japanese subsidiary in Europe in a given sector. The average Japanese subsidiary in the automobile industry has by far the largest size (1132 employees per subsidiary). It is followed by the stone, clay and glass industry (675) and the rubber and plastics industry (564).

Old and New Japanese Direct Investment in European Countries and Industries

Thus far the descriptive analysis has been static. The two tables that follow (Tables 3.6 and 3.7), introduce a dynamic element to the study. Japanese direct investment up to 1993 has been divided into two groups: investments made before the Single European Act (agreed late in 1985 and signed in 1986) on the one hand, and those from 1986 onwards. We have chosen the beginning of 1986 as the turning point because of the importance of the Single European Act for the building of what

Table 3.5 Average size of Japanese plants in Europe by region and industry, 1993

	FE	ST	CH	ME	MA	IN	EL	AU	TR	FO	TE	PA	PL	AVE
BELGIUM	42	1090	144		89	87	197	78					33	220
Vlaanderen			102		120	87	279	30					38	109
Wallonie	42	336			27			125					33	113
Brussels		3352	186				33						25	899
DENMARK							131							131
GERMANY	386	841	414		276	302	460	20		60	68	220	1139	381
Schleswig-Holstein														0
Hamburg	102				267	365	301							316
Niedersachsen	670				1307	629	168	20						564
Bremen							174							135
N/rhein-Westfalen			82		115	163					68	220	59	194
Hessen		841			131								3300	1424
Rheinland-Pfalz														0
Baden-W/berg			912		200	219	69			60				137
Bayern					468		861							747
Saarland														0
GREECE			166											166
SPAIN	1053	64	70		96		249	1792	208		112			455
Noroeste	267	64							341					341
Nordeste	1839				55		110	509						201
Madrid					186			1535						1187
Centro					181									181
Este			79		51		277	2390	142		112			509
Sur			43											43
FRANCE	324	1234		42	144	170	189	803	36	98	51		1602	427
Île de France	324	1234	17		121	166	152			98	73		2388	508
Bassin Parisien					202	251	238		36				30	151
Nord-Pas de Calais														0
Est					13	134	81							76
Ouest					240		396							318
Sud-ouest							84	803						84
Centre-est					116		10				7			234
Méditerranée							13							13

	FE	NF	ST	ME	MA	IN	EL	CH	AU	TR	FO	TE	PA	PL
IRELAND	*128*	*190*												*135*
ITALY	*30*		*26*		*112*	*98*	*200*				*189*		*34*	*197*
Nord-ovest	30		134		283	327	342		270		158			517
Lombardia		88			404	564	1006		270		95			116
Nord est					40	143	106				159			143
Emilia-Romagna														0
Centro			35								188			111
Lazio							150							150
Campania														0
Abruzzi-Molise														0
Sud													34	34
Sicilia	*335*		*271*											*271*
LUXEMBOURG		*549*	*150*						*71*	*15*				*366*
NETHERLANDS		*549*	*243*		*77*	*76*	*614*	*2379*					*73*	*397*
Noord-Holland			273			77	92							0
Oost-Holland			351		53	16	90	57	51	15			19	300
Zuid-Nederland			68		100	190	93	4700	90				87	81
West-Nederland			125	80		102		2142			272			761
PORTUGAL			*68*		*128*	*213*	*614*	*713*		*84*	*588*		*503*	*846*
UK	*93*	*760*						*1121*						*339*
North	93		20				242							338
Yorks & H/side						216	281						1	281
East Midlands								36			533			197
East Anglia			155											0
South-East					134	90		655			1456	513	79	440
South-West				80				664				608		636
West Midlands		1500			95	92		824				1151	2600	906
North-West					323	88		431				646	141	337
Wales			17		51	11				139		273	66	214
Scotland			82			45				29	181		130	132
Northern Ireland						165								165
Industry average	299	675	154	61	151	165	309	1132	146	64	205	220	564	338

Notes: FE=Ferrous and non-ferrous metals; ST=Stone & glass; CH=Chemicals; ME=Metal products; MA=Machinery; IN=Instruments; EL=Electrical; AU=Automobiles; TR= Transport equipment; FO=Food; TE=Textiles; PA= Paper & pulp; PL=Plastics & rubber.

Source: As for Table 3.4.

Table 3.6   Japanese investment in Europe by country before and after
1 January 1986 ($US millions)

Country	JDI Pre-1986	%	JDI Post-1985	%
United Kingdom	14 060	24.2	29 566	39.1
Germany	10 638	18.3	15 475	20.5
Spain	13 657	23.5	2 371	3.1
France	8 555	14.7	7 534	10.0
Netherlands	1 569	2.7	7 126	9.4
Portugal	2 807	4.8	4 414	5.8
Belgium	4 919	8.5	1 967	2.6
Italy	860	1.5	4 798	6.3
Republic of Ireland	866	1.5	1 698	2.2
Luxembourg	0	0.0	575	0.8
Greece	166	0.3	0	0.0
Denmark	0	0.0	131	0.2
Subtotal: UK + Germany	24 698	42.5	45 041	59.5
Total	58 097	100.0	75 655	100.0

Source: As for Table 3.4.

later became the European Union, and the drastic changes that have occured after the mid-1980s.

Table 3.6 shows the distribution of JDI in Europe by distinguishing between *old* (up to the end of 1985) and *new* (from 1986 onwards) Japanese direct investment. The percentage share of Japanese direct investment after 1985 is greater than the period before for a group of European countries (United Kingdom, Germany, the Netherlands, Ireland, Italy and Luxembourg) which have been to some extent the recent preferred destinations of Japanese direct investment in Europe. In contrast to this group of host countries, France, Belgium and especially Spain, have experienced a drop in their respective share when we look to the new Japanese direct investment (after 1985) in comparison to old investment (up to the end of 1985). For Spain, this table suggests that its entry into the European Community in 1986 did not provide any new visible impetus for Japanese investors to choose the country as a host location for their manufacturing investments. Concerning the share of the two host countries with the largest stocks of JDI (the United Kingdom and Germany), Table 3.6 shows that when we look to new investment, the share of these two countries is substantially higher (59.5 per cent), than for the old JDI (42.5 per cent).

Table 3.7 outlines the distribution of employment in Japanese subsidiaries in Europe by manufacturing sector, both before and after the

Table 3.7 Japanese investment in Europe by sector before and after
1 January 1986 ($US millions)

Industry	JDI Pre-1985	%	JDI Post-1985	%
Electrical products	18 514	31.9	23 600	31.2
Automobiles	12 473	21.5	21 347	28.2
Machinery	1 892	3.3	10 495	13.9
Rubber and plastics	11 166	19.2	922	1.2
Stone, clay, glass	4 091	7.0	5 901	7.8
Chemicals	2 737	4.7	3 229	4.3
Instruments	1 475	2.5	4 561	6.0
Textiles	1 125	1.9	3 506	4.6
Ferrous and non-ferrous	2 083	3.6	1 272	1.7
Other transport	1 972	3.4	511	0.7
Food	349	0.7	189	0.2
Paper	220	0.4	0	0.0
Metal products	0	0.0	122	0.2
Subtotal: electrical + automobile	30 987	53.3	44 947	59.4
Total	58 097	100.0*	75 655	100.0*

Note: Aggregated totals may not total 100 per cent exactly.

Source: As for Table 3.4.

beginning of 1986. Japanese new investments have focused more upon the machinery, instruments and textile sectors, compared with patterns in previous years. The shares of the two largest industries in terms of the extent of Japanese direct investment (electrical products and the automobile industry) remained almost unchanged (53.3 per cent before 1986 and 59.4 per cent after) while the shares of the old manufacturing industries (metal products, paper, food, other transport, ferrous and non-ferrous) dropped dramatically in the case of Japanese direct investments made after 1985.

Japanese direct investment made after 1985 has been directed mainly at the two largest traditional recipients in terms of their share of JDI, the UK and Germany, while Spain, Belgium and to some extent France seem to have been more successful in attracting JDI before the end of 1985. The distribution of JDI among NACE 2-digit European industries did not reveal significant differences when old and new investments are distinguished, except in the case of the machinery, textile and instruments industries. Japanese direct investment in Europe has been directed towards these three sectors to a greater extent after the end of 1985, in comparison with previous years. By contrast, the rubber and plastics, and the ferrous and non-ferrous sectors, seem to have been neglected by Japanese investors in recent years

CONCLUSION

This paper has analysed the pattern of Japanese foreign direct investment in European manufacturing industries by using a unique data-set which interprets the locational decisions of Japanese MNEs across regions, countries and industries. The main conclusion of this descriptive study is that the distribution of Japanese direct investment varies greatly across countries, across regions and across industries. Furthermore, the average size of a Japanese subsidiary varies substantially between regions and between industries.

The most favoured host countries are the UK and Germany, while the regions of Bayern (D), the South-East (UK), Île de France (F) and Este (E) are the four regions which have the largest regional share of employment attributable to Japanese investment in Europe in 1993. The electrical and electronic products sector and the automobile industry are the two manufacturing industries where Japanese MNEs have tended to concentrate their investment activities.

Old Japanese direct investment tends to be concentrated in Spain, France and Belgium, at least in so far as we compare the shares of investment in the latter made before the end of 1985 with the share after 1985. By contrast, the UK and Germany have received a greater volume of Japanese direct investment after 1985.

Elsewhere,[9] the present authors have completed an econometric study of the locational factors influencing Japanese direct investment in the European regions. This study addresses the question of the relative importance of country-specific and region-specific characteristics. In fact, both country and regional factors determine the distributional pattern of Japanese direct investment in the EU. These country-specific factors are the corporate tax rate, R&D capability and trade union activity. For the region-specific factors, labour costs, the level of unemployment and the existence of dense airflight networks have a significative influence upon the choice of a host region for inward investment.

Japanese multinational activity is thus highly diversified within the regions and industries of the European Union, and forms an increasingly important element of foreign manufacturing activity within the regions.

NOTES

1. See C.C. Coughlin, J.V. Terza and V. Arromdee, 'State Characteristics and the Location of Foreign Direct Investment within the United States', *Review of Economics and Statistics* (1991), pp. 675–83; N.J. Glickman and D.P. Woodward, 'The Location of Foreign Direct Investment in the United States: Patterns and Determinants', *International Regional Science Review* (1988), pp. 137–54; S. Hill and M. Munday, 'The UK Regional Distribution of Foreign Investment: Analysis and Determinants', *Regional Studies* (1992), pp. 535–44; I.B. Kravis and R.E. Lipsey, 'The Location of Overseas Production and Production for Export by U.S. Multinational Firms', *Journal of International Economics* (1982), pp. 201–23; R. Veugelers, 'Locational Determinants and Ranking of Host Countries: an Empirical Assessment', *Kyklos* (1991), pp. 363–82; H. Yamawaki, 'Location Decisions of Japanese Multinational Firms in European Manufacturing Industries', in K. Hughes, ed., *European Competitiveness* (Cambridge: Cambridge University Press, 1993), pp. 11–28.
2. Toyo Keizai, ed., *Kaigai Shinshutsu Kigyo Soran* (Directory of Japanese Multinational Corporations) (Tokyo: Toyo Keizai Shimposha, 1994).
3. The NACE (Nomenclature générale des activités économiques dans les Communautés Européennes) classification is the official industrial classification defined by the Eurostat.
4. This includes employees of domestic firms and employees of subsidiaries of foreign firms, including Japanese-owned.
5. Data on total employment are for 1991 and the statistical source is Eurostat (1994), *Regions Statistical Yearbook*, Theme 1, series A, Luxembourg.
6. The Southern regions are in Italy, Spain, Portugal and Greece.
7. See note 4.
8. Aggregated to the two-digit industry level (NACE-2).
9. J-M. Thiran and H. Yamawaki, *Regional and Country Determinants of Locational Decisions: Japanese Multinationals in European Manufacturing*, IRES Discussion Paper 9517 (Département des Sciences économiques Louvain: UCL, 1995).

4 The Rising Sun? The Japanese Contribution to the Local Economy in Wales

Max Munday,
Jonathan Morris
and
Barry Wilkinson[1]

INTRODUCTION

Japanese manufacturing investment has had a relatively long history in Wales, with pathfinder firms such as Sony and Matsushita entering the region during the mid-1970s. As a result of a series of expansions, and the entry of *second-wave* component manufacturing firms, the Japanese presence in Wales has increased dramatically and in 1994 employed an estimated 15 000 people in 33 manufacturing companies. Around a quarter of Japanese transplant manufacturing sector (TMS) employment in the UK is now in Wales. The longevity and size of the Japanese TMS in Wales provide ample material for a consideration of contribution to the local economy and the extent to which the presence of such investment corresponds to regional economic needs.

This paper examines the Japanese contribution to regional economic development. In the first section it will place inward investment into Wales in the context of regional economic development needs. The second section considers the growth and development of the Japanese TMS. The third section examines recent evidence which highlights the direct and indirect Japanese TMS impact on the Welsh economy. The final section contains conclusions and some inward investment policy lessons relevant to future attempts to attract Japanese firms.

Figure 4.1 Wales: Industrial sector share in total GDP, 1971, 1980 and 1990

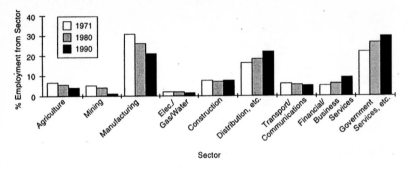

Sector

Source: Welsh Economic Trends, No. 15 (Cardiff: HMSO, 1994).

INWARD INVESTMENT AND THE WELSH ECONOMY

Wales, in common with many other peripheral regions of the UK, was subjected to considerable structural change during the 1970s and 1980s. For example, between 1975 and 1990 the number of employees within production and construction industries fell by some 125 000, reflecting significant losses in metal manufacturing and chemicals (68 000 jobs) and energy and water supply (38 000) jobs. The once dominant coal industry has virtually disappeared in terms of contribution to Welsh employment and GDP. Some consequences of the structural changes that have taken place in Wales are evident in Figure 4.1, which shows the contribution of key sectors to total Welsh employment for the years 1971, 1980 and 1990. The increasing share of employment taken by service sectors is evident, as is the decreasing share of employment in producer industries.

Recent history has seen some convergence of unemployment rates between Wales and the UK average. In spite of this convergence, Wales continues to be characterised by persistent disparities when considering other measures of economic well-being. Something of the nature of these disparities is shown in Table 4.1. On measures of personal wealth Wales is significantly behind most UK standard planning regions. GDP per head is some 15 per cent below average UK levels, with a fifth of household income in Wales coming from social security benefit. Whilst earnings in Welsh manufacturing are relatively high, the low rates of pay in the service sector mean that Welsh men are

Table 4.1   Welsh disparities, 1993

	Average Weekly Household Income	Share of Household Income from Social Security (%)	GDP per Head	Average Weekly Earnings for Males
Wales	£306	19.6	£7950	£308.3
UK	£353	13.9	£9385	£352.3
Wales as % of UK	86.7	n.a.	84.7	87.5

Source: Regional Trends 29 (London, HMSO, 1994); *Economic Trends* (Newport, CSO, 1995).

firmly at the bottom of the mainland pay league. The information in Table 4.1 also hides intra-regional disparity, with GDP per head figures in South Glamorgan significantly above those in the industrial South Wales valleys, West Wales and the rural counties. The remaining elements of regional policy for Wales are broadly set in this context of a need for well-paid employment in specific areas.

Significant regional policy resources in Wales have been devoted to marketing the regions to inward investors, providing factory units, financial assistance and after-care services. The policy objectives are clear. The Welsh Affairs Committee (1988) has stated that

> the policy of the Welsh Office and the agencies for which it is responsible is to seek to increase the flow (of inward investment) to improve the general prosperity of Wales, and in particular to increase employment opportunities. These benefits come from jobs provided or safeguarded by inward investment projects, through providing additional trading opportunities for industry already located in Wales, and through the stimulation of local industry through new ideas.[2]

Available statistics show that Wales has been particularly successful in attracting new foreign manufacturing. Hill and Munday have shown that between 1982 and 1992, Wales succeeded in attracting 545 new foreign projects,[3] which were connected with nearly 37 000 planned new jobs. Clearly, some care is required with these planned employment estimates, but on this basis Wales attracted some 16 per cent of the new foreign projects/jobs entering the UK over that period. A number of studies have attempted to show why it is that the region has performed so well in attracting new inward investment. Survey work based

Figure 4.2. Wales: Foreign manufacturing employment/real gross value added, 1983–91

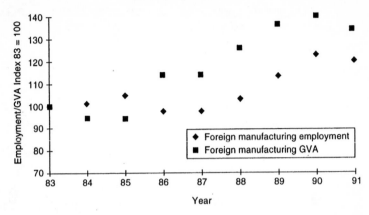

Note: 1983 = 100.

Source: Derived from Census of Production, PA1002 (various years).

on questionnaires has shown that factors such as labour availability and quality, infrastructure, financial assistance, plant availability and development agency after-care service have all been important. Empirical research points more to differences in relative levels of regional preferential assistance and infrastructure spending, together with Wales:UK manufacturing earnings ratios, as the most likely determinants of Welsh success.[4]

Foreign manufacturing firms employed some 68 000 people in Wales, or 32 per cent of the region's manufacturing employment, in 1994. Something of the scale of the growing contribution of the foreign sector to Wales is shown in Figure 4.2, which charts growth in foreign manufacturing employment and real gross value-added (GVA) between 1983 and 1991. While the growth of foreign manufacturing has historically been associated with firms of North American origin, the period 1983–91 saw increased involvement by firms of European and Japanese origin. For example, in the early 1970s over 85 per cent of foreign manufacturing employment in Wales was in firms of North American origin. By 1993, the proportion of foreign-owned company manufacturing employment attributable to North American firms had dropped to half (35 800 jobs), and nearly 40 per cent of foreign manufacturing employment was in firms of EC and Japanese origin. Between 1983 and 1991 firms from these two latter sources committed over £1.5 billion of investment to Wales, compared to £1.8 billion for North American firms. Regional dependence on one geographical source of foreign inward investment is clearly undesirable, and this diversification in geographical source, aided by Japanese (and EC) investment, has been a significant recent development.

THE GROWTH OF JAPANESE TMS IN WALES

The rapid growth of Japanese TMS employment in Wales is of comparatively recent origin. At the start of the 1980s Japanese firms employed just 2500 people. By 1985 this figure had risen to 3500 or 8.2 per cent of total foreign-owned manufacturing employment (1.7 per cent of Welsh manufacturing employment). Between 1985 and 1992 the total employed within Japanese subsidiaries grew at its fastest rate reaching just over 13 000 by 1992. Morris et al.[5] estimated that over 85 per cent of this employment was new as opposed to safeguarded. By 1994, employment in 33 Japanese manufacturing plants has been estimated at 15 000 people, with moderate increases forecast in the medium term.

Between 1980 and 1994, Japanese manufacturing employment came from a situation of not being separately listed in Welsh statistics, to a situation where it is estimated that Japanese firms account for around a fifth of regional foreign manufacturing employment. The growth of the Japanese TMS investment is shown in Figure 4.3, which also highlights the very recent nature of growth. The development of Japanese plants and projects essentially came in two phases. Between 1972 and 1985 there was slow growth in the number of new projects, but with this initial period witnessing pathfinder investments by firms such as Sony, Hitachi, Matsushita and Sharp. The growth of investment during the late 1980s reflected the large number of expansions projects in the existing Japanese OEMs (original equipment manufacturers) together with the entrance of second-wave component suppliers. Expansions projects were largely caused by increases in product lines manufactured by pathfinder plants. For example, during the 1980s Sharp at Wrexham moved from production of video cassettes only, towards manufacture of electronic typewriters, plain paper copiers and microwave ovens. The entrance of the second wave to some extent confirms the growing maturity of local Japanese investment and the need to increase local sourcing of key components (see Munday, 1995).[6] The growth during the 1980s also reflected an increase in the number of

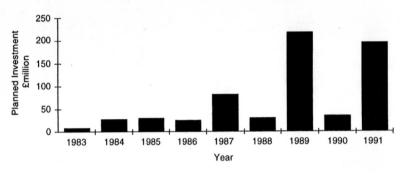

Figure 4.3 Growth of Japanese investment in Wales, 1983–91

Source: Welsh Development Agency.

plants each Japanese OEM had in Wales. For example, the Matsushita group moved from one to five separate plant locations in the region between 1986 and 1990.

The spectacular growth in employment caused by expansions projects is a singular characteristic of Japanese inward investment. Table 4.2 shows projects secured as well as associated employment by international source. Japanese projects accounted for nearly 30 per cent of foreign planned new jobs announced in Wales during the period 1983–91, and nearly 20 per cent of planned capital investment. Every Japanese project had on average a higher number of connected new jobs associated with it than projects from either North America or Europe, i.e. on average each Japanese expansion project was connected with planned employment of 154 people. The Far Eastern average capital expenditure per expansion project is also higher than that for North America and Europe, at £9.43 million per project. The table also shows that a high proportion of jobs connected with Japanese projects are new as opposed to safeguarded, reflecting the high proportion of greenfield Japanese manufacturing sites, rather than takeovers of domestic firms.

The Japanese TMS sector in Wales in terms of products and employment is shown in Table 4.3. A breakdown of this Japanese manufacturing employment by broad industrial sector shows that 60 per cent of employment provided has been in consumer electronics and office equipment production, and nearly 75 per cent of employment in these sectors is with Sony, Matsushita (Cardiff), Sharp and Hitachi. Over time, however, the number employed in other sectors has increased, with Wales attracting Japanese producers of automobile components.

Table 4.2 New foreign investment in Wales by nature of project

Source	Project Type	Number	Planned Jobs	New Planned Capital Investment (£m)
N. America	New	77	8 794	1 021.8
	Exp.	113	5 948	709.4
	Acq/JV	29	212	92.7
	Total	219	14 954	1 823.9
Europe	New	92	5 965	340.4
	Exp.	72	3 306	445.1
	Acq/JV	27	312	138.2
	Total	191	9 583	923.7
Japan	New	30	3 135	232.2
	Exp.	40	6 164	377.4
	Acq/JV	8	973	35.3
	Total	78	10 272	644.9

Source: Welsh Development Agency.

Table 4.3 Japanese companies in Wales: Product sector and employment, 1994

Sector	No. of Companies	Employment
Consumer electronics	6	7 485
Office machinery	4	1 507
Electronic components	5	1 699
Other electrical components	6	570
Automotive components	5	2 697
Other manufacturing	7	1 013
Total	33	14 971

Note: Employment figures are estimated and based upon survey data from Morris et al. (1993). Companies are characterised by their main product sector. The office machinery sector includes Star Micronics which went out of business during 1994, and the electronics components sector includes Race, which went into receivership in 1995.

Source: Based on Morris et al. (1993), adjusted for various company announcements during 1993–4.

The most notable examples are Calsonic, who took over the Llanelli Radiators facility in 1989, and Toyota at Deeside producing engines for the Toyota assembly plant in Burnaston, England. The majority of subsidiaries are wholly-owned by either one Japanese parent or a combination of Japanese interests, and the historical pattern until the late 1980s was for Japanese firms to enter through greenfield ventures. The one exception was the GEC – Hitachi joint venture at Hirwaun, which suffered innumerable problems and ended in 1984 with the Japanese partner taking over the operation. However, the period 1989–93 has seen more diversity in methods of entering the Welsh economy. During this period there have been two takeovers (Calsonic and Race), and a number of joint ventures: Ilbruck Koike, Gooding Sanken, Lucas SEI and R-Tek. The Gooding Sanken venture has since been taken over by the Japanese partner, and RACE electronics went into receivership in May 1995.

The subsidiaries encompass a broad spectrum of operations. Of the 25 Japanese plants in Wales responding to the survey of Morris et al.,[7] the following breakdown of activities was given: assembly (11 plants), assembly and manufacture (3), assembly, manufacture and development (7) and process (4). The majority of Japanese investments in Wales have gone through an assembly stage, before operations have matured and deepened, to assembly and manufacture, with development work in some well-established cases. One illustration is Sony at Bridgend, which initially assembled televisions. However, by 1994 the plant not only assembled, but also manufactured critical components such as cathode ray tubes and deflector yokes and a number of other components. The plant is considered to be a relatively vertically·integrated television plant.

THE JAPANESE CONTRIBUTION TO THE LOCAL ECONOMY?

In Wales, as in other peripheral regions, there is a desire for inward investment that diversifies and stabilises the local industrial base, creates local purchasing linkages, locates in areas of greatest economic need and engages in high value-added activities, rather than simple assembly operations. It was noted earlier that Wales also required high incomes in specific localities, so that pay levels within inward investors are an important consideration. Does Japanese investment meet these regional economic needs? This section reviews evidence from a number of studies that have examined the quality issues surrounding Japanese firms in Wales, particularly a survey completed by the authors between 1992–3, which sought to shed light on the economic and social consequences of Japanese manufacturing.

With regard to employment there is little doubt that Japanese firms have met the initial objectives of policy, creating a relatively large number of jobs in a short period. At the same time, the attraction of this employment has involved considerable public funding. Morris et al.[8] estimated that total financial assistance to Japanese manufacturing enterprises between 1981 and 1991 totalled around £42.5 million or approximately £7486 per job created. This is based on regional preferential assistance in terms of regional development grants and selective assistance, and it is clear that the true costs in attracting such investment go far beyond these figures. A number of studies in Wales have also addressed the issue of the quality of new employment created by Japanese investment (e.g. Morris, 1989;[9] Munday et al., 1995[10]). The main areas of concern with respect to the quality of employment are that inward investors from Japan (or elsewhere) may enter the local economy simply to take advantage of low factor costs, while gaining access to core markets in the South-East (see also Young, 1989[11]). The corollary is that this could lead to a high proportion of new employment for females and school-leavers (i.e. low-cost labour), and that employment provided is of an unskilled and routine nature, which in turn reduces the job experience of employees and the economic regenerative potential of inward investments.

Undoubtedly, females make up a considerable proportion of the Japanese company workforce in Wales. In overall terms, Morris et al.[12] reported that females made up some 50 per cent of the Japanese company workforce in Wales, with a high ratio of female to male employment in the plants involved in high-volume assembly operations. Such a high proportion is expected given that many of the Japanese manufacturers in this sector require dexterous skills in electronic goods assembly. Yet it was also shown that female employment as a percentage of total Japanese subsidiary workforces was declining over time as automation removes many assembly tasks and as some component production has been brought in-house by major manufacturers. Few Japanese manufacturers used a high proportion of school-leavers. While six companies reported that they had begun operations by taking on a high proportion of school-leavers, they had since developed more balanced workforces to promote stability. This had occurred because firms had suffered problems of high turnover, indiscipline and absenteeism. Hence, in 1992, Japanese company workforces were characterised by a greater range of ages than had previously been the case, with some new firms being scared off from using school-leavers due to the problems of established firms.

The jobs provided by the Japanese subsidiaries cover a number of levels from unskilled through to professional. The majority of jobs provided could be described as being of a semi-skilled nature. There are opportunities within the larger factories to rotate jobs and to learn other skills on the line. Multi-skilling is a precursor to further shop-floor promotion in many factories and is also a factor looked upon favourably during internal appraisal. In these cases the job experience of factory personnel is widened to a limited degree. With the continued automation of routine assembly tasks some of the most boring jobs will vanish in the near future. However, a large element of the routine survives in many of the larger Japanese factories.

The nature of employment provision is also reflected in pay levels. Japanese subsidiary financial reports for 1993 show that annual pay in 19 subsidiaries ranged from £9119 to £17 601. Lowest levels of pay are found in the more recently established producers of electronic components. The large consumer goods OEMs paid around £11 500 to £12 500, with the highest annual pay, i.e. above £13 000, being in the automotive, other manufacturing and process sectors. Hill and Munday,[13] reviewing similar data for 1992, found that 12 Japanese firms paid an average £10 191 per annum as compared to average foreign earnings in Wales of £15 374, and concluded that such disparities were largely due to sectoral differences in the makeup of the Japanese sample, i.e. a high proportion of Japanese employment in SIC 33/4, where pay levels nationally were relatively low.

Moving to a consideration of the location of Japanese investment, around 60 per cent of the employment created by Japanese manufacturing investment is clustered around Newport, Wrexham, Cardiff and Bridgend. In South Wales at least, the location of new Japanese enterprise would seem to be reinforcing existing spatial divides in the Welsh economy, with much of the investment clustered around what is essentially the M4 corridor. Such a placement pattern is to some extent inevitable given the infrastructure and labour requirements of such firms. It is also noted that some of the larger firms draw workforces from the large geographical area surrounding plants. In the case of Japanese manufacturers in Cardiff and Bridgend the labour catchment area includes some of the South Wales valleys hit hardest by structural readjustment during the 1970s and 1980s.

One additional policy objective in bringing foreign investment to Wales was the creation of trading opportunities for local firms. The existence of trading opportunities is important because payments made in the local economy to suppliers and service firms will have a beneficial multiplier effect. In addition to these possible trading opportunities, linkages with Japanese investors may provide the basis for the transfer of new ideas and best practice in operational technique to local suppliers.

Precise detail on the extent of local trading linkages and multiplier effects is difficult to assess because firms will rarely divulge their levels of local spending. Local Japanese firms are not required to purchase in Wales to meet either present or perceived future pressures on local content levels. In fact, Japanese firms, by purchasing only certain types of selected components within the EC, are normally able to meet EC requirements on local content levels. In practice this means that while electronic products such as power supplies, modulators, tuners, integrated circuits and discrete semiconductors are sourced in Europe, other goods such as capacitors, switches, relays resistors, less-basic semiconductors, magnetrons, crystals and PCBs may come from the Far East (see Intermatrix, 1991).[14] The majority of Japanese manufacturers in the Welsh economy have been shown to have fairly high levels of EC content. For example, Morris et al.[15] showed that the larger Japanese makers of consumer electronics equipment all had local content in excess of 50 per cent, with the common range being 60–80 per cent, varying by product. The highest levels of local content were found in those firms within the plastic processing/chemicals sector, where local content was as high as 95 per cent in three cases. Lowest levels of EC content were found in recently established Japanese enterprises producing either electronic components or sub-assemblies for the consumer electronics and office automation goods sectors. While Japanese firms reported that a high proportion of products came from Europe, many smaller electronic components were still purchased in the Far East. The Far East remains an important source for smaller select components because of purchasing economies, and the high search costs associated with redirecting business for a multitude of small parts.

The purchase of components in Wales is fairly limited. This is a common factor in foreign subsidiaries with Hill and Roberts[16] showing that on average local purchases made up 12 per cent of the total non-wage spending of sampled foreign firms in Wales (see also Turok, 1993).[17] For the Japanese, the most commonly bought locally made components included products such as plastic components and mouldings, metal pressings, metal parts, cartons and packaging, and printed materials. A limited number of more complex components were being bought from Japanese suppliers who had come to Wales. It has been in the interests of some Japanese assemblers to purchase as much as possible within a close radius of the plant site. Pressures in both physical and financial terms upon factory space has ensured the use of systems emphasising the accelerated flow of material through plants, prompt delivery of components and limited inventory holdings. In such a productive environment concise management of the supply chain is essential, not least when supplies are heavy and bulky in nature. In these special circumstances geographical proximity of suppliers aids the management process. Thus some Japanese companies in Wales have actively worked to develop the local supply infrastructure, particularly with regard to bulky and low-technology products.

Local trading linkages with Japanese manufacturers do have a further economic significance. Such linkages are a possible means of transferring best practice operational techniques. The Japanese have been keen to develop the local supply base through partnership-based relationships, as opposed to the more traditional style of buyer–supplier relationship where links are short-term, with an emphasis on quoted price and little shared information. In practical terms the *partnership principle* tends to link the manufacturer to a smaller number of suppliers on a longer-term basis with information on components production and final usage shared to aid technical collaboration and development work. A section of suppliers to local Japanese industry was surveyed by Munday[18] to find evidence of the existence of this partnership principle and to find evidence of collaborative relationships between buyer and supplier. The survey found some benefits for local suppliers who had been able to meet Japanese requirements. For example, winning business with one Japanese manufacturer was often a prelude to winning contracts with other Japanese plants in both Wales and the wider UK, with some suppliers noting that once linkage was in place, volumes had grown very quickly.

In some circumstances such suppliers had no longer needed to advertise but had just to manage growth and quality. Local suppliers had also perceived a genuine desire amongst Japanese plants to aid them in problem-solving. Other benefits resulting from linkages with Japanese firms had included uptake of Japanese quality standards. The long-run nature of the purchasing linkages with Japanese transplants had also given some suppliers the stability to undertake longer-term investment decision-making and production/resource planning. Furthermore, where partnerships had developed the Japanese were often anxious to extend the nature of linkage, with, in some circumstances, component-makers becoming involved in additional sub-assembly work connected with their products. While Japanese purchasing links in the local economy have been somewhat limited, there is evidence of the creation of local indirect employment. In addition, local suppliers who have won contracts have benefited from their close linkages with the Japanese in operational and commercial terms.

Local purchasing linkages are only one indicator of embeddedness in the regional economy. Plant autonomy is another important consideration. A foreign plant that is run tightly by its corporate headquarters many thousands of miles away may not be operated with the full local economic context in view. This can result in decisions having a crucial bearing on the future of the local economy being taken with little consideration for the local impact of these decisions. At another level, independent plants may allow a wider array of corporate functions with implications for the quality of employment. In this context, when Japanese plants in the local economy are large enough, they will create significant local direct and indirect economic effects, as well as both social and environmental externalities.

There is no single indicator of local plant-level autonomy. It is possible, however, to get an indication of autonomy from an examination of the strength of communications linkages with corporate head offices, the presence of expatriate management in the local structure, and the extent of corporate monitoring of subsidiary activities. In the study by Morris et al.,[19] 20 Japanese manufacturers gave details of reporting links. In 14 cases these reporting linkages were straight back to Japanese head offices rather than to European offices. In three other cases reporting linkage was complex due to joint venture agreements. In the case of only three Japanese enterprises was the initial reporting linkage to a European office. It was concluded that few Japanese parent companies had gone far towards localising reporting structures. In the majority of cases communication with the Japanese head office or parent was on a daily basis, with communications dominated by Japanese expatriate staffs. The content of daily communications included communication on technical matters and problem-solving, component ordering, sales and marketing information and personal matters involving Japanese staffs. Actual plant performance monitoring by Japanese head offices was usually carried out on a monthly basis, although in one plant in North Wales monitoring was on a weekly basis. The main monitoring linkage was via a monthly report which, as well as giving details of financial ratios, profit and loss, budget variance and output, would also in some instances provide details on productivity, development work, reject rates, local component usage and a number of quality parameters.

The level of autonomy of decision-making in Japanese plants is typically limited to day-to-day running of plants, with major decision-making on items such as investment and product done in conjunction with Japan. Evidence on communication linkage and plant monitoring points to a set of Japanese subsidiaries in Wales with strong links to head office. This is further evidenced by the position of Japanese personnel within subsidiaries. There are a number of sound reasons for the presence of Japanese personnel at the local level. Expatriate management aid the communication process, are often needed to aid the transfer of technology and processes from the parent organisation and are also needed to manage change. Within the majority of plants, nevertheless, the number of Japanese expatriates is declining. It is expensive for the parent firm to retain expatriate personnel locally. However, Japanese personnel still retain a number of key positions in local plant hierarchies.

The study by Morris et al. found that in 25 Japanese enterprises giving details there were just over 200 Japanese staff.[20] In only six cases were there more than 10 Japanese in a plant. Larger concentrations of Japanese staff were found in the producers of consumer electronics goods. Within the 28 Japanese manufacturing enterprises in Wales at 1992, all but seven still had a Japanese expatriate manager at the helm. Other Japanese personnel appear in a variety of roles, usually in technical, developmental, financial and quality management functions. In some cases Japanese managers sit as advisers to local senior management, a policy which has caused problems. Japanese personnel have thus been retained in many key positions within subsidiary organisational structures. This is further evidenced by the composition of the boards of directors of Japanese plants. The boards of directors of 20 Japanese subsidiaries in Wales in 1993 sampled from the subsidiary financial reports showed that out of 96 directors only 20 were non-Japanese. In 17 subsidiaries Japanese directors made up the majority, and in 8 cases there was no UK presence on the board.

In conclusion, the evidence on plant monitoring, reporting linkages and placement of expatriate personnel has indicated that Japanese plants have low levels of autonomy and decision-making authority. In this context, the scale of research and development carried out by Japanese plants in Wales remains limited. The presence of extensive R&D functions within subsidiaries can add greatly to the quality of subsidiary involvement and long-term prospects. R&D requires substantial investment in facilities and people, and importantly the presence of such functions can lead to significant technically based spin-offs in the local economy. Morris et al. reported that while the majority of surveyed plants were involved in development or design work, a low proportion exhibited extensive R&D work.[21] Design and development normally involved modification of Japanese-designed models for local usage, together with test and adaptation of locally produced components, and tooling. The absence of more basic research functions was also underlined by the small number of graduates employed. This absence of basic R&D may go some way towards explaining the generally low level of technical collaboration/industrial co-operation between local Japanese subsidiaries and local organisations in the region (excluding suppliers) which was brought out in the authors' survey.

CONCLUSIONS

Japanese manufacturing has certainly made a measurable economic contribution to the Welsh economy. The key economic benefits include stable manufacturing employment and a diversification of capital sources and products. It is also noted that the Japanese impact goes far beyond the economic, with significant demonstration effects in terms of new management techniques, industrial relations practices and methods of work organisation (see, for example, Wilkinson et al., 1993).[22] Yet, set against positive economic benefits are the substantial costs involved in attracting Japanese firms, and continuing questions about the long-term development potential of such investment, and its underlying quality. However, these latter concerns have been directed to inward investment from other sources in Wales, and are in no way criticisms specific to Japanese investors.

Wales faces a number of challenges with respect to the future attraction of inward investment from Japan. At one level the financial resources available to market the region to foreign investors and to provide appropriate services/grants have been dramatically reduced during the late 1980s and early 1990s. For example, government expenditure on regional preferential assistance to industry in Wales fell by some 50 per cent in money terms between 1988/9 and 1992/3. At one level the shortage of resources means that inward investment should be carefully targeted to ensure that the local economy attracts those foreign investors that contribute most to the cause of regional development. Yet this sort of targeting is problematic because forecasting future development potential is extremely difficult, as is measuring inward investment quality. This noted, some element of targeting has already taken place in Wales with agencies such as the WDA seeking second-wave Japanese components suppliers that have the potential to embed the Japanese OEMs more into the local economy and to provide the nexus for subcontracting clusters. However, even this policy has been shown to lead to problems because it may counter those local schemes that are attempting to develop the indigenous supply base (see Munday, 1995).[23] At another level, targeting is made difficult in practice by the excessive competition among an ever-widening array of European localities concerned with attracting Japanese inward investment.

In the face of these dual pressures policy prescriptions are somewhat muted. However, with special regard to Japanese inward investment we should note the following. First, in the light of a growing number of joint venture projects there may be a role for local development agencies to act as brokers between Japanese firms and potential local partners. Joint venture agreements may provide an effective method for skill and technology transfer, and may counter some of the negative aspects of plant dependence. Second, in the context of increasing competition to attract international capital, there may be a need for some policy resources to be devoted to those Japanese firms that are already in Wales. Correct after-care service may lead on to further expansions in existing facilities. Indeed, the growth of Japanese manufacturing employment in Wales has largely come from expansions in a small number of well-established OEMs. Finally, some policy resources might be used to attract other types of Japanese inward investment. Already by 1994, Wales had succeeded in attracting a number of Japanese service industry investments, including 12 firms in areas such as distribution, sales and marketing, freight-forwarding and the leisure industry. Although employment in these firms is relatively small, such investments can lead on to manufacturing or assembly work at a later date (see Collis and Roberts, 1992).[24] It may then be worthwhile for development agencies to attract and maintain relationships with these firms in the hope of fostering future expansions. By way of conclusion it may be noted that the steep decline of regional policy resources committed to Wales is of considerable concern, given the importance of financial aid and development area status in the location decision of firms of Japanese and other national origin.

NOTES

1. Max Munday and Barry Wilkinson, Cardiff Business School; Jonathan Morris, University of Glamorgan.
2. Welsh Affairs Committee, *Inward Investment into Wales and its Interaction with Regional and EEC Policies* (London: HMSO, 1988), p. 20.

3. S. Hill and M. Munday, *The Regional Distribution of Foreign Manufacturing in the UK* (London: Macmillan, 1994), pp. 38–9.
4. Welsh Affairs Committee, pp. 102–6.
5. J. Morris et al., *Working for the Japanese* (London: Athlone, 1993), pp. 37–9.
6. M. Munday, 'The Regional Consequences of the Japanese Second Wave', *Local Economy*, 10.1 (1995), pp. 4–20.
7. Welsh Affairs Committee, pp. 27–8.
8. Ibid., pp. 39–40.
9. J. Morris, 'Japanese Inward Investment and the Importation of Sub-Con-tracting Complexes', *Area*, 21 (1989), pp. 269–77.
10. M. Munday et al., 'Factories or Warehouses? A Welsh Perspective on Japanese Transplant Manufacturing', *Regional Studies,* 29.1 (1995), pp. 1–17.
11. S. Young, 'Scotland v. Wales in the Inward Investment Game', *Fraser of Allander Institute Quarterly Economic Commentary*, 14.3 (1989), pp. 59–63.
12. Welsh Affairs Committee, p. 43.
13. S. Hill and M. Munday, 'A Tale of Two Regions', *The South West Economy Trends and Prospects* (Plymouth: SWERC, forthcoming), pp. 45–59, at p. 56.
14. Intermatrix, *Market Opportunities for Electronic Component Manufactur-ers* (London: Department of Trade and Industry, 1991.
15. See Welsh Affairs Committee, p. 46.
16. S. Hill and A. Roberts 'Inward Investment and Regional Economic De-velopment', Paper delivered at the 17th annual ANZRSA Conference, New South Wales (December 1993).
17. I. Turok, 'Inward Investment and Local Linkages: How Deeply Embed-ded is Silicon Glen?', *Regional Studies*, 27.5 (1993), pp. 401–18.
18. M. Munday, 'The Financial Consequences of Linkages with Japanese Manufacturers', *Management Accounting,* 68.7 (1990), pp. 42–3.
19. Welsh Affairs Committee, pp. 51–4.
20. Ibid., p. 53.
21. Ibid., p. 29.
22. B. Wilkinson et al., 'Japan in Wales: A New IR?', *Industrial Relations Journal*, 24.4 (1993), pp. 273–83.
23. Morris et al., p. 18.
24. C. Collis and P. Roberts, 'FDI in the West Midlands: An Analysis and Evaluation', *Local Economy*, 7.2 (1992), pp. 114–31.

5 Learning From Japan: The Yeast for Britain's Manufacturing Regeneration?

Colin Haslam and Karel Williams,
with Andy Adcroft,
Sukhdev Johal and John Williams[1]

Learning from Japan is the title of a Department of Trade and Industry initiative, launched in 1993, to improve the performance of the UK auto components industry. The working assumption is that the Japanese production paradigm is different and is founded upon new manufacturing techniques which have transcendent virtues. These can therefore be accessed by British manufacturing industry and will work in the UK economy just as they do in Japan. Japanese parent firms and their transplant affiliates are identified *a priori* as centres of high performance and objects of emulation for host economy employees, who are then encouraged to participate in a process of self-criticism and value-reformation. Indeed, representatives of British component companies have featured prominently in a series of public meetings to disseminate the 'progress on steps they have taken in order to become world class, the benefits they have gained and their experience in implementing lean manufacturing principles'.[2]

Learning from Japan is also the title of this present paper about Japanese parent companies and their transplant affiliates in the UK, but with an element of scepticism or irony contained therein. Our paper presents the results of empirical work on both company accounts and official statistics, set in a simple framework which emphasises the importance of structural factors. Its working assumption is that firms which operate in one national economy will, in so far as they operate under similar structural conditions, produce broadly similar results regardless of differences in technique or ownership. This has a dual relevance for the issue of Foreign Direct Investment (FDI) in manufacturing.

First, and most obviously, it introduces empirical issues about the performance and prospects of transplant manufacturing affiliates to test the common presumption that these are sector leaders. Secondly, our approach redirects attention towards the parent economy and parent firm, together with structural factors influencing the generation of an investable surplus in the parent and its movement offshore into cost-recovering market access and/or cost-reducing low labour-cost production. As we shall argue, Japanese parents are now increasingly emerging as cash-strapped, high-wage companies which need to re-evaluate their foreign manufacturing strategy.

This paper returns to the themes of an earlier survey,[3] which observed a gross contradiction between the *a priori* assumption of high performance in foreign manufacturing transplants in both the US and UK, and the observable reality of mediocre performance. In the case of Japanese investors both sectors were relatively small and consisted of affiliates which were unprofitable, had unimpressive productivity levels and did not create significant numbers of jobs in the host economy because they relied heavily on components imported from Japan. The present paper, in effect, focuses upon *what has changed since then* and attempts to set these answers in a broader structural context, and in so doing reflects the conclusions of more recent work by the present authors.[4] This is concerned with the automobile industry and contains a methodology for analysing performance by deconstructing company reports and accounts. The first and most obvious effect of this new emphasis is that we begin by considering parent companies before turning, in the second half of this paper, to transplant performance.

JAPAN AFTER THE *HEISEI* BOOM

From a structural point of view, two basic points can be made about manufacturing direct investment. First, this kind of investment, like any other, requires the parent firm or sector to realise a cash surplus for capital over and above internal conversion costs, after purchases and labour have been paid for. Secondly, the capital surplus can be applied strategically to cost-recovery through investment in market access and/or to cost-reduction through low-wage production. These distinctions are important because they allow us to make the point that the end of the *Heisei* boom in Japan and the onset of recession marked the end of a trajectory; the Japanese manufacturing sector of the 1990s has a much smaller cash surplus and this must reinforce cost-reduction

Table 5.1 Per capita labour costs: Manufacturing sectors of selected countries ($US)

	France	Germany	Italy	UK	US	Japan	Korea
1983	17 288	19 088	14 026	12 793	23 099	14 518	5 162
1987	28 669	25 257	25 257	18 125	32 493	26 620	7 199
1989	29 423	31 857	28 630	21 301	30 829	30 963	12 464

Source: Eurostat, Series 4C, *Industrial Statistics Yearbook*; United Nations; *Yearbook of Labour Statistics* (International Labour Office, various years).

against the cost-recovery motives, which led to the opening of transplants in Europe and America.

In the period when the Japanese were particularly feared competitors, making large inroads in Western high-income markets, they benefited from a combination of low costs and high prices which generated large cash surpluses. As has been previously demonstrated,[5] the Japanese physical advantage over the Americans in terms of sectoral *build hours* was usually modest, but their financial advantage was overwhelming for two reasons. First, in every year up to and including 1985, the wages paid by Japanese assemblers were half or less of those paid in Detroit. Also, the prices obtained in the American market reflected the cost-recovery requirements of high-wage producers, which made the low-wage Japanese highly cash-generative. And it has been pointed out recently that the next generation of Asian new entrants has replicated this strategy: in cars, the Koreans have reduced build hours so that they are physically competitive, and thanks to low wages, hugely cash-generative. All through the 1980s, in both the auto and electrical/electronics sectors, Korean firms were realising 70 cents in the dollar as a cash surplus over labour costs, which precisely reverses the 30/70 split between capital and labour which is usual in Western manufacturing.

Japanese firms, in their heyday during the 1970s, were never as cash-generative as Korean companies in the 1980s, and Japanese cash generation was beginning to falter during the early 1990s for a variety of reasons. The first and most fundamental of these reasons has been rising real wage costs within the firm: indeed, the main lesson to be learned from the experience of Japanese firms so far is that rising real wages will, in due course, eliminate the competitive cost advantages of successful new entrants, as is evident in the case of Japan's domestic manufacturing industry as a whole, as shown in Table 5.1.

In the period of the high yen or *endaka,* the effects of rising wages were compounded by a rapid appreciation of the Japanese currency

Table 5.2 Value-added per employee, cash flow to sales and break-even point of operations in selected Japanese manufacturing sectors, 1983–93[a]

	1983	1988	1993
Automobile Industry			
Cash flow as % of sales	8.6	7.9	4.7
BEP as a percentage of operations[b]	73.1	84.1	95.0
VA/employee (million yen)	10.0	11.2	10.0
Domestic Electrical Appliance Industry			
Cash flow as % of sales	9.1	8.3	5.1
BEP as a percentage of operations[b]	67.8	76.3	93.6
VA/employee (million yen)	8.2	9.6	9.5
Industrial E&E Equipment/Computers			
Cash flow as a % of sales	10.0	9.8	6.0
BEP as a percentage of operations[b]	68.8	73.2	95.6
VA/employee (million yen)	9.6	10.8	9.7

Notes:
(a) The 44 Japanese companies surveyed account for 22 per cent of total Japanese manufacturing output.
(b) Break-even as a percentage of operations is calculated as labour costs plus depreciation as a percentage of the value added fund in each year.

Source: *Handbook of Industrial Financial Data* (Japan Development Bank, 1993); *Quarterly Survey* (Industrial Bank of Japan No. 100, 1994 IV).

against the dollar, with the yen trading steadily at 100 to the dollar, or lower, by early 1995. The Industrial Bank of Japan had in the previous year observed that every appreciation of 1 yen against the dollar reduced manufacturing net earnings by 5 billion yen. The effects of yen appreciation were also intensified due to earlier export success resulting in very high export/sales ratios: indeed the export/sales ratio was 50 per cent in cars, 55 per cent in consumer electronics and 70 per cent in electronic components.[6] And as exports became increasingly unprofitable, the competitive effects were compounded by a loss of capacity utilisation as the Japanese domestic market contracted after 1991, in the first serious recession since the mid-1970s. By 1994, in electrical and electronic engineering, in motor vehicles, and in general machinery, volume sales within the home market were 20 per cent down on the cyclical peak year of 1991.[7]

The Japanese manufacturing sector was ill-placed to meet this combination of demand difficulties and rising supply side costs. Table 5.2 illustrates this point by summarising the operating performance of 44 large Japanese corporations which are involved in the manufacture of cars and car components, electrical equipment or domestic electrical and electronic appliances. In each of the three sectors we have calculated the average value-added per employee in yen (millions), cash flow as a percentage of sales and the break-even point as a percentage of current operations.

The first observation must be that nominal value-added per employee, for all sectors, shows little if any increase between 1983 and 1993. Over this period Japanese corporations conceded increases in nominal pay levels and maintained (or increased) the level of employment. The only adjustment since the downturn in 1991 has been a reduction from 41 to 38 in the number of hours worked per week in manufacturing, although this reduction may also have been nominal.[8] Stagnant value-added productivity growth combined with gently rising labour costs to increase labour's share of value-added and reduce the level of internally generated cash flow from operations. In this 10-year period, cash flow generated as a percentage of sales revenue has, in all cases, been halved. Most of this decline has taken place in the Japanese recession of the early 1990s, although cash generation had deteriorated slightly by the late 1980s, when underlying problems were concealed by very high rates of capacity utilisation at the end of the boom period. The underlying deterioration in the operating characteristics of Japanese businesses is clearly illustrated from a calculation of the break-even point of current operations. This calculation establishes the level of capacity utilisation which has to be sustained before a positive contribution to net income is made from free cash after labour costs and depreciation have been covered. Significantly, in every major manufacturing sector the break-even point shifted upwards by 5–10 per cent during the 1980s due to the fact that the trajectory of nominal value-added growth was lower than the increase in nominal wage costs (numbers employed by the rise in nominal wages).

The irony is that by the late 1980s, as the uncritical adulation of Japanese production systems was reaching its peak in Europe and North America, it was becoming increasingly difficult to distinguish between the performance of many major Japanese manufacturers and their embarrassed Western competitors. Like the Germans, the Japanese were becoming high-cost producers who just managed to recover their costs by selling premium products, and only generated a cash surplus if high levels of capacity utilisation could be maintained. By 1993 in Japan, as throughout most of the 1980s in Germany, domestic manufacturers needed a 93–5 per cent rate of capacity utilisation before any cash

Table 5.3 Cumulative value of Japanese FDI, 1951–93

	Manufacturing ($US millions)	Non-Manu-facturing ($US millions)	% Manu-facturing	% Non-Manu-facturing	Total ($US millions)
Asia	28 350 (24.6)	36 975 (12.3)	43.4	56.6	65 325
North America	54 514 (47.3)	128 637 (42.8)	29.8	70.2	183 151
Latin America	7 277 (6.3)	42 562 (14.1)	14.6	85.4	49 839
Europe	19 372 (16.8)	61 859 (20.6)	23.9	76.1	81 231
Other regions	5 599 (5.0)	30 260 (10.2)	15.6	84.4	35 859
Total	115 112	300 293			415 405

Note: Figures in parentheses are the percentage regional shares of Japanese FDI.

Source: JETRO (Japanese Ministry of Finance) figures.

was generated. As a result, Japanese manufacturers, like their German counterparts, were desperately vulnerable to minor market downturns or shifts in the exchange rate. The lesson to be learned from this is that quite simply the internal techniques and management systems of Japanese manufacturers do not infallibly deliver super-profits and cash flow regardless of structural circumstance: these techniques may be a necessary condition for the maintenance of a financially robust business activity, but they are not in themselves sufficient. Changes in the overall context can negate gains (if any) from differences in management systems.

JAPANESE DIRECT INVESTMENT IN MANUFACTURING

Against this background we need to ask how, if at all, patterns of Japanese Foreign Direct Investment (FDI) and, more particularly, Manufacturing Direct Investment (MDI) have changed in character and direction. Table 5.3 looks first at long-run trends from 1951 to 1993. The first point to notice is that for Japan, as for other countries, most FDI is directed towards property, finance and other services, and not into manufacturing ventures: indeed, over the period in question 72 per cent went into sectors other than manufacturing. This is true of each of the main host regions with the significant partial exception of Asia, where a much higher proportion of Japanese FDI (43 per cent) went into manufacturing.

For our purposes we need to concentrate on MDI from Japan. When

Table 5.4   Global distribution of total Japanese manufacturing FDI: percentages

	Asia	Latin America	North America	Europe	Other Regions
1975	39.3	29.6	15.6	5.4	10.1
1980	36.6	21.3	19.3	7.0	15.8
1985	30.5	17.9	34.5	8.4	8.7
1990	23.6	8.5	50.7	12.0	5.2
1991	22.8	6.5	49.2	15.3	6.2
1992	27.2	7.4	45.3	21.6	−1.5
1993	32.9	3.3	37.3	18.3	8.2

Source: JETRO (Japanese Ministry of Finance) figures.

we do so it is not surprising to find that the lion's share (47 per cent) went to North America, but it is perhaps more surprising to find that over the entire period Asia (25 per cent) absorbed more Japanese manufacturing investment than Europe (17 per cent). One reasonable interpretation is that most Japanese MDI (over 70 per cent) is directed towards the Pacific Rim, a geographical expression which very loosely includes both the adjacent high-income markets of North America and the adjacent low-wage production areas of East Asia. The first area offers opportunities for cost recovery and the second area offers the possibility of cost reduction.

If we then consider the variation of MDI shares in more recent years, the basic picture is unchanged in its overall aspect: in these years after 1985 Asia and North America continue to account for between 65 and 75 per cent of the total. The main difference arises from the increased share going to Europe in the early 1990s, mostly at the (apparent) expense of Latin America. But even at its peak in 1992 the European share was relatively modest, and the really big shift in manufacturing location which took place during these years was the vast expansion into transplants in North America during the boom of the late 1980s. Less dramatic, but no less indicative, has been the restoration in the early 1990s of Asia's share (Table 5.4).

The motivation behind the recent switch to Asia reflects the problems referred to earlier for Japanese firms: they need to recover costs in a period of sharp recession and, as one response, they shift MDI to low-wage Asian countries which serve as sources for components. In the 1980s, when underlying weaknesses were less evident, Japanese firms could afford transplant investments in high-income regions like

North America as a way of reducing trade friction and investing in market access. Indeed, this motive has been repeatedly mentioned in corporate responses to official questionnaires right up to the end of the *Heisei* boom, prompting MITI to note that 'if the reasons for the movement by Japanese enterprises offshore are looked at, it can be seen that "expansion of local overseas markets" is the dominant reason given in the USA and Europe, with rates of 70.1 per cent and 76.4 per cent respectively'.[9]

With the Japanese economy entering a recession, this kind of transplant investment in market access was one which many Japanese parents could ill afford. Moreover, it was a form of investment which American subsidiaries could not sustain from their own resources because Japanese transplant manufacturing in America had never generated significant profits. This point emerges very clearly from the US Bureau of Commerce series (1994) on transplant profitability, which shows that Japanese manufacturing affiliates in the US have generally done no better than break-even, while at the same time their European counterparts have earned a respectable return on sales. By 1991, the American recession had taken its toll and Japanese affiliates were then making a net loss on sales of 5.4 per cent, while EU subsidiaries were containing their net loss on sales to just 0.32 per cent, and the British affiliates were still healthily profitable. If Japanese affiliates operating in the US had world-class performance characteristics, this was not reflected in a bottom-line profit surplus (Table 5.5).

The presence or absence of operating losses recorded by Japanese manufacturing affiliates in the US is of questionable significance due to the fact that Japanese distribution subsidiaries have traditionally been made to break even, usually through manipulation of input prices, so that cash and profits are directly realised in Japan by the parent for the purposes of minimising tax liability and reducing exchange-rate risk. If transfer-pricing is being used in the same way in Japanese manufacturing affiliates, it needs once again to be set in a 1990s context, given that Japanese corporations, by the early 1990s, needed this kind of support to buttress their fading internal surplus. And there is further scope for increasing this cash surplus if overseas MDI is redirected towards offshore production in low cost East Asian countries. The most recent JETRO White Paper on Foreign Direct Investment raises the spectre of a hollowing-out of domestic Japanese manufacturing industry as activity shifts to lower wage Asian sites, whereby

Table 5.5 Sales and profits of foreign manufacturing subsidiaries operating in the United States

		Sales ($ million)	Net Income ($million)	Profits/Sales %
Japanese Parent	1978	2 621	3	0.11
	1984	9 914	25	0.25
	1989	39 262	−460	−1.17
	1991	64 908	−3 526	−5.43
EU-12 Parent	1978	46 482	1 473	3.17
	1984	105 812	2 117	2.00
	1989	181 112	3 142	1.73
	1991	259 246	−837	−0.32

Sub-division of EU-12		Sales	% of EU-12	Net Income	Profit/Sales %
German Parent	1989	42 542	23.4	441	1.04
	1991	46 741	18.0	−653	−1.40
UK Parent	1989	73 802	40.7	2 327	3.15
	1991	83 449	32.2	2 084	2.50

Source: Foreign Direct Investment in the United States (US Dept of Commerce, various years).

the overseas business activities of Japanese corporations will lead to increased production overseas and a rise in the rate of overseas production in view of the probable absence of any major growth of exports. Further, international procurement involving imports from overseas production bases and imports of parts and materials from more cost advantageous regions is expected to be aggressively promoted and boosted.[10]

The Japanese electronics sector has long sourced entry-level products and simple components from Taiwan, Malaysia, Singapore and more recently China; the fear is now that 'Japanese high-tech manufacturing is on the move out of Japan'.[11]

While these important developments take place in East Asia, Europe remains relatively peripheral for Japanese manufacturers in their role as direct exporters and direct investors. With a population of 350 million, the EU contains as many high-income consumers as the United States. But, because it is half-way across the world, and a more diverse market, Europe has always been very much less important to Japanese multinationals. Japanese imports and transplants have 10 per cent of the European car market against 30 per cent in the US, and the Japanese have never succeeded in effectively eliminating indigenous

Table 5.6 Japanese manufacturing investment (MDI) as a percentage of merchandise exports (ME) to Europe

	MDI ($ million)	ME ($ million)	MDI/ME %
1987	852	45 544	1.9
1988	1 547	55 690	2.8
1989	1 545	55 968	2.8
1990	1 545	62 531	2.5
1991	4 593	68 263	6.7
1992	4 791	71 397	6.7
1993	2 041	64 012	3.2
Cumulative			
1987–93	16 914	423 405	4.0

Source: JETRO; OECD.

manufacturers of certain consumer electronic products as they did in the US. Consequently, the EU has received a much lower share of Japanese manufactured exports. Transplant manufacturing in Europe has emerged, as a result, as a small-scale supplement to this relatively low-key direct export effort. As Table 5.6 shows, the Japanese have in recent years sent less than 5 yen of direct investment for every 100 yen of direct merchandise exports.

Japanese parent firms have tried less hard with European transplants because the motive of market access operates much less strongly in what is for them a distant, relatively minor market. The strength of the access motive is confirmed by responses to official questionnaires, as well as by the geographical distribution of their manufacturing plants within the EU, as outlined in Table 5.7. Japanese transplant manufacturing operations have been generally located in or near the high-income markets of Northern Europe. By 1994, more than two-thirds of the total were located in the high-income markets of the UK, France, Germany and the Benelux countries. Within this favoured grouping, the UK transplant sector has the largest number of plants and the lion's share of automobile assembly plants established after the mid-1980s, with Nissan, Toyota and Honda now manufacturing in Britain. Clearly, therefore, the consequences of this influx upon the prospects and performance of British manufacturing are a major consideration in any analysis of Japanese investment in Europe.

Table 5.7 Growth of Japanese manufacturing plants in Europe by region, 1985–94

Country	No. Plants (1985)	No. Plants (1994)	Change 1985–94
UK	32	206	+174
France	30	121	+91
Germany	35	106	+71
Netherlands	16	45	+29
Belgium/ Luxembourg	15	43	+28
Spain	22	64	+42
Italy	8	52	+44
Others	31	91	+60
Total	189	728	+539

Source: JETRO.

THE JAPANESE TRANSPLANT SECTOR IN THE UK

The key questions about Japanese transplant manufacturing in the UK are relatively straightforward, with the first set of issues concerning the size of the sector and its backward linkages through purchases to the British economy and to the Japanese parent company. The second set of issues concerns the subsidiaries' performance in terms of profitability and value-added productivity. The answers to these questions are contentious, even though the empirical conclusions presented in an earlier paper by the present authors,[12] based on the statistical evidence of the late 1980s, have offered overwhelming evidence that the Japanese transplant sector was then small in size, mediocre in productivity, lacking in profit and probably heavily import-dependent. If the evidence was difficult to refute, its significance was challenged by a variant on the infant industry argument being used to suggest that the current size, linkages and financial performance of the UK's Japanese transplant sector was irrelevant because the sector was in its infant or start-up phase and could be expected to grow rapidly, develop local linkages and improve its performance. With the lapse of time and the change of circumstance since this debate began, we can now return to the evidence and consider whether our critics' optimism about the infant sector's prospects has been justified by the sector's subsequent development.

The first awkward fact is that the sector remains small in size and is no longer growing fast. Table 5.8 summarises the most up-to-date,

Table 5.8 Foreign affiliate shares of total UK manufacturing employment and value-added, 1991 (000s)

Ownership	Total Employment	% Total Employment	% Value-Added
Total	4506.4	100.0	100.0
UK-owned	3731.6	82.9	72.3
Foreign-owned	774.8	17.1	27.7
French	56.0	1.2	1.5
German	37.0	0.8	0.8
Japanese	56.6	1.3	1.6
Dutch	33.7	0.7	0.7
US	374.0	8.3	11.2
Others	217.5	4.8	11.9

Source: Business Monitor PA1002 (CSO, 1991).

publicly available and comprehensive evidence taken from the 1991 Census of Production. The table shows that in 1991, after a period of rapid growth from a very small base, the Japanese transplant sector employed just 57 000 workers or 1.3 per cent of the manufacturing workforce. This made it roughly comparable in size to the French affiliate sector, which is the largest of the EU transplant sectors and one sixth the size of the US affiliate sector, which still remains the only statistically significant foreign presence in UK manufacturing. The gap between the publication and collection of Census data is such that the evidence in Table 5.8 is, of course, four years out of date. But it is fairly certain that the sector has not expanded significantly in the intervening period because many Japanese transplants have been badly hurt by a recession which has caused parents to defer expansion plans and sack workers. In a 1994 JETRO survey of Japanese manufacturing affiliates operating in Europe, more than 80 per cent of respondents admitted they had been *hurt in one way or another* by the recent recession; when asked to be more specific about their responses, 38.7 per cent had *dismissed employees*, 36.6 per cent had *scaled back their manufacturing plans* and 31.8 per cent were *obliged to give up their intended capital investments*. Significantly, also, the British record may well be worse in the medium term because of the reliance on transplant car assembly by firms that are losing share or selling output by discounting their product.

The Japanese transplant sector in the UK is small for the same reason as the European transplant sectors are small; in a world of relatively free trade, just as in a region of relatively free trade, most manufacturing sectors prefer to serve foreign markets with direct exports from their

Table 5.9 UK–Japan balance of trade deficit, 1987–93 ($ millions)

Year	UK Imports from Japan	UK Exports to Japan	Balance of Trade
1987	5464	1495	3969
1988	5531	1743	3788
1989	7108	2260	4848
1990	6726	2596	4130
1991	6754	2258	4496
1992	7444	2227	5217
1993	8536	2740	5796

Source: PA 1023 UK Trade Statistics.

home base rather than establish overseas branch manufacture. Significantly, as Table 5.9 shows, the UK's trade deficit with Japan has not fallen since the establishment of transplant operations, although recession normally dampens the demand for imported manufactures; in the three recession years of 1991–3 the bilateral UK deficit on manufactures with Japan averaged $US5.1 billion, which was nearly 25 per cent higher than the average deficit of $US4.2 billion in the three boom years of 1987–9. The prospect of the appreciation of the yen against the pound sterling may now make direct exports from Japan less attractive, but that does not favour the transplants because they are heavily dependent upon imports of components from Japan.

The dependence on component imports is an important issue because it weakens the backward linkages to the domestic economy; a transplant sector with a high propensity to import is economically undesirable because it diverts added-value and employment from the host economy to the parent company. In an earlier paper on transplants a calculation of the Japanese transplants' propensity to import into the US could be derived from Bureau of Commerce data, but it could only be inferred that the position might be similar in the UK given that Japanese manufacturing transplants in the UK had a suspiciously low value-added/sales ratio.[13] A recent MITI survey does, however, now allow us to confirm earlier assumptions, using data presented in Table 5.10.

The broad position is that Japanese manufacturing plants in Asia, the US and the EU all import around 40 per cent of their procurement requirement from Japan. We are still not all that far from the situation of Japanese auto assemblers in the US in the early 1980s where two transplant units incorporated parts equal in value to one finished car directly exported from Japan. As for the level of local procurement from within the region, that is unusually low in the case of the EU,

Table 5.10   Procurement sources of Japanese manufacturing affiliates by
region, 1992

Regional Location of Japanese MFDI Affiliates	% Local Procurement	% Imported from Japan	% Imported from Third Country	% Total Import Content
Asia	48.5	37.9	8.9	46.8
US	51.7	42.1	6.2	48.3
EU	29.0	44.4	21.8	66.2
World	46.5	40.9	12.6	53.5

Source: MITI, *Overseas Business Activities of Japanese Corporations* (1992).

due in part to a significant amount of components and products originating in Asian subsidiaries of the Japanese parents; thus only 29 per cent of the value of EU sales is locally sourced against approximately half in the American and Asian cases. The key point to consider is that only one third of Japanese transplant purchases in Europe are sourced from the EU, and it is hard to see this changing given that, first, European electronic parts are an expensive substitute for low-wage Asian output; and, second, the capacity of the auto transplants to source within the EU is limited by the fragmented, low-volume nature of their operations. In the UK, three Japanese motor manufacturers build five models whose total output is less than 500 000 units per year. Low local procurement is a structural fact of life for the UK's Japanese transplants, engendering as it does more tied imports and less employment for the local economy.

If the Japanese transplant sector in the UK remains limited in scale and heavily dependent upon imported components, the profit and productivity performance has changed, albeit marginally, for the better. During the recent recession, profitability has undoubtedly deteriorated from the break-even position which was the norm in the late 1980s. According to a 1994 JETRO survey, 51.2 per cent of Japanese transplant affiliates in the EU were by 1992 making operating losses. The position in the UK is unlikely to be any better, so that in overall terms the transplant operations are now no longer a market opportunity, but more of a financial problem for Japanese parents themselves facing difficulties. Operating losses by UK affiliates must be covered by Japanese parents, which are chronically short of cash for the basic tasks of product and process renewal. This is the background against which the current round of redundancies, investment cutbacks and postponements of expansion in the UK's Japanese transplants may be understood. For many Japanese parents, damage limitation is now the name of the transplant game.

Table 5.11 Value-added per head and relative value-added per head of UK-based foreign and domestic affiliates (Manufacturing Divisions 2–4)

Location of Parent's HQ	Value-Added per Head (£) Nominal			Relative Value-Added per Head US-Owned Affiliates = 100		
	1983	1989	1991	1983	1989	1991
UK	12 947	20 149	23 657	72.3	59.0	75.2
EU-12	14 331	26 148	25 010	80.0	76.6	79.5
France	12 073	30 524	28 707	67.4	89.4	91.2
Germany	16 035	27 750	24 916	89.6	81.3	79.2
USA	17 906	34 153	31 464	100.0	100.0	100.0
Japan	13 880	23 523	30 572	77.5	68.9	97.2

Source: PA 1002 Census of Production, Table 18 (1983, 1989, 1991).

The one cause for optimism is an improvement of value-added productivity in the UK's Japanese transplants which is documented in Table 5.11. In the two years between 1989 and 1991, the UK's Japanese transplants substantially closed the gap with the US subsidiaries operating in the UK, whose productivity performance has long been one third better than that of indigenous, British-owned manufacturing firms. The performance improvement is not, however, without parallel and the observed improvement should not be attributed to superior techniques. As Table 5.11 shows, the French transplant sector managed much the same kind of productivity improvement over the period 1989–91, and that should make us cautious about attribution in relatively small sectors employing fewer than 60 000 as in the Japanese or French cases. Often, acquisition or expansion which takes the affiliates into new sectors is likely to be the main influence on productivity. The Japanese have in recent years built up a position in car assembly and component manu- facture which have traditionally been high-productivity sectors and this reduces the drag from electricals and electronics which are traditionally low-productivity sectors. A sectoral shift towards inherently high- productivity activities vindicates the structural interpretation, rather than the alternative, which emphasises world-beating innovative techniques.

Overall, the pattern of Japanese transplant performance confirms the structural prediction that affiliates which operate in a host economy under the same structural conditions as local firms will perform much as indigenous firms do. Large differences in hours worked and wages paid, just like differences in market access or product position, will produce large differences in performance. But the Japanese transplants in Europe cannot find advantage in this way because they must operate under the terms of national social settlements which put a floor under wages and a cap on hours. They have a marginal advantage from relocating to the peripheral regions of Britain where the writ of the Social Chapter does not apply, but they cannot escape the saturated and cyclical markets for autos and electronics in which they and indigenous firms must sell their output. If they cannot find cost-reduction advantage in the factory or cost-recovery advantage in the marketplace, it is hardly surprising that so many Japanese transplants turn in average performances.

CONCLUSION

The flood of Japanese manufacturing exports, especially in the very visible areas of cars and electricals, made it increasingly clear in the 1980s that Japan was outstripping its Western competitors. Not surprisingly, it gave rise to a similar flood of social scientific research and texts offering explanations. A popular and hitherto dominant conclusion was that Japanese industry had evolved a superior system of management and production. Perhaps the most influential of these texts was *The Machine that Changed the World*,[14] which popularised the term *lean production* and dubiously claimed to have discovered a 2:1 superiority in Japanese-style car production that was valid in manufacturing generally. On this reading what was to be learnt from Japan was a new and better paradigm of production. The same lesson has been fostered by management consultants claiming to introduce UK firms to the benefits of Japanese world-class production.[15] The gains from emulation are equally stressed in the DTI's *Learning from Japan* initiative.

One particularly direct way of securing renewal in Western national manufacturing centres thus seemed to be through the opening of Japanese transplant factories. These would bring with them both the productive practice and management knowledge behind these new and superior manufacturing techniques, and thus serve as the yeast for economic regeneration.

Our evidence questions the assumptions behind these interpretations and expectations. The uncomfortable experiences of Japanese industry apparent in the recent recession, epitomised by the high break-even point facing firms in many key sectors (Table 5.1), emphasises the extent to which Japanese success was dependent upon particular market and social conditions, as well as improved methods of production and management. There *were* improved techniques and there *were* better management practices, but much of the internal gain from these in terms of productive flow and cash generation stemmed from different structural conditions: typically an assured and growing home market, lower labour costs and longer hours. All this is quite graphically illustrated when the experience of transplant manufacturing subsidiaries is examined. As a consequence, far from effecting the direct transfer of Japanese productive virtues, their relatively ordinary performance in the UK and the US illustrates the extent to which operating in a common social and market environment tends to produce results which are more notable for their similarities than their differences.

NOTES

1. Colin Haslam, Royal Holloway College, University of London; Karel Williams and John Williams, University of Manchester; Andy Adcroft and Sukhdev Johal, University of East London.
2. Andersen Consulting, *World-wide Manufacturing Competitiveness Study: Implications for UK Companies* (London: 1995).
3. K. Williams, C. Haslam, J. Williams, A. Adcroft and S. Johal, *Factories v. Warehouses: Japanese Foreign Direct Investment in the UK and America*, University of East London Occasional Paper No. 6 (1992).
4. K. Williams, C. Haslam, S. Johal and J. Williams, *Cars: Analysis, History, Cases* (Oxford: Berg, 1994).
5. See William et al. (1992).
6. Industrial Bank of Japan, *Report on Currency Appreciation* (Tokyo: 1994).
7. Industrial Bank of Japan, *Monthly Report* (Tokyo: August 1994).
8. JETRO, *Nippon Business Facts and Figures* (Tokyo: 1994).
9. MITI, *Survey on Globalisation of the Japanese Economy* (Tokyo: 1991).
10. JETRO, *White Paper on Direct Investment* (Tokyo: March 1995), p. 35.
11. *Tokyo Business Today* (October 1993).
12. See Andersen Consulting (1995).
13. Ibid.
14. J. Womack, D. Jones and D. Roos, *The Machine That Changed the World* (New York: Rawson Associates, 1990).
15. Andersen Consulting, *The Lean Enterprise Benchmarking Project Report* (London: 1992); *World-wide Manufacturing Competitiveness Study* (Boston: 1994).

6 The Origins and Growth of Japanese Manufacturing in Ireland

James Darby
and
Max Munday[1]

The Republic of Ireland has been characterised as a *dependently industrialising peripheral economy.*[2] The same is true of Northern Ireland, despite the province's legacy of traditional industries and the strong political and financial support for industrial development extended by the British government. For potential investors it is true that Ireland has attractions as a point of entry into European markets, particularly to non-EU firms,[3] although the small size of the two economies, lack of locally available inputs and higher transportation costs are all disincentives. Nevertheless, as export platforms within the EU, both the Republic and Northern Ireland seem well suited to the type of investment which Japanese manufacturing firms have been making in other developed economies.

The externally-owned manufacturing sector is a vitally important component of industrial employment in Ireland, and it therefore seems worthwhile to investigate the limited but real success of attempts to attract Japanese manufacturing plants to sites in Ireland. In particular, the discontinuous pattern of Japanese establishment deserves attention as a source of insight into the dependent status of the Irish economies.

EARLY JAPANESE PROJECTS IN IRELAND

The Republic of Ireland had actively pursued a policy of attracting foreign-owned manufacturing subsidiaries since the late 1950s, in an attempt to change the country's status as one of the most under-industrialised and peripheral of the developed economies. The first two Japanese manufacturing investors in Ireland – Morinaga Milk Industry Company and Mitsui Mining and Smelting Company, each investing jointly with the Mitsui general trading company – established themselves in Ireland at the beginning of the 1970s. Morinaga chose in July 1971 to acquire a minority shareholding in a dairy products company in Donegal, while two years later the Mitsui Mining and Smelting Company, which like Morinaga had been involved in a major industrial poisoning case in Japan in the late 1960s, established a plant just east of Cork city to produce electrolytic manganese dioxide. This project was intended in part to 'save energy at home and eliminate the pollution costs of smelting',[4] and was followed by plans for another electrolytic smelting plant in 1978, again near Cork, this time involving the production of copper foil in a short-lived venture by Nihon Denkai.[5]

Early Japanese projects in Europe typically involved smaller, recently established and entrepreneurially led firms, with the larger, bureaucratic and hierarchical combines, mainly originating in the Meiji period at the end of the nineteenth century, following at their own pace. In Ireland the presence of the very largest Japanese companies among the early investors, which included Mitsui group affiliates and later Asahi Chemical and Nippon Electric projects, was noteworthy.

In Ireland in the early and mid-1970s Japanese manufacturing investors were expanding overseas in some cases to dissociate themselves from the environmental crisis in Japan which they had helped to create. In other cases they were attracted by potential market opportunities and the availability of suitable sites and resources, which were becoming more expensive, as well as environmentally questionable, in their own country. Although potential barriers to highly competitive Japanese imports were subsequently to emerge as the principal motivating factor behind the establishment of Japanese factories in Europe, in Ireland projects by firms in some of the less competitive sectors of Japanese industry, such as the food processing and chemicals sectors, were nevertheless prominent in the early years. Indeed, the early pattern of Japanese manufacturing investment in Europe has been characterised by a significant number of projects which were in less competitive sectors, or in chemicals-related industries, or involved in pollution-related activities, or by firms with a recent history of pollution in Japan, and this is clearly evident when the early history of Japanese manufacturing in Ireland is considered.

In the manufacture of synthetic fibres, unlike other parts of the chemicals industry, Japan had achieved a globally competitive status,[6] despite the fact that this was an industry which has continued to be both environmentally unattractive and unprofitable in its domestic operations. The third Japanese manufacturing project in Ireland, with

acrylic fibre and yarn produced at sister plants on the Atlantic coast of
Mayo, saw the Asahi Chemical Industry Company, supported by the
general trading company C. Itoh and the IDA, investing heavily in an
ambitious, capital-intensive venture. Unfortunately for Asahi, a major
recession in synthetic fibres was getting underway as the firm began to
establish its Irish operations, and the 1100 jobs forecast for 1981[7] never
fully materialised, and the venture incurred considerable losses. To the
credit of the Asahi management, great efforts were made to ensure
that the operation continued, unlike many of the foreign investors in
Ireland at this time, who were content to close down loss-making
operations.[8]

According to the influential Telesis Report,[9] which reviewed industrial
policy in the Republic of Ireland and was critical of the cost-effectiveness
of many of the procedures employed to attract inward investment, the
grant cost per job between 1973 and 1980 was highest in the textile
and chemicals sectors. Projects by Japanese manufacturers in this period
were particularly capital-intensive, although the Asahi project may have
accounted by itself for almost 40 per cent of the accumulated total at
the end of the decade.[10] With only a handful of sites, therefore, Japanese
manufacturing firms came to account for over 10 per cent of cumulative
inward investment in the Republic of Ireland by 1977.

At the beginning of the 1980s Japanese manufacturing plants in the
Republic of Ireland employed over 2000, and according to Japanese
Ministry of Finance figures, the investment totals were surpassed by
only three other EC member-states, and in no case by more than 20
per cent.[11] Together with the short-lived Nihon Denkai project, and
twin ventures by Noritake to produce ceramic tableware in Wicklow,
the late 1970s saw the emergence of Japanese electrical and electronics
sector investments in Ireland. Nippon Electric Corporation (NEC) in
1975, and Fujitsu in 1980, began to assemble and test integrated circuits
in greenfield plants which were located in, or close to, Dublin. Two
other short-lived projects also involved the production of audio equipment
by Toho after 1980 and computer accessories by Sord after 1981. Notably,
it was possible for the IDA to boast of Ireland's status as 'the leading
location for Japanese investment in Europe' at this time,[12] but the merits
of this claim were soon to be questioned.

Both Britain and France sought to attract Japanese investors in the
1980s as a means of creating jobs, particularly in peripheral regions,
and perhaps in so doing promote some transfer of process or product
technology, or the improvement of a secondary aspect of the monolithic
trade imbalance. The competitive pressures caused by the expansion

Table 6.1 Loss of employment in the earliest Japanese plants in Ireland, 1983–93

Company	1983	1993	Net Change
Donegal Dairy Products (Morinaga)	45	0	−45
Mitsui Denman	147	226	+79
Asahi	477	323	−154
NEC	250	354	+104
Noritake/Arklow	602	189	−413
Toho	150	0	−150
Sord	39	0	−39
Fujitsu	74	200	+126
Total	1784	1292	−492

Source: JETRO (September 1983), pp. 214–19; JETRO (October 1993), pp. 118–20.

of Japan's international business activities were also of greater direct concern to Britain and France than the Republic of Ireland, which was much less reliant upon indigenous firms for industrial growth. The French government, with some of the world's largest firms in the consumer electronics and automobile sectors to protect, was not afraid to try to constrain Japan to modify its trade and investment strategies in Europe, and the British government came to regard the establishment of Japanese manufacturing plants as a major tool of industrial relations reform in the UK, if not a major source of employment.[13]

As a consequence, the importance of multilocational policies by Japanese investors in Europe,[14] together with the high price the British government was prepared to pay for Japanese factories, meant that new Japanese projects were not common in Ireland until the late 1980s. By this time Japanese-owned manufacturing plants had also begun to appear in Northern Ireland, and the countdown to 1992, the establishment of a single market in the EC, had begun. Furthermore, existing Japanese firms in the south had also failed to expand according to earlier estimates and expectations.

Noritake closed one of its two plants with the result that only 150 were employed in 1987 in the remaining operation, down from 500 in 1975. Fujitsu and Sord both failed to approach anticipated employment totals of 1100 and 500 respectively, never achieving even a quarter of these target figures,[15] with Toho also failing to come close to the 630 jobs forecast for 1983.[16] By the mid-1980s, as a consequence, employment in Japanese-owned factories was down to around 1500 in total, following the additional closure of Toho, Sord, Nihon Denkai and the Morinaga joint venture, as well as redundancies at the Asahi operations in Mayo after 1982.[17] The decision by NEC in 1982 to build a semiconductor factory in Scotland which would eventually engage in wafer fabrication, rather than just the assembly and testing of integrated circuits,[18] was another stultifying factor in the attempts of the IDA to bring major Japanese projects to the Republic of Ireland, despite their willingness in this case to offer a larger investment subsidy.[19]

The Industrial Development Authority in Dublin has been given considerable discretionary powers, and with the opening of the Irish embassy in Tokyo in 1973 the IDA was able to begin a three-year promotional campaign in the following year directed towards Japanese firms. In view of the number of project decisions that were taken before 1974, problems with the 'defensibility of employment' in Japanese plants,[20] as well as the scarcity of viable new projects after 1975, meant that this cannot be viewed as a particularly successful initiative, however. The same could not be said of the four-year period which ran from the beginning of 1987 to the end of 1990, during which a promotional strategy to attract 35 new Japanese projects was implemented, with the greater part of this ambitious target achieved by the end of 1993.[21]

The climate for Japanese manufacturing in Europe in the mid-1980s was dominated by imbalances between the European Community and Japan in visible trade. It was assumed that local production in Europe would entail import substitution, in keeping with existing conceptions of the nature of inward investment, and in furtherance of this an EC draft proposal to extend the scope of anti-dumping duties to imported components used in local assembly appeared at the beginning of 1987.[22] An investigation of the dumping of photocopiers had begun in August 1985, resulting in the imposition of duties upon nine Japanese exporters.[23] This was followed by investigations of the export of typewriters, printers, excavators and microprocessors, and in all cases an increase in the number of Japanese plants assembling these products in Europe was the immediate result.

In host economies eager to attract inward investment, efforts were made to reassure potential Japanese investors that attempts would be made to curb the influence of new and existing trade laws, with the Irish Minister of Foreign Affairs, Gerard Collins, promising to restrain French-sponsored protectionism within the EC as part of a campaign to attract Japanese manufacturing investors.[24] The Industrial Development Board for Northern Ireland (IDB), for its part, addressed the issue of the impact of EC anti-dumping legislation as part of its promotional

Table 6.2 New investments in Europe by Japanese office equipment firms involved in EC anti-dumping investigations, 1985–8

Firm	UK	France	Germany	Italy	Ireland	Spain
Canon (C)	1991*	1984*	1973*	1987*		
Fuji (C)			1988			
Konica (C)			1987*			
Kyocera (C)	1989	1989				
Matsushita (C)	1988	1987	1987*			
Minolta (C)		1990*	1986*			
Ricoh (C)	1984*	1987*				
Sharp (C)	1987*	1989*				1986
Sanyo (C)	1988		1984			
Toshiba (C)	1991	1986*	1986			
Brother (P)	1985*				1989*	
NEC (P)	1987*		1990			
Fujitsu (P)	1990*				1989*	
Seiko Epson (P)	1987*	1988*	1986*			
Tokyo Electric (P)	1986		1986*			
Oki (P)	1987*					
Citizen (P)	1988*		1992			
Star Micronics (P)	1988*		1992			
Brother (T)	1985*				1989*	
Sharp (T)	1985*	1989				
Matsushita (T)	1987*	1987	1987			
Silver Reed (T)	1984*					
Canon (T)	1988	1984				

Notes:
Copier (C); Printer (P); Typewriter (T).
*Investments to produce same product.

Source: Calculated from JETRO (October 1993), pp. 67–137.

strategy,[25] and arranged seminars in Japan on the same subject to potential investors, highlighting the issue jointly with discussions of 1992.[26]

Following a small and now defunct investment in 1983 by the computer component firm Aval, and another project in Dublin two years later by Munekata to produce injection moulding equipment, Japanese-owned factories in Ireland began to emerge with much greater frequency after 1986. Dainippon Ink, with no fewer than 30 small manufacturing operations in Europe by 1993, was to establish its first Irish operation in south-west Dublin in 1987. At around the same time, the first Japanese firms in Europe involved in the manufacture of health-care products were establishing themselves in the Republic of Ireland, following continuing efforts by the IDA to target internationally mobile projects in this sector.

Table 6.3 Japanese manufacturing plants in Europe established after 1984 with more than 100 employees in 1993

Sector	UK	France	German	Italy	Ireland	Spain	Portugal	Netherlands	BL	NO	Austria	Total
Office automation	14	5	7	1	5			1				33
Consumer electronics	5	4	6			1			1			17
Electronic components	9	2	6	2	1						1	21
Electrical equipment	5	1	2	1		3	1			1		14
Vehicle assembly	5					1	1	1				8
Vehicle component	14	2	1			1			3			21
Construction equip.	1	1	3	1		1		1		1		9
Chemicals-related	8	3	6	2		2		2	1	1		25
Other industrial products	9	5	5	2		1	1		1		1	25
Other consumer products	9	3	1	4		2	1	1			1	22
Total	79	26	37	13	6	12	4	6	6	3	3	195

Notes:
BL = Belgium and Luxembourg; NO = Denmark, Norway and Finland.
Office automation includes copiers, typewriters, computers and related components.
Electrical and electronic components does not include OA components.
Vehicle components includes car audio and tyres.
Chemicals-related includes plastics, pharmaceuticals, cosmetics and synthetic fibres.

Source: Calculated from JETRO (October 1993), pp. 67–137.

Table 6.4 Wholly-owned Japanese manufacturing operations in computers and office automation in the Republic of Ireland, 1988–90

Japanese Company	Product	Location	Year	Employment
Alps Electric	Computer parts	Cork	1988	238
Fujitsu Isotec	Printer parts	Dublin	1988	176
Brother	OA components	Drogheda	1989	113
Oshima Kogyo	Printer parts	Dublin	1989	61
Mitsumi Electric	Computer parts	Cork	1990	223
Hitachi Koki	Computer printers	Dublin	1990(A)	232
Mitsubishi Kasei	Floppy disks	Limerick	1990(A)	496

Note: A = Acquisition.

Source: Calculated from IDA Ireland (February 1994), mimeo.[28]

In the decision of Yamanouchi to invest in a greenfield project near Dublin, and the choice of the acquisition method by Fujisawa Pharma–ceutical Company to acquire a plant in County Kerry, we can detect two continuing trends in the pattern of Japanese manufacturing establishment in Ireland. First, acquisitions are becoming more common, especially outside Dublin and surrounding counties. Despite the larger numbers of existing employees involved in many of these takeovers however, and their typically more peripheral locations, job-creation rather than job-preservation may be more clearly linked to greenfield plants, which are becoming more common in Dublin, the Pale around Dublin and the city of Cork. For this reason much of the rise in the numbers employed in Japanese-owned plants in Ireland after 1985 may be attributed to the growth of acquisitions, and this may in turn be largely attributed to the approaching single market in Europe, and the desire of Japanese companies to establish a local manufacturing presence.

In a parallel process, most of the greenfield projects that emerged in the same period are involved in the assembly of electronic equipment used in computers, printers, and typewriters, and may be linked to the EC anti-dumping campaigns of the mid-1980s, and Ireland's response to EC–Japan trade disputes. Seven of the 13 Japanese manufacturing operations that started between the beginning of 1988 and the end of 1990 may be connected to this development, according to IDA figures, and together they account for the greater part of job creation by Japanese firms in Ireland during the last 5, 10, or 15 years.[27]

Although foreign manufacturing firms were said to be favouring peripheral regions of the Irish Republic after the mid-1980s, rather than the Dublin area and Cork,[29] the reverse is true for Japanese investors.[30] This may be linked to the growing importance of electronic component assembly, which benefits more from access to international airports and higher-level communications facilities. These advantages are of lesser importance in the case of the heavier processing industries which were more likely to be established in the early years of Japanese manufacturing in Ireland. Only the UK, France and Germany have more Japanese electrical and electronic equipment and component plants than Ireland, and unlike every other country in Europe with the exception of the Netherlands, Ireland has more component than equipment operations among the Japanese-owned firms in this sector.

It is therefore surprising in a sector of manufacturing which mainly involves semi-skilled assembly work,[31] with labour costs as a critical factor, that competition from sites in Spain, Portugal and Greece has not been more evident, despite predictions based on the discernibly increasing attractiveness of more southerly locations for inward FDI in the EC in the 1980s.[32] Considering the status of Ireland as a food-exporting country it is also surprising that no Japanese projects in this sector have appeared since the demise of Morinaga in the early 1980s, especially as there are now no fewer than 20 Japanese food-related projects in France, including a recently established Morinaga joint venture to produce cheese.

It is also curious that the growth of Japanese vehicle assembly and vehicle component plants in Europe, and particularly the UK, has not resulted in any projects in the Republic of Ireland in this important area of industrial activity, even though firms like Brother and Mitsumi had made contemporary investments in electronic equipment on both sides of the Irish Sea in the late 1980s. Despite their absence south of the border, however, Japanese vehicle component projects did begin to appear in Ireland after 1988, but were to establish themselves in Northern Ireland, where they form a significant part of the small but growing number of Japanese manufacturing firms in that province.

EARLY JAPANESE PROJECTS IN NORTHERN IRELAND

There are differences in the pattern of Japanese manufacturing operations in Northern Ireland and the Republic of Ireland which cannot easily be explained by differences in local conditions such as access to markets and the cost and availability of the factors of production. As open, peripheral economies within the EC, disadvantaged by higher transport and energy costs, both parts of Ireland have a restricted industrial base. This narrow base is in turn highly dependent upon trade and exhibits a very high degree of external ownership, particularly in technologically intensive and export-oriented sectors. Demographic features are also similar in some important respects, with increasing populations on both sides of the border, high dependency ratios and high levels of un-employment.[33] From the viewpoint of a potential Japanese investor, therefore, these are important similarities, which might have produced identical patterns of manufacturing investment, were it not for certain features associated with politics or international political economy.

Northern Ireland's continuing political problems certainly inhibited and delayed the early appearance of Japanese manufacturing operations in the province. Some of the projects which were established in the Republic of Ireland, or Wales, or Scotland, would have come to Northern Ireland in the 1970s if The Troubles had begun a decade later. The politics of trade and investment in the EC in the mid-1980s nevertheless encouraged an appreciable number of projects to establish themselves on both sides of the border after 1985, with some specialisation according to sector suggesting that the IDA and their counterparts the IDB in Belfast were not in direct competition for all types of Japanese inward investment.

As well as the intensification of EC anti-dumping investigations in the mid-1980s, preparation for a single European market in cars, as it affected Japanese car exports and local production, became a major preoccupation for Japanese interests. The strong support for Japanese trade and investment strategies in Europe, which was extended by both the British and Irish governments during this crucial period, resulted in the growth of Japanese-owned operations in Northern Ireland and the Republic in the late 1980s. Along with information and medical technology, and clothing and textiles, auto component investments are a targeted sector for the IDB.[34] Of the five Japanese manufacturing projects in Northern Ireland in 1993, three are concerned with producing automotive components, one operation acquired by Kyocera in 1989 makes components associated with integrated circuits, and the longest-established Japanese firm, Canyon, produces plastic spray guns. Northern Ireland has also benefited recently from a number of investments originating in other parts of the Asia-Pacific region, notably four Korean consumer electronics plants, and in this respect, at least, seems to compare favourably with recent experience in the Republic of Ireland.

In 1985 there were no plants in Northern Ireland owned by Far Eastern companies, but by 1990 5 per cent of plants and 8 per cent of employment in foreign-owned manufacturing operations was attributable to this source, compared to totals of 4 per cent and 5 per cent respectively for Scotland.[35] The total number employed in these plants had in the process risen from a handful in 1986 to around 1500 in 1990.[36] Before 1985, however, the efforts of the IDB and the British government had not succeeded in attracting any investment from this source, after a series of apparently unsuccessful overtures to the representatives of Japanese big business.

The first Japanese company to invest in the province, Iwax, began pilot production of disposable cigarette lighters in Ballymoney in 1985.[37] The IDB stressed that Iwax had received 'no special favours'[38] in addition to £2 million grant assistance, but the project was never to reach the anticipated employment total of 120, and despite a growing market in Europe, was to fold after only three years of production. The first two products to be manufactured in Northern Ireland by Japanese firms were unglamorous and low-tech, like many of the early projects that appeared in Britain in the mid-1970s. After Iwax, the Canyon Corporation began producing plastic trigger spray guns at a site just north of Belfast in 1987, in another greenfield venture which was to create more than 100 jobs.

Employment in Japanese-owned plants was to expand considerably in 1988 and 1989, however, mainly as a result of two acquisitions of companies with sizeable existing workforces, at plants located in East Belfast, Coleraine and Larne. In 1988 Takata acquired a plant formerly owned by a General Motors subsidiary, and now with over 800 employees produces car seatbelts and door and window locks in Dundonald, a few miles east of Belfast. The following year the Kyocera Corporation, which had been involved in an EC anti-dumping action between 1985 and 1987,[39] purchased a 100 per cent stake in the European operations of the American company AVX, which produced ceramic capacitors in England and France, as well as at two plants in Northern Ireland.

Until the mid-1980s Japanese manufacturing investors in Europe seemed reluctant to acquire European capacity, preferring to invest in subsidised greenfield projects with hand-picked and under-unionised workforces. In Northern Ireland, however, the acquisition method permitted largely non-Japanese management teams to remain in control, and reduced the necessity of posting Japanese managers and engineers to the province. Even so, the fifth Japanese manufacturer to invest in Northern Ireland, the automotive castings firm Ryobi, appointed an American manager from the company's Indiana plant to take charge of their new plant in Carrickfergus in 1990, despite the project's greenfield status.

Ryobi produce aluminium castings, mainly for Ford of Germany, in a highly automated plant with fewer than 50 employees.[40] Takata, as Japan's largest producer of air bags as well as seatbelts, has recently begun to manufacture air bags for passenger cars at a new plant in the Kennedy Way Industrial Estate, just off the upper Falls Road. The locations of the previous Japanese investments, in Ballymoney, Newtownabbey, Larne, Coleraine, Dundonald and Carrickfergus, have all been close to the largest concentrations of Protestant population in the province. Clearly, persuading foreign firms to invest in north or west Belfast is one of the most difficult tasks facing the IDB,[41] while the cost of attracting firms to the province as a whole, and the scale of benefits that they bring have also been seen as problematic.

COSTS AND BENEFITS

The question of costs and benefits associated with Japanese investment in both Northern Ireland and the Republic of Ireland is a matter of considerable concern, in so far as the attraction of Japanese investment involves significant expenditures on items which include overseas regional promotion, and capital grants. For example, IDB promotional efforts in the Asia-Pacific region involved spending of £6.3 million in the period 1988–91, which accounted for around 40 per cent of total IDB promotional expenditure, following the opening of new premises in Tokyo and a new office in Seoul in 1987.[42]

Figures which reveal the cost of persuading foreign firms to create jobs in Northern Ireland and the Republic of Ireland are not available for Japanese investment specifically, but aggregate calculations suggest a figure of £115 564 per job for the Republic between 1983 and 1989, and £20 344 per job in Northern Ireland for the period 1986–91.[43] Although there is no indication that jobs which have been created or maintained through Japanese investment would have cost any less than this, it is important to recognise that the time and money spent on promoting Ireland and providing grants to Japanese firms has been associated with significant opportunity costs, inasmuch as financial assistance and advisory services could equally have been used in the support of indigenous industry and related initiatives. However, it has been suggested elsewhere that the opportunity costs associated with attracting foreign investment to the Republic of Ireland have not been substantial, in that there has been little indigenous displacement and that domestic firms have not been excluded from grant aid. In effect, overseas industry has produced a substantial economic return in output, employment, foreign exchange earnings and presence in high-technology sectors [and] given the weakness of indigenous industry it is difficult to be confident that the diversion of funds from overseas industry to indigenous would have produced comparable returns, even in the longer term.[44]

How far such a conclusion can be extended to Japanese subsidiaries is questionable, however, and requires some reference to the costs and benefits particularly associated with investment from this source, even though the relatively small number of firms involved may make this separate evaluation problematic. Among the key questions to be considered, the choice of location is the first key indication of likely long-term impact, not only in terms of country choice, but also in relation to the size of local markets and the quality of locally available inputs.

Secondly, there is the question of what investors actually do in terms of assembly, manufacture, product development and research, bearing in mind that regional authorities normally prefer investment which is characterised by a wide range of skilled functions. This then raises the question of the correspondence between foreign operations and local economic development needs, which typically include job-creation in particular localities, as well as raising income levels, earning foreign exchange, promoting industrial stability and diversification, and developing local supply linkages. Furthermore, Japanese investment may be particularly associated with the dissemination of new types of work organisation, personnel management techniques and industrial relations practices to domestic firms.

In the majority of cases, Japanese manufacturing investment in the Republic of Ireland has been shown to have been attracted primarily by attractive tax and capital incentives, together with the availability of a suitable labour force.[45] This motivation pattern has been consonant with the initial Irish policy objective of attracting investors wishing to export a substantial proportion of their output. Clearly, motivations based solely on cost criteria, such as a desire to minimise costs of production whilst gaining access to both product and factor markets, has been representative of many Japanese projects in the Republic. These have been typically based around the processes of final assembly, testing, inspection and packaging for export.

Japanese investment in the Republic of Ireland has created employment, although compared to direct investments from North America and the

Table 6.5 Japanese investment in the Republic of Ireland: employment in February 1994

Type of Investment	Number	Employment
Manufacturing companies	27	3612
Financial services	6	65
Japanese school	1	48
Non-manufacturing companies	6	n.a.
Japanese minority holdings	7	1123
Joint ventures/technical agreements	4	n.a.

Source: IDA Dublin.

UK, the Japanese contribution has been relatively small. In 1990 15 Japanese manufacturing establishments provided around 2140 jobs, or some 1 per cent of manufacturing employment.[46] In relative terms, Japanese penetration of the Irish economy was similar in scale to its presence in the UK, where in 1990 104 Japanese enterprises employed just under 40 000, representing not quite 1 per cent of UK manufacturing employment.[47] Yet the number of establishments in the Republic of Ireland has grown rapidly since 1990, and IDA data indicated that by 1994, 27 majority-owned Japanese manufacturing companies employed more than 3600.

From the point of view of local economic development it is important to distinguish between jobs that are created by new projects and those maintained through acquisitions. However, judging true additionality is made problematic by the fact that some takeovers of existing operations do lead to genuine job safeguards or further expansions. Bearing this in mind, it is apparent that among the 3600 jobs in Japanese subsidiaries, approximately 1000 are the result of six acquisitions which have mostly taken place since 1990.

Table 6.5 summarises job-creation by Japanese companies in the Republic of Ireland and indicates that the process has not been limited to the manufacturing sector. Several Japanese financial services firms have branches in Dublin, including Daiwa, Mitsubishi Trust and Sanwa Bank. The non-manufacturing sector also contains three firms involved in the high-technology sector, including a Hitachi laboratory in Dublin engaged in information technology research and development, and Sumitomo at the University of Limerick conducting lightwave technology research. The employment generated in the non-manufacturing and financial services sectors is at present fairly small, but together with a number of technical agreements and minority holdings in manufacturing

Table 6.6 Location of Japanese manufacturers in the Republic of Ireland, 1994

Region	Number of Plants	Employment*
Dublin	11	1045
South-east	1	12
South-west	3	561
Mid-west	5	747
West	2	345
North-west	0	0
Midlands-east	5	902
Total	27	3612E

Note: *Employment total includes two small firms where employment is estimated.

Source: IDA Dublin.

concerns, it indicates a diversified Japanese presence in the Irish economy, with the emergence of R&D facilities being of particular note.

Other questions regarding the nature of job creation have focused upon plant location, project durability and the choice of industrial sector. The Irish government has attempted since the 1950s to encourage inward investment to locate away from the more populous and developed Dublin and eastern coastal areas, and towards the western periphery of the country, where there is a need for stable non-agricultural jobs and the raising of income levels. Indeed, a perceptible shift towards the western periphery during the 1980s, led by foreign firms who accounted for nearly 50 per cent of employment in the western periphery by 1989, has been detected.[48] It would seem, however, that the Japanese firms operating in 1994 have shown more of a preference for the east of the country, with the Dublin area hosting nine establishments, as well as two takeovers (Table 6.6).

There is a concentration of Japanese manufacturing investment in the mid-west region, mainly attributable to acquisitions involving Fujisawa in Kerry and Mitsubishi Kasei near Limerick. Other areas in the west have not, however, benefited significantly, particularly in recent years, suggesting that Japanese firms now have a tendency to avoid the least developed areas of the Irish Republic. However, analysis of the spatial distribution of foreign establishments highlighted the plight of the Dublin area with respect to the loss of manufacturing employment, with nearly 27 000 jobs lost between 1981 and 1989. In so far as the western periphery lost relatively fewer manufacturing jobs than eastern areas in the period 1981–9, then the arrival of Japanese manufacturers after 1985 in Dublin county is of some economic significance, despite the small net employment contribution.

It has been demonstrated that foreign manufacturing in Wales and the south-west of England has contributed to a greater stability in overall local manufacturing employment, with foreign manufacturers in these regions less prone to the effects of recession.[49] In Wales, for example, Japanese manufacturing employment was found to be particularly stable, with only one major closure in a history of Japanese investment spanning two decades. Declining traditional sectors in peripheral areas make the stability of jobs resulting from inward investment, and more importantly the incomes they provide, of correspondingly greater value to the economy. Nevertheless, there is a prevailing fear that heavily subsidised branch plants, with their choice of location determined mainly by the size and availability of grants, will only provide employment for limited periods.

The foreign sector in the Republic of Ireland generally performs well in this respect, with the survival rate of foreign jobs, generated after 1978 and still in existence in 1988, being around 52 per cent compared to just 43 per cent in indigenous firms.[50] It would seem, however, that Japanese investment in the Republic of Ireland is less durable than other parts of the foreign-owned sector. By 1993, eight Japanese manufacturing plants had closed with the loss of approximately 730 jobs. When it is considered that Japanese plants had only created around 2600 additional jobs by 1994, these losses are relatively high, with the largest losses occurring as a result of closures at Noritake, Toho, Sord and Atari, whose combined peak employment levels by 1986 had been 590 jobs.[51] Added to this there has been an erosion of employment at Noritake Arklow Potteries and Asahi Spinning, totalling around 560 jobs. Closures in the electronics sector are perhaps testimony to the marginal nature of these plants, with more rapid investment and disinvestment encouraged by the routine assembly-based nature of operations.

In terms of industrial sector, Japanese manufacturing establishments have contributed significantly to Irish employment in electronics and engineering (Table 6.7), and in so doing have to some extent furthered sectoral diversification. Between 1981 and 1990 over 8500 jobs were added to the electronics and office automation sector in the Irish Republic, with Japanese firms making an important contribution of approximately 7 per cent to employment in this sector.[52] The remaining major industry is chemicals and pharmaceuticals, where Japanese firms employ nearly 700 people, or approximately 5 per cent of employment in this sector.

Table 6.7   Japanese manufacturing in the Republic of Ireland by industry, February 1994

Sector	Number	Employment
Non-ferrous metals	1	100
Ceramics	2	210
Chemicals	6	696
Metal products	1	61
Electrical/electronic engineering	12	2159
Instrument engineering	2	112
Other	3	274
Total	27	3612

Source: IDA Dublin.

The Irish Census of Production provides information which can be used to analyse, in comparative terms, the productivity, pay and linkages of Japanese manufacturers in the Republic of Ireland. Data from the Census of Production is summarised in Table 6.8. The information on earnings is clearly disappointing, with average Japanese earnings below that of Irish firms in 1990. However, it should be noted that earnings reflect the industrial sector of investments, and the large number of Japanese jobs in the electronics sector may partially explain lower relative earnings, with higher average earnings expected in general engineering and transport. Even so, the low average earnings are of some concern and hint at the routinised nature of semi-skilled operations in electronics plants, as well as gender imbalance in workforces, and the relative absence of higher level functions.

It is also worth noting that these data refer to 1990, and there may be some expectation that earnings differentials will converge as the Japanese sector matures. The table also shows that earnings levels in Japanese plants in the Irish Republic were very similar to earnings levels in Japanese subsidiaries in the UK at the same time. Measures of net output per head tell us something of employee productivity, as well as relative capital intensity. Net output per capita in Japanese subsidiaries is relatively high at £147 500, and well in excess of that in the domestic sector. Interestingly, it is also higher than net output per head in Japanese subsidiaries in the UK at 1990, hence relative to the domestic Irish sector, Japanese subsidiaries are shown to be more productive.

Net output as a percentage of gross output tells us something about the extent to which firms add value to their industrial inputs. On this

Table 6.8 Japanese investment: key manufacturing statistics from the Irish Census of Industrial Production and the UK Census of Production

	Average earnings (£I & £Sterling)	Net output per employee	Net output Gross output	% Domestic materials
Irish-owned firms	£I11 585	£I26 500	31.1%	68.3%
All foreign firms	£I13 844	£I69 100	55.9%	29.4%
Japanese firms (ROI)	£I11 539	£I47 500	51.0%	16.9%
Japanese firms (UK)	£11 980	£42 990	37.4%	n.a.

Source: Irish Census of Production (1990); UK Census of Production, PA1002, Summary Tables (1990).

measure Japanese firms compare favourably with the overall foreign sector average. A low ratio of net to gross output is one possible indicator of assembly operations using a high proportion of bought-in materials. Figures in Table 6.8 should be treated with extreme caution due to the ability of foreign firms to adjust the prices of interdivisional transfers.

A critical feature of linkage to the host economy is the extent to which foreign companies purchase local products, and in so doing support employment in other firms. Table 6.8 shows that domestic firms source nearly 70 per cent of their materials locally, with Japanese sourcing levels considerably lower. It may be noted, however, that many of these subsidiaries are fairly new, with the expectation that buyer–supplier linkages will intensify over time. In addition, the specialised nature of some components used by Japanese electronic assemblers are unlikely to be available in the Republic of Ireland, and must therefore be imported.

Japanese transplants in the Republic of Ireland have therefore had a limited economic impact, although some jobs have been created, and Irish manufacturing industry has become a little more diversified. Against this, only a fraction of employment has been newly created or additional, with the stability of employment in Japanese manufacturing subsidiaries remaining a matter of concern. Some Japanese plants have been present in the Republic of Ireland for over two decades, with the employment outlook in long-established plants uncertain in the face of product maturity, as in the case of the Asahi project.

Indirect employment creation has also been limited by the nature of supplier linkages between the Japanese-owned sector and local firms, while the small size of this sector has tended to mitigate against significant transmission effects in terms of work organisation and personnel management. There is, for example, very little evidence that Japanese firms have been the agents of industrial relations change in Ireland that they have been suggested to be in some areas of the UK.[53] Nevertheless, in its favour Japanese investment in the Republic of Ireland can be shown to be relatively productive as well as an earner of foreign exchange, given that the majority of products are produced for overseas markets. Furthermore, there has been some success in attracting Japanese investment in industrial sectors where other peripheral regions of the UK and Europe have hitherto failed to secure projects, such as pharmaceuticals. In addition, the Irish Republic has also received some R&D investment involving leading Japanese firms.

Turning to Japanese investment in Northern Ireland, it is perhaps too early to comment upon its economic impact. The Japanese sector in the province comprises six firms employing just over 2000 people, although the creation of additional employment has been limited inasmuch as well over 80 per cent of jobs in the Japanese sector are the result of acquisitions by Kyocera and Takata. Northern Ireland differs from the Republic of Ireland in so far as three investments, Ryobi, Takata and ESS Automotive, are concerned with manufacturing auto components, while no Japanese plants in this sector have chosen to locate south of the border. The redistribution of foreign manufacturing employment to the periphery that occurred in the UK during the 1970s and 1980s was not felt in the province, as foreign manufacturing employment fell to a low of 13 600 in Northern Ireland by 1989. Nevertheless, since then, Japanese investment in the province has helped to stabilise foreign manufacturing employment, although in terms of locational choice, jobs in Japanese plants have tended to mass around the largest concentrations of new investment in Northern Ireland, rather than the remoter areas of the province and the most intractable unemployment blackspots.

The question of costs and benefits is an important issue for these two small economies, given that the attraction of inward investment must ultimately be paid for by British and Irish taxpayers, whose income is ultimately determined by the size and growth of their national economies. These efforts need to be realistically linked to the likely scale of the benefits which inward investment might bring to either the Republic of Ireland or Northern Ireland, or to any region where the attraction of inward investment is a basic industrial policy. Inevitably, the singular features of Japanese manufacturing investment and the importance of European economic integration must be recognised as powerful influences upon the success of these policies.

CONCLUSION: JAPANESE FIRMS AND THE EUROPEAN PERIPHERY

The discontinuous pattern of Japanese investment in Ireland and its reliance upon external factors for growth can be best explained in terms of economic dependence and changes in the global political economy. There is a large dependence on imported inputs in Ireland, and the typical foreign manufacturing subsidiary exports 90 per cent of output, imports 80 per cent of material inputs, and is therefore engaged in assembly or processing work which involves low levels of local content.[54] Indeed, between 1988 and 1992 the import of materials for further production accounted for 56–9 per cent of the value of total exports of industrial produce for the Republic of Ireland.[55]

A manufacturing environment which typically involves low levels of local content, and where linked trade and investment strategies are unlikely to undermine domestic firms, would therefore seem to offer ideal locations for the Japanese investor within Europe. The volume of Japanese manufacturing investment in Ireland, with just over 5 per cent of operations and about 3 per cent of employment in all subsidiaries in Europe with Japanese investment, can therefore be regarded as surprisingly low. To explain this apparent insufficiency, objective operating criteria and the efforts of promotional agencies within Ireland can be at least partly discounted, with external economic and political factors recognised as significant influences upon the pattern of establishment. For the Republic of Ireland this has meant that the UK's status as the most likely alternative location for inward investment[56] has been reinforced by British support for Japan's economic expansion in Europe, and some projects have been diverted to Britain as a consequence. In the case of the auto components industry, for example, no Japanese projects have been established in the Republic of Ireland, even though domestic employment in this sector tripled between 1980 and 1987,[57] and three Japanese plants in this sector appeared after 1988 in Northern Ireland.

Both the United Kingdom and the Republic of Ireland receive most of their inward investment from countries outside Europe,[58] and this might seem to suggest that the successful attraction of Japanese manufacturing firms would be continuing a well-established tradition. However, the changing global climate for mobile investment projects, and in particular the end, in the 1980s, of the strongest phase of US multinational expansion,[59] may have come to question the merits of a full-blown industrial policy strategy of *industrialisation-by-invitation*.

Japan's choice of investment locations in Europe may be more carefully chosen, as well as increasingly restricted to the more important and larger markets, because of the importance of linked trade and investment strategies which differ from those of other multinationals.

The strategy of increasing the value and sophistication of products manufactured in Japan, and developing markets for these products overseas, requires a measure of tolerance and support in potential foreign markets, and in Europe this means that the countries with larger economies or more problematic trade deficits are those that receive a greater share of Japanese manufacturing investment.[60] Despite a positive attitude to Japanese interests, and a manufacturing environment which is highly appropriate for the Japanese type of assembly operation in Europe, the Republic of Ireland nevertheless had in 1992 more plants owned by Swedish firms than by Japanese companies, with more jobs.

The small size of the Irish economy, and its consequent limited influence upon European policy-making in the areas of trade and industrial policies, seems to be a limiting factor in any campaign for more Japanese investment. Political factors may divert Japanese projects to other countries in Europe, and those that establish themselves may engage in the assembly of products with low levels of local content, with more sophisticated components sourced from Japan. The role of inward investment from other countries may also be limited, with a dependence upon existing subsidiaries likely to become more pressing as the supply of mobile projects decreases.[61] Diminishing prospects for higher-value marketing and engineering operations engendered by the Republic of Ireland's status as a tax haven,[62] as well as a likely imitation of Japanese multilocational policies by non-Japanese firms, could also serve to confirm the gloomy conclusion of the Telesis Report that the role of overseas industry in industrialisation is ultimately limited.[63]

Although the prospects for a great increase in Japanese manufacturing investment in Ireland are therefore not considerable, some positive transfers have taken place, and some jobs have been created, particularly since 1987. In both Northern Ireland and the Republic of Ireland, nevertheless, only 2 per cent of manufacturing employment, and 5 per cent of externally-owned manufacturing employment, is attributable to Japanese-owned firms, with comparable figures for the UK as a whole of just over 1 per cent, and 7 per cent, respectively. Perhaps surprisingly, also, the UK, the Republic of Ireland and Northern Ireland have broadly similar numbers of manufacturing jobs in local Japanese firms, when adjusted for population. Compared with other European countries they are all receiving considerable shares of Japanese investment, although the absolute totals of jobs created or maintained may be seen to be disappointing when the size of domestic manufacturing sectors, the scale of mass unemployment, and the volume of existing American- and European-owned plants is considered.

The evolution of Japanese manufacturing in Ireland is instructive mainly in so far as it reveals the indirectness of the influences which both increase and decrease the flow of new projects, and control the form which they ultimately take. Largely due to environmental problems in Japan in the 1960s, Ireland received its first batch of Japanese manufacturing operations in the 1970s. Largely due to the European Commission's anti-dumping actions of the mid-1980s, as well the desire of Japanese firms to establish themselves in Europe before 1992, Ireland started to receive a significant number of new Japanese projects once again after 1985. Furthermore, because of the UK government's support for minimal restrictions on the growth of Japanese trade and investment in Europe, particularly in the automobile sector, Japanese firms began to consider establishing themselves in Northern Ireland in the late 1980s. Hence, after a long period of obvious hesitation, and helped by a new willingness to acquire existing concerns, the efforts of the IDB and the British investment lobby came to be rewarded by the appearance of Japanese-owned factories.

Northern Ireland and the Republic of Ireland are both wholly peripheral regions of Europe. In considering the impact of Japanese manufacturing upon these two small economies, therefore, a wider question concerning the consequences for the more developed core and less developed periphery in Europe begins to present itself. The UK is at the same time one of the larger European economies, a strong supporter of free trade, and part of both the core and the periphery of the European economy. For these reasons a disproportionate amount of Japanese manufacturing investment in Europe establishes itself in the UK. The attraction of core locations may increase as the complexity of Japanese involvement increases in the years to come, and this might not be to the disadvantage of the UK as a whole, unless of course it becomes an entirely peripheral part of the European economy. For Northern Ireland and the Republic of Ireland, however, such a change would further marginalise economies which already face the twin challenges of development and modernisation.

The positive transfers associated with inward investment depend upon the level of local content in assembly plants, as well as the scale of operations, and there is evidence that these benefits are undergoing a structural change, as all foreign multinationals come to be influenced by the example of Japanese strategies for global expansion. While Japanese manufacturers seem no less willing than other foreign investors to choose peripheral locations for their plants in Europe, the scale of their contribution to industrial development strategies, except at the local level, is never likely to be more than marginal. For peripheral regions of Europe, therefore, especially where the attraction of inward investment is the basis of industrial development policies, the direct and indirect impact of Japanese economic growth in Europe is likely to be equivocal, questioning the basic strategy of industrialisation-by-invitation.

NOTES

1. Dr James Darby, Queen's University of Belfast; Dr Max Munday, Cardiff Business School.
2. D. Jacobson, 'Theorising Irish Industrialisation: The Case of the Motor Industry', *Science and Society*, Vol. 53, No. 2 (Summer 1989), p. 187.
3. D. O'Hearn, 'Global Competition, Europe and Irish Peripherality', *Economic and Social Review*, Vol. 24, No. 2 (January 1993), p. 179.
4. T. Ozawa, *Multinationalism, Japanese Style* (Princeton: Princeton University Press, 1979), p. 177.
5. Industrial Development Authority (IDA), *Annual Report* (IDA: Dublin, 1978), p. 16.
6. *The Economist*, 7 April 1979.
7. *Irish Times*, 25 April 1974, 3 October 1975.
8. *Sunday Tribune*, 24 April 1983; P. Breathnach, 'Japanese Manufacturing Investment in the Republic of Ireland', *Area*, Vol. 29 (1989), p. 28.
9. National Economic and Social Council (NESC), *A Review of Industrial Policy* (*Telesis Report*), Report No. 64 (1982), Section 6.2.
10. *Financial Times*, 8 December 1981.
11. Ministry of Finance, Government of Japan, *Direct Overseas Investment Registered During Fiscal 1982* (Tokyo, May 1983).
12. *Financial Times*, 8 December 1981.
13. F. Peck and I. Stone, 'Japanese Inward Investment in the Northeast of England: Reassessing "Japanisation"', *Environment and Planning C*, Vol. 11 (1993), p. 66.
14. R. Mayuya and D. Jacobson, 'Japanese Direct Investment in Ireland', *Irish Business and Administrative Research*, Vol. 12 (1991), p. 122.
15. Breathnach (1989), p. 30.
16. IDA, *Annual Report* (1978), p. 16.
17. Breathnach (1989), p. 30.
18. *Financial Times*, 2 September 1980, 11 August 1981.
19. *Financial Times*, 2 June 1980.
20. NESC (1982), p. 149.

21. *Irish Times*, 25 September 1989; Breathnach (1989), p. 31.
22. *Financial Times*, 2 January 1987.
23. *Financial Times*, 24 February 1987.
24. *Irish Times*, 18 May 1991.
25. Industrial Development Board (IDB), *Annual Report*, 1990/1, p. 53.
26. IDB, *Annual Report*, 1988/9, p. 48.
27. IDA, *Japanese Investment in Ireland* (February 1994), mimeo.
28. IDB, *Annual Report*, 1988/9.
29. P.J. Drudy, 'The Regional Impact of Overseas Industry', in A. Foley and D. McAleese, eds., *Overseas Industry in Ireland* (Dublin: Gill and Macmillan, 1991), p. 166.
30. Breathnach (1989), p. 31.
31. J. Wickham, 'Dependence and State Structure: Foreign Firms and Industrial Policy in the Republic of Ireland', in O. Höll, ed., *Small States in Europe and Dependence* (Vienna: Bramuller, 1983), p. 170.
32. Breathnach (1989), p. 33; B.G. James, *Trojan Horse* (London: Mercury Books, 1989), p. 238; D. Jacobson and B. Andréosso, 'Ireland as a Location for Multinational Investment', in A. Foley and M. Mulreany, eds., *The Single European Market and the Irish Economy* (Dublin: Institute of Public Administration, 1990), p. 312.
33. Department of Finance and Personnel, *Northern Ireland Structural Funds Plan 1994–99* (Belfast: 1993), pp. 77–8.
34. IDB, *Forward Strategy 1991–93* (Belfast: December 1990), p. 18.
35. Northern Ireland Economic Council (NIEC), Report No. 99, *Inward Investment in Northern Ireland* (Belfast: November 1992), pp. 39–40.
36. D. Hamilton, 'Foreign Investment and Industrial Development in Northern Ireland', in P. Teague, ed., *The Economy of Northern Ireland* (London: Lawrence and Wishart, 1993), p. 197.
37. IDB, *Annual Report*, 1985–6.
38. *Financial Times*, 3 November 1984.
39. *Financial Times*, 24 February 1987.
40. *Financial Times*, 2 March 1994.
41. *Financial Times*, 17 January 1994.
42. NIEC (November 1992), p. 62; IDB *Annual Reports* (1987–8, 1990–1).
43. NIEC (November 1992), p. 53; D. McAleese and A. Foley, 'The Role of Overseas Industry in Industrial Development', in A. Foley and D. McAleese, eds., *Overseas Industry in Ireland* (Dublin: Gill & Macmillan, 1991), p. 18.
44. Ibid., p. 23.
45. R. Mayuya and D. Jacobson, in *Irish Business and Administrative Research* (1991), p. 115; Breathnach (1989), p. 28.
46. *Census of Industrial Production* (Dublin: Central Statistical Office, 1990).
47. *Census of Production*, Summary Tables PA1002 (London: Central Statistical Office, 1990).
48. P.J. Drudy, 'The Regional Impact of Overseas Industry', in Foley and McAleese (1991), pp. 156–7.
49. S. Hill and M. Munday, 'Foreign Manufacturing Investment: A Tale of Two Regions', *The South West Economy and Trends* (Plymouth Business School: SWERC, 1995).

50. F. Ruane and A. McGibney, 'The Performance of Overseas Industry 1973–89', in Foley and McAleese (1991), p. 69.
51. Breathnach (1989), p. 29.
52. Census of Industrial Production (1990).
53. B. Wilkinson, J. Morris and M. Munday, 'Japan in Wales: A new IR?', *Industrial Relations Journal*, 24.4 (1993), pp. 273–83.
54. L. Tsoukalis, *The New European Economy* (Oxford: Oxford University Press, 1993) p. 251; S. Nolan, 'Economic Growth: Theory and Analysis', in J.O'Hagan, ed., *The Economy of Ireland* (Dublin: Irish Management Institute, 1987), p. 268.
55. Central Statistics Office, *Economic Series* (Dublin: Stationery Office, February 1994), p. 29.
56. R. Mayuya and D. Jacobson, in *Irish Business and Administrative Research* (1991), p. 116.
57. IDA, *Annual Report* (1987), p. 31.
58. S. Thomsen and S. Woolcock, *Direct Investment and European Integration* (London: Pinter/RIIA,1993), p. 13.
59. D. O'Hearn, in *Economic and Social Review* (January 1993), p. 180.
60. Breathnach (1989), p. 33.
61. D. O'Hearn, in *Economic and Social Review* (January 1993), p. 188.
62. NESC (1982), p. 152.
63. Ibid., p. 185.

7 The Spatial Impact of Japanese Direct Investment in France

Bernadette Andréosso[1]

INTRODUCTION

It has only been since the late 1980s that France has wholeheartedly promoted itself as an attractive location for foreign direct investment (FDI).[2] Foreign-controlled firms now represent 22 per cent of the French workforce, and account for 27 per cent of capital expenditure, 30 per cent of production and 30 per cent of exports.[3] In 1993, these firms created 15 425 jobs in 270 different operations.

Germany and the North American countries have traditionally been the leading sources of foreign investment in France. In 1993, German-controlled firms ranked first in terms of employment (15 per cent of the 15 425 new jobs), whereas North American-controlled firms represented the largest group of operations (89 out of 270). In the same year, Japanese firms constituted the 6th largest group of new firms (13 operations), but with only 4.86 per cent of new jobs.[4] It should be noted that in spite of a recent revival of interest in France by Japanese investors, employment in new Japanese operations during that year was exceeded by projects involving Hong Kong firms. The latter were responsible for 1378 new jobs, compared with 750 jobs in firms with Japanese equity participation.

It is difficult to separate the issue of (foreign) firms' location from that of regional development, especially in a country where disparities in terms of economic development have been historically so pronounced.[5] In France, the famous Caen–Marseilles line still separates a relatively urban and industrialised north-east from a more rural and less developed western half of the country. The objective of our study is to determine whether Japanese FDI has led/leads to specific spatial ordering within the French economy.

In the case of Japanese investment, spatial ordering can be the result of two somewhat interrelated phenomena. First, the predominance of the strategies of *central location* over the strategies of *peripheral location*,

111

or vice versa. Secondly, the inherent features of the *keiretsu* system, according to which Japanese firms tend to have very close relationships with their domestic suppliers and distributors. The strategies of central location tend to focus upon the market as the major explanatory variable in the choice of a given location by a MNE (multinational enterprise). For example, firms locate in the core of the EU, in order to exploit maximum benefits associated with servicing a large, high-income market. The strategies of peripheral location, however, focus on production costs. They are aimed at servicing the entire European market through the exploitation of low labour costs in peripheral regions.

Before examining the issue of *keiretsu* linkages, it will be useful to introduce the individual features of Japanese manufacturing in the light of recent patterns of Japanese investment in France.

FEATURES OF JAPANESE INVESTMENT AND RECENT FDI TRENDS IN FRANCE

Characteristics of Japanese Investment in France

The variables that explain FDI are, *inter alia*, market size of the host country or distance to nearest markets, labour costs, intensity of trade relations, the technological level of the investing country and any advantageous fiscal regimes prevailing in the host country. The explanatory power of these variables varies broadly according to (1) the type of the investor, and (2) the nature of the host country, and within these two categories, it varies according to the nature of the industry, as well as the time that the investment takes place.

It has been customary to distinguish Japanese and US strategies of foreign investment, inasmuch as US investment has been characterised as more sensitive to financial incentives, such as capital grants, regional grants and advantageous fiscal regimes. Typically, the US firm prefers a quick return on its investment, whereas the Japanese firm gives higher priority to other location-specific advantages such as the quality and availability of human capital. Furthermore, Japanese FDI has been depicted for the most part as *trade-oriented* (to use Kojima's terminology), whereas American FDI has been characterised as *anti-trade-oriented* (or *tariff-jumping* FDI).[6]

The fact that France is 'geographically, politically and culturally in the core of Europe'[7] explains why the country is *naturally* regarded as one of the two or three major destinations for Japanese investment in

Europe. Classified as the 13th most competitive country by the World Competitiveness Report in 1994, France has a labour productivity rate that has increased more rapidly than that of all other OECD countries since the early 1960s, as well as moderate labour costs, a quality infrastructure and relatively low transport costs.[8] In addition, the size of the country and its proximity to end markets are important considerations for would-be Japanese investors.

Fiscal incentives are seldom considered the primary deciding factor in the choice of France as an investment location. However, they do play a pivotal role in deciding on a short-list of potential sites. Tariff jumping, or the avoidance of market restrictions, has, however, achieved a special importance in the case of France. Before the changes engendered by the completion of the internal market, heavy quotas and administrative restrictions penalised imported electrical products (such as video recorders). Consequently, for some Japanese firms, the creation of a joint venture with a local French partner was the only way to bypass these restrictions. For investing firms, nevertheless, concern has been expressed about inadequately trained workforces,[9] and in particular the unsatisfactory level of computer literacy and its impact on prospective investment in the electronics sector.

Recent Japanese Investment Trends in France

The purpose of this sub-section is to outline briefly the distribution of Japanese investment throughout Europe, and to emphasise France's relative position in this scheme. Although according to the French National Accounting system, a French firm is assumed to be under foreign control in the large sense when a foreign firm holds more than 33.33 per cent of its capital stake,[10] we may define a Japanese firm as being any firm located in France, in which there is a certain degree of Japanese participation (in excess of 10 per cent of equity). A firm defined in this way will be referred to as a *firm with a Japanese equity participation* (FwJEP).

When compared with other European countries (a handful of which are broadly similar in terms of size and distribution of wealth) France is currently host to the second biggest group of Japanese manufacturing firms in Europe, after the UK (Table 7.1). By January 1994, 121 of the 728 Japanese manufacturing ventures in Europe had established themselves in metropolitan France. This total figure of 728 Japanese manufacturing projects corresponds to a 2.7 per cent net increase compared with the previous year. By comparison, the yearly increase

Table 7.1 Intra-European distribution of Japanese manufacturing, January 1994

	Manufacturing firms			Companies with R&D Bases	
	Total	% Share	1993 Net Change	Total	% Share
France	121	16.6	+2	34	12.9
Germany	106	14.6	–2	53	20.0
Italy	52	7.1	+7	14	5.3
UK	206	28.3	+9	83	31.5
Others	243	33.3	+3	80	30.3
Total	728	100*	+19	264	100*

Notes: Europe is here taken to be the EU-15 + the three ex-EFTA countries (Iceland, Norway and Switzerland). The net increase corresponds to the number of new firms minus disinvesting firms in the 12-month period after January 1993.
*Aggregate totals may not total 100 per cent exactly.

Source: JETRO (1994).[11]

in 1984 was nearly 62 per cent. Although the UK is still the preferred destination for Japanese manufacturing investment (with a net figure of +9), it is also apparent that France (+2) and Italy (+7) are becoming increasingly attractive locations. Although France is demonstrating a stronger comparative dynamism in attracting foreign mobile capital, it still performs rather poorly in terms of suitability as a location for R&D-based firms. With less than 13 per cent of the European total for Japanese investing firms with a R&D base, France lags well behind Germany (20 per cent) and the UK (31.5 per cent).

At the European level, Japanese manufacturing presence is strong in chemicals, electronic and electrical equipment, machinery and food, as can be seen from the data given in Table 7.2. These industries also correspond to the 'European poles of competitiveness', mentioned by Androuais.[12]

Japanese interests in the food industry, a competitive area of French manufacturing, are quite pronounced. Indeed, the Japanese presence in this sector in France is proportionately four times as great as for Europe as a whole. Examples of Japanese interests in the French food industry include:

• Ezaki Glico Co. Ltd, a joint venture (1982) with Générale Biscuit Glico France SA
• Meiji Seika Kaisha Ltd, a joint venture with Beghin and Say to produce fracto-oligosaccharide

Table 7.2 Japanese firms in selected European countries by industrial sector as a percentage of total Japanese firms operating in the same country

Industrial Sector	Total Europe	France %	Germany %	Italy %
Chemicals	17.0	14.0	10.4	13.5
Electronic and electrical equipment	14.5	18.2	17.0	11.5
General machinery	11.4	9.1	18.8	19.2
Electronic components	10.6	6.6	16.1	1.9
Food	4.5	17.4	2.8	–
Clothing and textiles	2.4	2.5	–	17.3
Others	39.6	32.2	34.9	36.6
Percentage total	100	100	100	100
Total number of companies	728	121	106	52

Note: Totals are calculated as the number of Japanese firms in one industry related to the total number of Japanese firms established in that country.

Source: JETRO (1994).

- Okura & Co. Ltd (a minority participation since 1991 in Société Aquacole D'Ouessant, involved with the cultivation, R&D and marketing of sea weed for food)
- Mercian Corp, (which bought the Chateau Reyson vineyard in 1988) and
- Suntory France SARL, a joint venture between Suntory Ltd and Grands Millésimes de France SA to produce and market wine.

Another industry where Japanese investment is well represented is the electronic and electrical equipment industry, an industry which in France is generally less competitive globally except in the area of telecommunications equipment. Significantly, it is in this particular segment of the industry that the Japanese investors have focused most of their attention.

In the largest EU countries with a high GDP per capita and a significant legacy of non-EU inward investment, Japanese investment has concentrated on the particular competitive strengths of each country, as a means of benefiting from accumulated experience and competitive advantage. Hence, Japanese investment has a noticeable presence in the strong German and Italian machine-tool industries, and has established itself also in the competitive and dynamic Italian clothing industry. Empirically, it would seem, therefore, that at the intra-EU level, the distribution of Japanese investment has been guided by profiles of national competitive advantage.[13]

A spatial ordering of Japanese investment at the intra-EU level is also noticeable in the services sector as a whole, and particularly in the financial services industry (banking, investment, securities). As is clearly apparent from statistics compiled by the Japanese Ministry of Finance, France (and Germany) lagged well behind the UK in that area. Cumulative data in dollar terms for the years 1951–89 show that the UK has taken up the lion's share of Japanese investment in financial services. Indeed, nearly 40 per cent (38.9 per cent) of all Japanese investment in this industry in Europe took place in the UK during this period. Luxembourg, with its financial services centre, accounted for 24.4 per cent of the total, while the Netherlands, with 23.9 per cent, is the third most important destination for Japanese financial service investment in Europe. It seems that France, with only 1.4 per cent, and Germany, with only 2.1 per cent, have not been targeted as major investment locations by Japanese financial institutions.[14]

In 1993, according to JETRO figures, 62 per cent of all Japanese manufacturing operations in France were greenfield operations,[15] and this percentage is close to the corresponding figure for all foreign-owned companies investing in France.[16] However, another 22 per cent were Japanese acquisitions of French companies (usually those in difficulties), a figure which is substantially above the 15 per cent for total foreign investment in France. Examples of French firms rescued by Japanese companies are Toyoda Machine Works Ltd taking over the machine tool producer Ernault Somua in 1985, and the acquisition of tyre-maker Dunlop by Sumitomo Rubber in 1983.[17] A third type of Japanese investment involved capital participation in French firms, with 14 per cent of Japanese investing firms using this method of establishing a manufacturing presence in France. It should also be noted that three-quarters of employment in firms with Japanese equity participation is derived from projects which were originally acquisitions or joint ventures. Only one quarter of jobs in Japanese subsidiaries in France can be linked with projects that began as greenfield operations.[18]

Concluding Remarks

Japanese investment flows have altered the spatial ordering of industry at the global level and at the intra-European level. For France as a whole, this is most evident in the prominence of Japanese investment in the food and telecommunications industries. Unlike in other comparable

EU countries, there has been a relatively low penetration rate of Japanese (and non-EU) capital in French industry. This can in part be explained by inhospitable and discriminatory investment laws, which persisted until the late 1980s. Indeed, it is only since the year 1987 that greenfield investments by foreign (EU and non-EU) multinationals have been freely permitted.[19]

The modification in French investment law finds its roots in the radical change in the attitude of the French business and political communities in the 1980s towards international capital movements. The increase in the intensity of regional integration in the EC, as it then was, manifested itself in preparations for the *1992 programme*, and gave an impetus to many French firms which were starting to investigate more closely European markets and industries. As a result, a large exodus of capital weakened the balance of payments in the late 1980s, and led the French government to repeal the stringent investment legislation. Another factor was that the French authorities has come to accept that discarding their *General Motors syndrome* (chasing away mobile projects to neighbouring countries) was a more appropriate strategy in the context of an increasingly integrated EU.[20]

DISTRIBUTION OF JAPANESE MANUFACTURING INVESTMENT IN FRANCE: CENTRAL AND PERIPHERAL LOCATION STRATEGIES

The objective of this section is to describe the way total Japanese direct investment has been distributed between the core and the periphery of France, and to analyse whether or not Japanese investment naturally contributes to regional disparities in France. We can suggest that Japanese direct investment contributes to regional disparities in France if we observe that:

1. The relative distribution of Japanese firms and of employment in firms with Japanese equity participation (FwJEP) is uneven within national boundaries, and reinforces the Paris/provinces (and/or northeast/south-west) divide. This occurs if a strategy of central location is preferred to a strategy of peripheral location.
2. The level of corporate integration existing within and between FwJEP through extended relationships, leads to the loss or elimination of market share for French firms.

Spatial Distribution of Japanese Investment in France

Historically, there has been a high propensity for multinational firms to locate in the core regions of advanced industrial economies. For example, Blackbourne found that in the UK in 1968 50 per cent of US manufacturing plants were located in the South East of England.[21] It may well be asked if the location of Japanese investment in France has followed this classical pattern, or whether strategies of peripheral location have been favoured.

Before the geographical distribution of Japanese firms and employment in France is discussed, the distribution of subsidiaries by economic sector can be usefully outlined. In 1993, there were 321 firms with Japanese equity participation in France, employing nearly 28 000. These firms were present in all economic sectors, with the manufacturing sector accounting for only 102 firms, but with approximately two-thirds of total employment.[22] Only one firm was operating in the agricultural sector as such, with Cérécole SARL, in which the Japanese stake is 50 per cent, involved in the production and distribution of corn in Normandy. The agri-food sector is nevertheless well-represented by a number of firms in the wine (Bordeaux region), and spirits (Poitou-Charentes region), industries. These include Grands Millésimes de France SA, a joint venture between Suntory Ltd (40 per cent participation) and Grands Millésimes de France (60 per cent).

Probably the most striking fact emerging from Table 7.3 is the large number of wholesale firms. There were 113 such firms, employing more than 7000 people, and all situated near the major markets (essentially Paris, with four near Lyons, two near Rouen, etc.).

The services sector has grown to encompass 105 firms, with slightly fewer than 2000 employees. As has been mentioned previously, the French services sector, excluding distribution, has been relatively unsuccessful in attracting Japanese investment, a feature shared with the less sophisticated Spanish economy.

However, in the early 1990s, France caught up with the UK to some extent. Among the 105 Japanese services firms located in France in 1993, 17 were operating in the Banking/Investment/Securities area (i.e. large financial services). It is well to note that these financial services companies are all located in Paris (near the Champs Elysées area). Furthermore, of the remaining 88 services companies, only five were not clustered around metropolitan Paris.

As a result, only 20 per cent of all firms with Japanese equity participation are located outside the Paris/Île-de-France region, with

Table 7.3 Firms with Japanese equity participation in France, January 1993

Sector	Total	Number of Firms Paris	Provinces	Employment
Total	321	254	67	27 735
Wholesale	113	99	14	7 078
Manufacturing	102	54	48	18 702
Services	105	101	4	1 953
Agriculture	1	0	1	2

Source: Toyo Keizai (1994);[23] JETRO (1994).

only 10 per cent of all Japanese *non-manufacturing* firms similarly dispersed. It follows, therefore, that the establishment of Japanese *manufacturing* firms in France helps in part to reduce the concentration of firms with Japanese equity participation in and around the Paris region.

But even if these polarising trends connected with both services and wholesale industry projects are removed from the analysis, the Paris/provinces divide still holds true. In 1993, the Paris/Île de France region accounted for more than 56 per cent of all manufacturing employment in FwJEP, and yet the region sustained less than 19 per cent of total manufacturing employment. On the other hand, the *provinces*, with 81 per cent of total manufacturing employment in France, have attracted less than 44 per cent of manufacturing jobs in FwJEP. Table 7.5 presents this statistical information in aggregate, and Table 7.4 introduces it by describing the relative involvement of the[e] French regions in total manufacturing together with Japanese manufacturing activity. The GDP per capita and the unemployment rates by region are also recorded, as these totals can be used as general performance indicators.

The French system of national accounting allows for the computation of value-added on a regional basis. This is calculated in the same way as the national value-added (VA), i.e. for any region *I*,

$$VA_i = \sum_{j}^{n} (P_j - IC_j),$$

where P_j and IC_j refer to the production and to the intermediate consumption respectively, at market prices, of a given industry *j* producing in region *i*.

The Paris/Île-de-France region, as is evident in Table 7.4, is the wealthiest French region and combines with this also the highest activity rate (63 per cent against 55 per cent for France in average), with the highest regional share of investment (58 per cent) in high-tech sectors (computers, pharmaceuticals, aircraft construction).[24] In this region, three-quarters of jobs are in the services sector (two-thirds for France), and only 33 per cent of non-executive jobs are unskilled (40 per cent for France).[25]

At the other extreme end of the spectrum of regional development in France lie the less advanced regions (Limousin, Languedoc, Auvergne and Poitou-Charentes), all regions where the Japanese manufacturing presence is either minuscule or completely absent. The most appropriate way to analyse the relative concentration of manufacturing employment in FwJEP on a geographical basis is through the use of location quotients (LQ). For our purposes, such a quotient is defined as:

$$LQ_i = \frac{N_i^J}{N_i^T},$$

where N_i^J is region i's share of manufacturing employment in firms with Japanese equity participation, and N_i^T is region i's share of total manufacturing employment. Table 7.5 ranks the various regions in decreasing order of totals for Japanese manufacturing employment.

Outside the Paris/Île-de-France region, the location quotient is rarely above the critical value of 1. It does assume a value of 2.32 in Franche Comté, 1.86 in Picardie, 1.45 in Basse Normandie and 1.31 in Alsace, and in the case of Brittany, the quotient is close to 1. In every other region, however, the quotient is low. Interestingly, it would seem that the regions to the south of Paris have been the most neglected of all by Japanese manufacturing investors.

For some particular regions, these quotients should, however, be read with caution. In the Franche Comté and in the Picardie regions, the extremely high value of the quotient is almost entirely explained by the presence of one large firm only.[26] In the case of the Franche Comté, it is explained by the presence of Peugeot MTC SA (employing 1110 people, and in which Honda Motor Co. Ltd holds a 25 per cent capital stake), and in the case of Picardie, by MBK Industries (controlled by Yamaha Motor Co. Ltd, and representing 1196 employees). The high quotients achieved by these two regions are biased, therefore, and should be distinguished from that of the Alsace region.

Additionally, the values of the quotients for the Brittany, Normandy

Table 7.4 Regional distribution of Japanese investment in France,
January 1993

Region	Unemployment rate (%)	GDP/Capita	Regional Share of Total Manufacturing Employment (%)	Manufacturing Employment in FwJEP
Paris/Île-de-France	7.2	149	18.92	10 578
Provinces	n.a.	n.a.	81.08	8 124
West				
Aquitaine	10.7	92	4.17	253
Bretagne	8.4	83	4.25	754
Basse Normandie	8.0	85	2.49	679
Haute Normandie	9.8	101	3.00	228
Poitou Charente	9.9	82	2.51	37
Loire	9.0	85	5.83	691
Centre-South				
Centre	8.4	92	4.89	415
Limousin	8.0	77	1.06	–
Auvergne	8.7	82	2.30	–
Midi-Pyrenées	8.7	83	3.56	–
Languedoc	12.9	78	2.51	–
South-East				
Provence	11.0	91	5.27	25
Rhône-Alpes	7.2	98	11.56	1 021
East				
Bourgogne	8.1	89	2.95	–
Franche-Comté	6.7	92	2.55	1 110
North-East				
Alsace	4.5	104	3.71	912
Lorraine	8.0	83	4.54	601
Champagne	9.3	95	2.78	54
Picardie	10.0	87	3.84	1 344
Pas-de-Calais	11.8	80	7.23	–
France*	8.7	100	100.00	18 702

Note: *This excludes Corsica and the French Overseas *Départements*.

Source: Eurostat (1993); Toyo Keizai Inc. (1994); JETRO (1994).

and the Rhône-Alpes regions are somewhat unexpected. The value is
relatively high in Brittany (0.94), a less developed region by French
standards, and low in two of the wealthiest French regions, Haute
Normandie (0.40) and the Région Rhône-Alpes (0.47). It seems that
the provinces have tended to attract Japanese investment in a very
uneven manner, which does not easily correlate with the indicators of

Table 7.5 Regional distribution of Japanese manufacturing employment in France, January 1993

Region	Location quotient
1. Paris/Île-de-France	2.99
Provinces	0.53
2. Franche Comté	2.32
Picardie	1.86
Basse Normandie	1.45
Alsace	1.31
Bretagne	0.94
Lorraine	0.70
Pays de la Loire	0.63
Rhône-Alpes	0.47
Centre	0.45
Haute Normandie	0.40
Aquitaine	0.32
Champagne-Ardennes	0.10
Poitou-Charentes	0.07
Provence/Côte d'Azur	0.02
3. East	1.08
North-East	0.70
West	0.63
South-East	0.33
Centre-South	0.15

Source: Author's calculations based on Toyo Keizai and JETRO statistics.

economic performance. In other words, the relative economic performance of regions does not naturally explain the distribution of Japanese manufacturing investment outside the Paris region.

By contrast, the Paris/Île-de-France region has been a natural magnet for Japanese manufacturing investment from the outset. Indeed, well before it embarked upon a policy of attracting foreign manufacturing investment in the early 1990s, the Paris/Île-de-France region naturally attracted most of Japanese investment. In keeping with existing patterns of multinational involvement, Japanese firms would have gravitated to the core region of France because of its proximity to the principal French markets. In time, however, they may have considered other large cities because of their cultural and infrastructural attractions. In the Alsace region, for example, Colmar hosts the second largest Japanese community (after Paris), in no small part due to the setting up of a Japanese school nearby in Kayserberg.

According to Tandeau,[27] more than half of would-be foreign investors

Table 7.6 Local content of parts and materials for composite products: Selected countries, 1993

	Ratio >70%	Ratio >50%
Total*	52.0	73.7
France	45.3	67.9
Germany	44.3	72.2
Italy	78.9	84.2
UK	56.5	77.9

Notes: Figures show percentage of firms in each category; *EU-15 plus Norway, Iceland and Switzerland.
NB: These figures are based on a sample of 416 manufacturing firms in Europe; in the case of France, only 54 firms were considered, less than half the total population.

Source: Adapted from JETRO (1994).

in France do not consider the western part of the country at all, at least before any thorough location study is attempted.

As a result, and as evidenced by the locational choices of Japanese manufacturing investors in France, the strategies of central location have been predominant. This prompts the question whether or not this spatial ordering of the French economy, at least insofar as it refers to Japanese inward investment, can be partly explained by the *keiretsu* system of inter-firm relations.

Spatial Impact of Japanese Corporate Integration

As an associated feature of the *keiretsu* system, Japanese companies operating abroad tend to create very close relationships with their (Japanese) supplier firms. The implications for Ireland of these cohesive networking relationships has been illustrated by Mayuya and Jacobson[28] for the Japanese electronics industry, and by Andréosso and Jacobson[29] for the motor car industry. In the first of these papers, the authors write that when an equipment manufacturer 'sets up a subsidiary abroad, the supplier firm often follows'.[30] In the second paper, the authors point out the effects on Irish firms and on the Irish economy of Japanese manufacturing investment in the British motor car industry.

One way of measuring the extent of linkages with the local economy is by calculating the local content (of parts and materials) of output emanating from FwJEP in a given geographical location. Table 7.6

summarises this information. In 1993, half of the surveyed firms in Europe sourced more than 70 per cent of their materials and parts locally. Although this represents a decline compared with the previous year, the local procurement ratio of Japanese firms in Europe has increased continuously throughout the years. When asked about the reasons for this trend, the surveyed FwJEP mention the declining prices of parts and materials offered by companies in Europe, as well as the improvement in the quality of these goods (JETRO, 1994).[31] In short, the higher degree of integration of FwJEP in the national European economies seems to be related to the value of the yen rather than to the stringent local content requirements set up by the European Commission.

It is important to note that the increase of the local procurement ratio is due, to a large extent, to the setting up of Japanese suppliers in Europe, rather than to a switch from Japanese suppliers to non-Japanese suppliers. The national or local subcontractors are still typically and primarily packaging firms, and firms producing standardised mechanical parts and electronic components. In the case of key (high-tech) components, direct imports and the local establishment of Japanese subcontractors and component suppliers are still the preferred options.

In the case of France, concerns have been expressed about the building up of a self-contained network of FwJEP and its potentially destabilising effect on the French economy. According to Mazier,[32] this feature of the Japanese *keiretsu* system can weaken the cohesion and integrity of national manufacturing industry. In de Bernis' view,[33] Japanese direct investment in the intermediate goods sector (such as machinery) is aimed at setting up parallel and independent production systems. It is worth examining whether or not these concerns are well founded.

According to France Japon Eco,[34] it is estimated that each *direct* job created in a Japanese firm generates one other job in a local subcontracting firm.[35] Japanese FDI in France has also led to some perceptible technological and organisational spillover effects. For example, the takeover by Sumitomo Rubber of the main Dunlop plant in the Auvergne led to new patterns of work organisation, and to new ways of conducting business (such as higher quality, faster delivery, quicker responses, etc.), adopted not only by Sumitomo itself but also by its subcontractors. As a result, the subcontractors could venture into new markets. Canon in Brittany has also forged links with some 120 partners dispersed throughout Europe; and has developed a network of 32 subcontractors located in the Bretagne and Loire-Atlantique regions.

However, the Sumitomo example appears like an isolated case: most Japanese projects do not confer the same scale of spillover effects upon the local economy. Furthermore, the nature and quality of the relationship between Canon Bretagne and its 120 European subcontractors needs to be clarified. In 1988, the turnover of Canon was FF 1 billion; in the same year, the company sourced FF 300 million worth of parts from the European market (of which 80 per cent were from *privileged partners*), and it imported FF 450 million worth from Japan.

More importantly, the linkages, if any, are poorly distributed in geographical terms. The subcontractors that are located in France and which supply key products (electronic components) tend not to locate themselves on the western periphery of the country. For example, in the case of Canon Bretagne, 12 of the 15 packaging firms are local subcontractors, whereas only 5 out of 20 subcontractors supplying electronic components are Breton firms. An analogous situation prevails in SDK,[36] which had to suspend a contract with a local sub-contractor producing electrical cables, in favour of a Japanese subcontractor located in Alsace.

The most commonly advocated reason for this *état de fait* is, again, the unsatisfactory quality of the product supplied by local/national subcontractors. In SDK, 3 per cent of final products were found to be defective (against 0.5 per cent for a typical equivalent firm in Japan). The prevailing quality problem has often less to do with the quality of the labour force than with the organisational calibre of the subcontractor.[37] Because of a lack of communication within the same firm, contracts are agreed by the commercial department, without the assurance that the production department can meet the terms of the contract (delays, number of units to be supplied, etc.). In other cases, poor quality is explained by the lack of adequate technology necessary for testing the quality of the parts and components produced on French territory.

However, and in the light of the information displayed in Table 7.1, some new trends can be detected by examining the evolution of business activities performed by Japanese firms in France. These trends are illustrated below:

Distribution → Assembly → Production → R & D Centre

> *(Assembled*   *(Made in France)*
> *in France)*   (key components still
> imported from Japan)

Some examples readily illustrate the above pattern: Mitsubishi Electric France (telecommunications equipment) moved from the assembly stage to the production stage; SDK (electronics) has been moving from a production base (with 60 per cent of local content) to a Research Centre; and Canon Bretagne has established its first independent European research centre in Rennes-Atalante, the Breton technopolis. Its first research project will be R&D in the area of telecommunications. However, it has been alleged that Japanese firms carry out very little R&D in the Japanese-owned research centres hitherto established in Europe, with the exception of Sony.[38]

To conclude, therefore, linkages created by firms with Japanese equity participation have been selective, both on a geographical basis and in terms of product. Also, it seems that Japanese subcontractors locating in France have not been influential or sizeable enough to bring about the systematic substitution of Japanese firms for local and traditional producers. Nevertheless, some encouraging trends have been noticed recently, in particular the move towards the creation of a research centre in Brittany, historically the most neglected French region in terms of industrial and economic development. It follows therefore that if the Paris/Île-de-France region has naturally attracted most of Japanese investment in France, regions such as Brittany may have been seen as attractive locations because of *artificial* elements, principally as the result of policy initiatives. We now turn to these elements.

CONCLUSION: FRENCH POLICY AND PERIPHERAL LOCATION

Following McDermott's pioneering study[39] which indicated a shift of new foreign establishments away from the core and towards the periphery of the UK, Hill and Munday[40] have corroborated this result, and further assert that the shift towards the periphery has been correlated with active periods of regional policy. Sekiguchi[41] suggested that the UK, Belgium and the Netherlands welcomed Japanese investment as a means of providing employment in depressed regions of structural unemployment and underdevelopment.

In the case of France, the historical Paris/provinces and east–west divides have given rise to a post-war *Politique d'Aménagement du Territoire* (Regional Policy). In 1963, the economic development and regional planning organisation DATAR[42] was created. DATAR has played a leading role in terms of regional policy at the national level,[43] administering the PAT (*Prime d'aménagement du territoire*), a government grant indexed to the scale of investment and job-creation, and as such a major tool of regional development. In the beginning, the geographical focus of DATAR was broader, concerned with fostering industrialisation in the western part of the country. Later, in the post high-growth era (after 1974), the organisation focused upon *conversion poles* in areas of structural decline, particularly those associated with the coal, steel, shipbuilding and textile sectors.

Since 1983, DATAR has been allocated an additional financial package specifically to attract Japanese investors to locations in France. Following the decentralisation law of 1982, which delegated increased powers from Paris to the regional authorities, DATAR has tried to direct Japanese investment towards the areas most hit by unemployment.[44] Subsequently, in 1992, the foreign representation of DATAR was consolidated through the creation of a network of Invest in France Agencies.

Since the early 1980s, France has benefited from patterns of inward investment comparable to other larger European economies, with foreign firms, including Japanese subsidiaries, tending to relocate in the most economically deprived regions. This has been due to a combination of factors, the most important being the active role undertaken by the regions themselves in terms of industrial development initiatives. Other factors have also contributed, notably the pressure exerted by political parties, the marked improvement of the transport network in the 1980s, and other infrastructural elements.

The local authorities of the regions (*Conseils Régionaux*) have initiated dynamic marketing strategies aimed at promoting their regions in Japan and elsewhere. Almost all regions in France are now engaged in heavy promotional campaigns, emphasising their specific locational attractions to potential Japanese investors, with a European pole located in Lorraine/Alsace, an aerospace-based agglomeration in Aquitaine, and the R&D-based technopolis in Sophia-Antipolis, near Cannes. One major criticism has, however, been directed towards all these of local initiatives insofar as they appear uncoordinated at the national level, and have been insufficiently planned. Clearly, a lack of institutional co-ordination can lead to duplication of effort and expense, perhaps leading to disenchantment with regional policy as whole.

Political interests played a substantial role in the location of Mitsubishi in Brittany, while remaining psychological barriers and remoteness were alleviated by the development of the high speed train the TGV *(Train à Grande Vitesse)* in western France. Permitting shorter commuting times between Brittany, the Loire Atlantique region and Paris, the TGV has placed the Atlantic arc of France within more comfortable reach of potential foreign investors.

The human capital aspect has also been significant as a determining factor in the attraction of foreign investment. Some public authorities have been very active in the retraining of inadequately qualified workers, as evidenced by the role of the National Employment Agency (ANPE) and the Chamber of Commerce prior to the establishment of the Mitsubishi electronics plant in Brittany. And while in some cases Japanese firms have been able to recruit a well-trained labour force on the spot, in other remote peripheral areas the choice of location has been facilitated by man-made locational advantages. The technopolis, combining research and telecommunication facilities has been one result of this type of policy initiative, and in Rennes (Brittany) the university, the business school, the Ecole Nationale Supérieure des Télécommunications and local research centres have had an important bearing upon the locational choice of Mitsubishi as well as the local establishment of Canon's first European Research Centre.

In conclusion, therefore, we may note that Japanese FDI is a relatively recent phenomenon in France. When it is not aimed at rescuing ailing companies, Japanese FDI tends to be heavily represented in the most competitive sectors of French industry (food, telecommunications and rubber industries). In line with the strategies of central location, Japanese FDI would have tended naturally to accentuate the Paris/provinces and east–west divides. Moreover, the local procurement ratio is lower for France than for other comparable European countries, and this suggests that Japanese FDI is still poorly integrated into the French economy. The dynamism of DATAR, of the Délégation aux Investissements Internationaux (DII) and of local authorities in some French regions has helped reduce the polarisation of foreign investment around the major urban centres. Nevertheless, in spite of these dynamic promotional initiatives, Japanese FDI remains heavily concentrated in the most developed cities and regions of France.

NOTES

1. The author wishes to thank Sean Cassidy (University of Limerick) and Jacques Jaussaud (Université de Poitiers) for their statistical assistance.
2. FDI is distinct from portfolio investment and refers to the ownership of assets by foreigners in a geographically defined area.
3. DATAR, *Foreign Investment Flows in France for 1993* (Paris: Invest in France Network, 1994).
4. Ibid.

5. See Jean François Gravier, *Paris et le désert français* (Paris: Le Portulan, 1947).
6. K. Kojima, *Japanese Direct Foreign Investment* (Tokyo: C.E. Tuttle, 1978).
7. This is based on a statement made by a Japanese executive working in Canon Bretagne SA, but as will be seen, this is not (yet) empirically supported.
8. F. Hatem and J.D. Tordjman, *La France face à l'investissement international* (Paris: Economica, 1995).
9. *France Japon Eco* (1990).
10. INSEE (Institut National de la Statistique et des Etudes Economiques), *Tableaux de l'Economie Française* (1994/5).
11. JETRO, *10th Survey of European Operations of Japanese Companies in the Manufacturing Sector* (Tokyo: Japan External Trade Organisation, October 1994).
12. A. Androuais, 'Les Investissements extérieurs directs japonais dans les pays de la C.E.E. – Vers de nouvelles formes d'implantation', in A. Androuais, ed., *L'Investissement extérieur direct* (Presses Universitaires de Grenoble, 1990).
13. At the global level, the spatial distribution of Japanese investment follows the logic of the Rostowian/Balassian models which are compatible with the *New International Division of Labour Model*: global enterprises locate their functions according to the characteristics of regions (i.e. standardised products in less skilled, labour-intensive and low labour costs countries, high quality/up-market products in countries with high disposable incomes; see, for example, Y. Nagamoto, *Japanese Investments Abroad: Past, Present and Future* (Louvain: Japanese Presence in Europe, 1990).
14. All figures are from the Japanese Ministry of Finance, *Report on Direct Foreign Investment* (1991).
15. The JETRO figure emerges from the results of a survey conducted in all European countries; in the case of France, there were 58 respondents, out of a total of 121 manufacturing firms.
16. DATAR (1994).
17. In the case of the takeover by Toyoda Machine Works, cumulative losses led to disinvestment in 1993.
18. *France-Japon Eco* (1990).
19. See in particular Decree No. 89-938, 29 December 1989 (in *Journal Officiel*, 30 December 1989, Paris), amended by the directive of the 15 January 1990 (*JO*, 16/01/1990). Note that non-EU investments of more than FF50 million, or undertaking a minimum participation of 20 per cent in the capital of a French firm, is still subject to a declaration to, and authorisation from, the French government.
20. In the early 1980s, after having been refused authorisation to set up a plant in the steel-making area of northern France, General Motors located in Spain, creating 3000 jobs. When Spain became a member of the EC, GM's products could cross the border tariff-free.
21. A. Blackbourne, 'Multinational Enterprise and Regional Development: A Comment', *Regional Studies*, 12 (1978), pp. 125–7.
22. The mismatch between the 121 manufacturing firms recorded in Table 7.1 and the 102 firms recorded here is explained as follows: (1) Some of

the 121 manufacturing firms recorded by JETRO would be classified as *wholesale* firms here, because their main business line is wholesale (for example, Toto Ltd (Ceramics) is listed as a manufacturer by JETRO, and as a wholesale firm by Toyo Keizai), see Toyo Keizai, *Kaigai Shinshutsu Kigyo Soran* (Tokyo: Toyo Keizai Shinposha, 1994). (2) With one exception, the agro-food firms are not listed by Toyo Keizai. (3) The Toyo Keizai list gives consolidated results; for example, Sumitomo Rubber Industries Ltd (listed as one big firm in the above list) refers to four different plants in the JETRO list.

23. Ibid.
24. Eurostat (1993).
25. L. Bisault, V. Destival, and D. Goux, 'Emploi et chômage des non-qualifiés en France', *Economie et Statistique*, No. 273 (1994), pp. 17–27.
26. In both cases in the motor car industry.
27. B. Tandeau, *Marché unique et stratégies de localisation des entreprises industrielles étrangères* (Communication au Colloque International sur le thème *Les groupes industriels et financiers et l'intégration européenne*, LEREP, Toulouse, 28–30 September 1989, p. 15).
28. R. Mayuya and D. Jacobson, 'Japanese Direct Investment in Ireland', *Irish Business and Administrative Research*, Vol. 12 (1990).
29. B. Andréosso and D. Jacobson, 'Le double processus d'intégration spatiale et industrielle à la lumière du cas irlandais', *Revue du Marché Commun et de l'Union Européenne*, No. 350 (September 1991), pp. 648–58.
30. Tandeau (1989), p. 16.
31. Determination of European standards in the context of the 1992 Programme has led to an improvement in the general quality level of European products.
32. J. Mazier, 'Intégration européenne, investissements directs étrangers et régimes de croissance', *Japon in Extenso*, Nos 32/33 (Poitiers: June/Sept 1994), pp. 25–45.
33. G. de Bernis, Investissement extérieur direct et systèmes productifs en France et au Japon', in A. Androuais, ed., *L'Investissement Extérieur Direct* (Presses Universitaire de Grenoble, 1990).
34. France Japon Eco (1990).
35. It should be remembered that only one quarter of all jobs in firms with Japanese equity participation are net creations (DATAR, 1994).
36. A joint venture created in 1985 by Trio-Kenwood and the Breton firm Sofrel (electronics).
37. In Brittany, the manufacturing firms which traditionally have been most aware of the quality dimension were subcontractors working for the armaments industry. These firms were accustomed to high quality, to precision and small production batches, with fewer worrries about low costs. With the arrival of Japanese firms in Brittany, local firms have to promote a strategy that can be best summarised as: Quality–Short Delivery Times–Low Costs.
38. C. Poitier, 'Les Unités de production asiatiques en Europe: quel contenu local de la production?' in F. Hatem and J.D. Tordjman, *La France face à l'investissement international* (Paris: Economica, 1995).
39. P.J. McDermott, 'Overseas Investment and the Industrial Geography of the UK', *Area*, 9 (1977), pp. 200–7.

40. S. Hill and M. Munday, *The Regional Distribution of Foreign Manufacturing Investment in the UK* (London: Macmillan, 1994).
41. S. Sekiguchi, 'Japanese Direct Foreign Investment', in L. Tsoukalis and M. White, eds., *Japan and Western Europe* (London: Frances Pinter, 1982), pp. 166–83.
42. *Délégation à l'aménagement du territoire et à l'action régionale.*
43. Another body with a national co-ordinating role is the DII *(Délégation aux Investissements Internationaux).*
44. France Japon Eco (1990).

8 Japanese Manufacturing Investment in Italy

Corrado Molteni

THE EXTENT OF THE JAPANESE PRESENCE IN ITALY

Italy is a large market for Japanese manufacturers but thus far Japanese multinationals investing in Europe have not shown a particular preference for locating in the Italian Republic as a whole, either in the highly industrialised north of the country or in the not so industrialised southern regions. All available data from Italian and Japanese sources confirm this fact.

According to Japanese Ministry of Finance (MOF) statistics (which record the amount of planned investments), up to March 1994 Italy had attracted less than 2 per cent of all postwar Japanese direct investment in Europe, with only a slight increase in relative share in recent years (see Figure 8.1 showing the Italian share in the annual flow of Japanese direct investment into Europe).

The MITI annual surveys on the overseas business activities of Japanese corporations[1] present a similar picture, showing that at the end of March 1992, of the 3528 affiliates overseas in the manufacturing sector covered by the survey, only 32 (less than 1 per cent) were located in Italy. These represented a total of 4520 employees and capital of about 40 billion yen invested in Italy (respectively 0.36 per cent and 0.7 per cent of the total number of employees and the total amount of Japanese capital invested worldwide). This survey also shows the clear preference of Japanese firms for locating in the United Kingdom, Germany, Spain, France and the Netherlands (see Figures 8.2, 8.3 and 8.4).

The lack of a strong Japanese interest in Italy can be detected also in a JETRO survey of the European operations of Japanese companies in the manufacturing sector.[2] According to this source, at the end of January 1994, Japanese firms had established only 52 manufacturing bases in Italy compared to 206 in the United Kingdom, 121 in France, 106 in Germany and 65 in Spain.

The relative paucity of direct investment, particularly in the manufacturing sector, is therefore the most immediate feature of Japanese involvement in Italy. This is also clearly reflected in Italian official statistics,

Figure 8.1   Japanese direct investment in Europe: Italian share, 1985–93

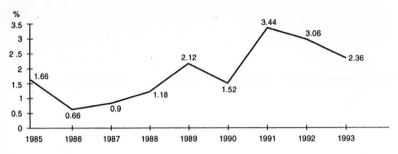

Source: Japanese Ministry of Finance.

Figure 8.2   Geographical distribution of Japanese direct investment in
Europe: Manufacturing sector, March 1992

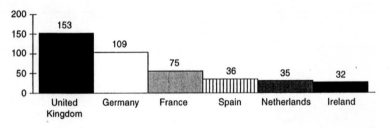

Number of Cases

Source: MITI (1993).

Figure 8.3   Geographical distribution of Japanese direct investment in
Europe: Manufacturing sector, March 1992

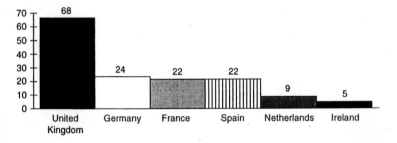

Number of Employees (thousands)

Source: MITI (1993).

Figure 8.4   Geographical distribution of Japanese direct investment in
Europe: Manufacturing sector, March 1992

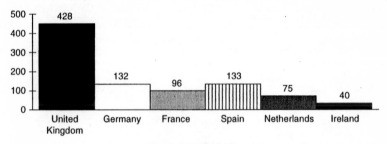

Invested Capital (billion yen)

Source: MITI (1993).

which reveal a negligible Japanese share (1.7 per cent) of the foreign
direct investment recorded up to the end of 1993 (see Table 8.1).

After turning to the causes of the limited nature of involvement in
Italy by Japanese firms, an examination of the specific evolution of
individual projects will be made. In so doing, the strength and origins
of the persistently negative perceptions of Italy as a location for Japanese manufacturing investment will be assessed. In a subsequent section the pattern of Japanese manufacturing investment will be analysed,
focusing particularly on sectoral composition, forms of entry, regional
distribution and the interrelationships between these aspects. In the
concluding section, the factors which limit the scale of Japanese involvement will be discussed, particularly Italy's traditional lack of a
consistent and effective policy towards foreign investment.

A CONCISE HISTORY

It is possible to divide the brief history of Japanese direct investment
in Italy into three phases: (1) the period of the pioneers, covering the
1960s and the first half of the 1970s; (2) the years from 1978 to 1983,
when Italy was almost entirely neglected; and (3) the stage from 1984
to the present, during which increased interest coinciding with a general global expansion of Japanese manufacturing activities became
apparent (see Table 8.2).

In the first stage, only a few companies decided to enter the Italian
market through direct investment. The first company in this group of

Table 8.1 Italy: Foreign direct investment by country of origin,
December 1993 (billion lire)

Country	Amount (Cumulative Value)
Switzerland	16 028
USA	9 913
France	9 897
Netherlands	8 196
UK	6 974
Luxembourg	6 481
Germany	5 355
Japan	1 518
Others	25 096
Total	89 458

Source: Bank of Italy.

Table 8.2 Japanese manufacturing operations in Italy: Period of entry,
September 1994

	1st Stage 1968–77	2nd Stage 1978–83	3rd Stage 1984–90	1991–	Others
Year of establishment	6	7	28	6	5
Start of operations	5	3	30	7	7

Source: Calculated from JETRO (1994), author's estimates.

pioneers was Ajinomoto, the largest manufacturer of amino acid products and monosodium glutamate (MSG), a food seasoning discovered by the founder of the company and sold under the company's well-known trademark *Aji-no-moto*. In 1961 Ajinomoto signed an agreement with an Italian state-controlled company – Breda of the EFIM group – for the establishment of a joint venture. The new company, INSUD S.p.A., started operations in 1966 in Manfredonia, a town in the southern region of Apulia. However, this undertaking was not successful, and it came to set an unfortunate example for other potential Japanese investors. Rising production costs, problems of oversupply in the European market and the unsettled state of Italian labour relations in the early 1970s adversely affected the company's performance. Even the incentives offered by the Italian government for investing in the South – albeit incentives that were provided late and were probably less than expected – could not improve the economic situation of the company. Moreover, in 1975 the Italian partner withdrew from the joint venture, leaving Ajinomoto alone and unable to manage a comeback. In 1977 the Japanese firm decided to put an end to this undertaking and this was to influence markedly the development and the pattern of subsequent Japanese involvement in Italy.

The second pioneer was Yoshida Kogyo K.K. (YKK), the world's largest manufacturer of zip fasteners, which arrived in Italy – at that time a country with many small and medium sized competitors of YKK – in 1968, and started operations in 1972. In this case, however, the investment, a wholly-owned subsidiary set up near Vercelli, between Milan and Turin, was quite successful. YKK rapidly conquered 60 per cent of the expanding Italian market, as competing Italian firms were too small to match the highly organised mass production system introduced by the Japanese firm. Profits accumulated, and, following the founder's philosophy of reinvesting profits locally, the company expanded its activities through the establishment of new subsidiaries, including a design centre located in Milan.[3]

Another successful investor in Italy is Toray Industries, a leader in the field of synthetic fibres and man-made leather, and a firm which has shown a strong preference for investing abroad, especially in South-East Asia. In 1974 the company set up a joint venture in Italy with Enichem,[4] a state-controlled firm, for the production of a woven fabric named *alcantara*, which had been developed in Toray's laboratories. Alcantara is also the name of the joint venture, which operates with 400 employees from a plant near Terni, in the central region of Umbria. This was the first investment made by Toray in a developed country,[5] and the choice of Italy and the joint venture as the form of entry were clearly determined by the strong tradition of Italian expertise in the field of leather goods. According to Mr Kobayashi, the chief Japanese executive employed at Alcantara, the success of the venture can be attributed mainly to two factors: Toray's advanced technology and Italian marketing expertise. When Toray first joined its Italian partner it possessed a very innovative spinning technology which had enabled it to create a new product very similar to natural suede. But its knowledge of European markets was fairly poor, and for this reason it had to rely on the marketing acumen of the Italian managers. This well-conceived scheme of co-operation has made the joint venture very successful indeed, both in terms of market share and of earnings,[6] and not only in Italy but also in foreign markets, where approximately 50 per cent of the production is sold.

The third successful pioneer has been Honda, which established in

Italy a subsidiary for the production of 125cc motorcycles in Atessa, a small town in the southern region of Abruzzo. Initially formed as a joint venture with an Italian-owned partner, in 1981 it became a wholly-owned company, which in 1993 ranked among the 300 largest corporations in Italy. The company, originally established with the aim of overcoming import restrictions, has now achieved a high local content ratio (more than 80 per cent), in no small part due to the acquisition of local suppliers of parts and components.

The success of these companies and a few other initiatives in the 1970s was not, however, enough to change the Japanese perception that Italy was a relatively unattractive location for direct investment: a perception based on the negative image of Italy's economic and social conditions during that period, and reinforced by the unhappy experience of Ajinomoto. As a result, in the second stage of Japanese firms' involvement in Italy, few investments were planned and even fewer undertaken: indeed from 1978 to 1983 only three new manufacturing firms actually began operations (see Table 8.2).

This period also witnessed the short-lived history of ARNA, the 50/50 joint venture between Nissan and Alfa Romeo. Established in 1980, this company was the second direct investment in Europe by Nissan, which in January of the same year had just acquired a 36 per cent stake in Motor Ibérica, Spain's largest manufacturer of commercial vehicles. Production in the ARNA joint venture started in 1983 at a greenfield plant in Campania, at Avellino, as well as at the existing Alfa Romeo plant of Pomigliano d'Arco, a few miles closer to Naples, where the final assembly took place. Nissan supplied the body panels and rear suspension system, directly imported from Japan, while Alfa Romeo provided the engine, the transmission system and the front suspension. The venture did not succeed however, due mainly to production and marketing difficulties, and in the spring of 1987 Nissan withdrew from ARNA following the acquisition of Alfa Romeo by Fiat.[7] This failure, however, seems to have had little impact on existing Japanese perceptions of Italy, as it is generally understood that both partners had entered the joint venture without having clearly defined the joint venture's objectives or the likely methods of achieving them. Nissan, in particular, was less than committed to this project and had by January 1981 announced its decision to undertake a feasibility study for a much more substantial greenfield investment in Britain, which led to the establishment of Nissan Motor Manufacturing in February 1984.

Starting around 1985, Japanese direct investment began to flow abroad much more rapidly, and Italy was also able to benefit from the general growth of establishments, although these still represented a small fraction of the total directed towards Europe. Many companies like Amada, Canon, Daihatsu, Ebara, Hitachi Kenki (Hitachi Construction Machinery), Komatsu, Nippon Denso, Nippon Zeon, Onward Kashiyama, Sanyo Electric, Seiko, Shimano, Sony, Takeda, Teijin, Unitica, Yamaha Motor, and the five major *sogo shosha* (C. Itoh, Marubeni, Mitsui, Mitsubishi and Sumitomo) invested either in greenfield operations or, more often, in joint ventures. Another company, Bridgestone, became a major employer in Italy as a result of its acquisition of the American tyre producer Firestone, which owned a large plant in the south of the country. Thus, from the second half of the 1980s to the present, 37 new ventures have been started, including the most significant and sizeable Japanese undertakings in the country.

Particularly significant was the decision, taken in 1990 by a company of the Ajinomoto group, to invest in another project in Italy, but this time choosing a location near Venice, in the northern part of the country. This decision seems to reflect a more confident and positive attitude towards Italy: an attitude that has gradually developed in the course of the last few years and was presaged by the investment mission sent to Italy by MITI in March 1988 and headed by Yo Kurosawa of the Industrial Bank of Japan. In the report published after his return to Japan, Kurosawa (after mentioning all the negative factors such as political instability, the high inflation rate, numerous strikes and absenteeism, which in the past have prevented foreign investment in Italy), emphasised:

> the great improvement in the investment climate . . . and the extremely high potential of [Italy's] economy [and, in particular] the large number of small and medium sized enterprises contributing as supporting industry to the development of the export-oriented machinery and transport equipment sectors.

Kurosawa concluded by advocating 'the matching of the Japanese firms' strength in production management with Italian creativity, flexibility and marketing skills; the fusion of two heterogeneous management styles'.[8]

While this new attitude has not, as yet, resulted in a significant increase in the overall Japanese presence relative to other European locations, it has evidently been reflected in the nature of the investment projects undertaken in the last decade in Italy, to which we will now refer.

Table 8.3 Japanese manufacturing operations in Italy: Sectoral
composition, January 1994

Sector	Number of Investments in Italy (A)	Number of Investments in Europe (B)	$\frac{A}{B}$ %
Machinery	10	83	12.0
Apparel	9	18	50.0
Chemicals	7	124	5.6
Electronics and electrical equipment	7	183	3.8
Transport equipment	6	69	8.7
Textiles	3	16	18.8
Metal products	3	35	8.5
Others	7	200	3.5
Total	52	728	7.1

Source: Calculated from JETRO (1994).

THE CHARACTERISTICS OF JAPANESE MANUFACTURING IN ITALY

Sectoral Composition

Japanese manufacturers in Italy have a distinctive sectoral profile. The 1994 JETRO survey reveals that only a limited number of companies – 13 out of 52 – have invested in the two sectors most popularly associated with the competitive strength of Japanese manufacturing and the expansion of Japanese production in Europe: electronics and motor vehicles (see Table 8.3).

In particular, no investment has been undertaken to produce consumer electronics products other than the Sony audio cassette plant, and the electronic musical instrument factory controlled by the Japanese company Roland. All other Japanese companies in this important sector have merely established trade and sales subsidiaries for the import and the distribution of products manufactured either in Japan or in other European countries.

Car and car component manufacturers have also been reluctant to choose Italy. The only project in this sector (following the demise of ARNA) is the minority participation of Daihatsu in a joint venture with Piaggio to produce small commercial vehicles. The other investments in the transport equipment sector involve the manufacture of motorcycles and bicycles: two industries in which Italian firms still maintain a competitive edge in the production of both finished products and parts and components.[9]

Japan's most competitive sectors have not invested heavily in manufacturing operations in Italy. Rather, a fairly large number of companies have invested in the so-called traditional sectors, in the machinery industry and in some scale-intensive sectors like chemicals and household electric appliances. Investment has therefore focused upon the sectors in which the Italian industry maintains a significant market share in other industrialised countries.[10]

In the apparel industry alone, Italy has actually attracted half of the Japanese investment projects in Europe (9 out of 18), while in the machinery industry Italy has been able to attract the same number of investments as France. Major companies, like Onward Kashiyama in the apparel sector and Amada in the metalworking machinery and robotics industries, have been among the most active investors, controlling several companies in their respective fields. What is interesting to note is that in the case of these two companies, all but one of the investments have been made either through the acquisition of existing firms or joint ventures with an Italian partner. The rationale behind these investments would not seem to be the transfer to the Italian partner of superior Japanese managerial resources in order to gain substantial direct access to the European market, but rather the acquisition of Italian technological and marketing know-how and expertise, or in the case of joint ventures the access and the development of complementary assets.

Form of Entry

The method of establishment is actually the second most distinctive feature of Japanese manufacturing investment in Italy: it has taken place mostly through capital participation (often with a minority stake) or acquisition of existing firms, together with a few greenfield investments. Indeed, in comparison with other European countries, there has been a stronger preference for joint ventures with local partners, irrespective of the size of the investing company. Table 8.4 shows that out of 52 investments recorded by JETRO only 20 are wholly-owned subsidiaries, 7 are majority-controlled joint ventures, and 23 (44 per cent of the total) are either 50/50 joint corporations or minority-controlled investment.

In another context, of the 530 European manufacturing subsidiaries

Table 8.4 Japanese manufacturing operations in Italy: Capital share, September 1994

Majority-controlled			Minority Investment			Other
100%	99–51%	Total	50%	49–10%	Total	
20	7	27	5	18	23	2

Source: Calculated from JETRO (1994) and author's estimates.

participating in the 1992 MITI survey, almost 80 per cent were majority-controlled and 62.6 per cent wholly-owned, with the highest percentage (90.4 per cent) of majority-controlled affiliates in the electronics and the electric machinery industry.[11] In these two high-tech sectors, wholly-owned greenfield investment is, in fact, the best way to keep and exploit effectively the relevant advantages already owned by Japanese firms.

On the other hand, as we have already seen, Japanese investment in high-tech, science-based sectors in Italy is very limited. Investment tends rather to be concentrated in the traditional and specialised supply sectors, in which Italian companies are competitive but often lack the capacity and resources for both the autonomous and (most importantly) timely development of new products and new production systems. For this reason the joint venture is regarded by Italian firms as an effective means to acquire new assets, especially new technologies and/or new products, as well as a means to control a potential competitor.

For the Japanese partner it is, instead, a means of gaining rapid access to a market and to human resources, and, in several cases, of overcoming or circumventing existing or anticipated protective barriers such as local content regulations. The joint venture allows both sides to reduce their share of the costs and risks involved, and just as importantly, it secures the economies of scale necessary to compete in the European market in a relatively limited period of time. In other words, the joint venture is a preferred option whenever the advantages deriving from the acquisition of new, complementary assets and the reduction of investment and risks are higher than the costs caused by the loss of *ownership advantages*. This is also the rationale behind many co-operative ventures between Italian and Japanese firms, from the large ones started by industrial groups like Fiat and Hitachi in the construction machinery sector, to the smaller ones like the joint venture established by Fiamm and Nippon Denchi for the production in central Italy of small sealed lead-acid batteries.[12]

A good example of the motivation and the strategic issues associated with Japanese investment in Italy is the joint venture between Piaggio and Daihatsu (P & D S.p.A.).[13] This is a fairly recent undertaking, established at Pontedera near Pisa in February 1991, with the objective of manufacturing small (1000cc) four-wheeled commercial vehicles to be sold throughout Europe using both partners' sales networks. This was a completely new business for Piaggio, a group with 9500 employees and about 50 companies with a strong specialisation in the production of scooters (Vespa) and motorcycles, but with no experience in the manufacture of four-wheeled motor vehicles. Whilst Piaggio had been producing and selling a three-wheeled commercial vehicle (APE) since 1948, the market was limited and has shrunk rapidly. Moreover, the company was facing increasing competition, even in Italy, as a result of the on-going integration of the European market. The need to add a new product was thus strongly felt by Piaggio management, which had two options available: the autonomous development of a four-wheeled vehicle or obtaining access to already existing technology through an acquisition or a cooperative agreement. The first option was rejected because of financial considerations and, most importantly, because of the long development time required; an acquisition was not considered a viable proposition: thus, the only remaining option was to find a suitable partner. Since Japanese producers have had a long, successful experience in the manufacture of small, versatile vehicles, the choice of a Japanese partner was a natural one, and eventually Piaggio opted for a joint venture with Daihatsu – a leader in this segment of the market – who also happened to be looking for European partner.[14]

In November 1989, Daihatsu and Piaggio began to negotiate. For Piaggio the objectives were:

1. the acquisition (in a relatively limited period) of suitable production capacity (about 30 000 vehicles annually);
2. use of the existing facilities in Pontedera; and
3. access to new technological, managerial and organisational resources.

For Daihatsu, the main goals were:

1. establishing a production base in Europe;[15]
2. attaining high levels of local content; and
3. partially overcoming Japanese voluntary export restraints.

After lengthy and complex negotiations the two parties reached a first agreement in December 1990 and two months later the joint venture was established, with 51 per cent of the shares controlled by Piaggio and 49 per cent by Daihatsu.

The arrangement agreed upon by the two partners is somewhat unique as the joint venture is not the owner of the plant, which remains an asset of Piaggio; rather, the venture subcontracts the production of all the vehicles to be purchased and sold by the two parties. For this reason, the joint venture has only 10 employees: 6, including the president, from Piaggio, and 4 from Daihatsu in charge of production and quality control. As for Daihatsu, it provided the technical assistance required for the construction and the start-up of the plant, whose layout is entirely based on a Japanese model, and it sold the moulds to the joint venture, which is leasing them to Piaggio. The Japanese company also transferred its technological, organisational and managerial know-how to the Italian partner, by sending more than 60 technicians and engineers to the Pontedera factory and through the training in Japan of Piaggio's workers (all these costs were borne by P&D and Piaggio). The Italian company, for its part, took charge of all the other equipment investment, including building, presses, robots, and the facilities for assembly and painting of the final product.

The production process is actually the assembly of the components imported from Japan – components which include the engine, the gearbox and the suspension – and the parts and components produced in Pontedera or supplied from other Italian or European producers.[16] The final product is then sold by Piaggio at an agreed transfer price to P&D, and from P&D to Daihatsu and the sales division of Piaggio, which are marketing the vehicle under two different brandnames: Hi-jet in the case of Daihatsu and Porter in the case of Piaggio. The two companies are indeed competitors in the European market, especially in some countries like Switzerland and France, where the two dealers networks can overlap. This may be a source of potential conflict, but can also operate as a stimulus to improve the quality and the efficiency of sales and distribution activities.

In this way, through the attainment of economies of scale, the exploitation of complementarities and the beneficial effects of competition between the two partners' sales networks, the new company has equipped itself to become a successful enterprise. The final outcome is, however, still dependent upon how extensive and how effective will be the transfer of Japanese manufacturing techniques. The results achieved so far seem to be rather contradictory. In particular, notwithstanding the efforts by the Italian and Japanese managers, Piaggio, like other joint ventures (and greenfield investments as well), appears to be still

Table 8.5   Japanese manufacturing plants in Italy: Regional distribution,
September 1994

	North	Centre	South	Other
Total	34	12	5	1
(of which Piedmont and Lombardy)	21			

Source: Calculated from JETRO 1994 and author's estimates.

facing serious difficulties in the adoption of Japanese working practices like teamwork, job rotation and quality control: difficulties well
reflected in the relatively low level of workers' productivity.[17]

Regional Distribution

The sectoral composition and the form of entry have also affected the
regional distribution of Japanese manufacturing investment in Italy (see
Table 8.5).

As can be readily perceived, the location of Japanese plants is mainly
concentrated in northern Italy, and in particular the regions of Pied-
mont and Lombardy, the industrial heartland of the country, where many
of the joint venture partners are based. In similar vein, 7 of the 12
Japanese manufacturing ventures in the central regions established themselves in this part of Italy to be close to the headquarters or the main
plants of their partners. Consequently, in keeping with this trend, only
a few investors have chosen the south, despite the generous and sophisticated system of incentives provided by the central government.

Altogether only 5 manufacturing units are located in southern Italy,
the Mezzogiorno, and of these 5, 1 is the result of the acquisition by
Bridgestone of an American multinational (Firestone) and 2 are located in the most developed region of the south, Abruzzo. The other 2
projects are based in Sicily (Takeda Italia), and in Basilicata (Emblem
Europe, a joint venture between Snia Tecnopolimeri, Unitica and
Marubeni).

In the south 3 unsuccessful attempts to establish manufacturing ventures have also been undertaken: the above-mentioned cases of Ajinomoto
and ARNA and, more recently, the joint venture between Olivetti, Sanyo
Denki and Mitsui for the production of facsimile machines which was
set up in June 1989. It proved to be a short-lived venture, however,
after being initiated by Olivetti who wished to utilise an idle plant in
Pozzuoli, near Naples. The venture received strong support from the

Italian government, but was hampered from the outset by the absence in the south of efficient sub-component suppliers and by the inadequacy of Naples' harbour facilities (the company had to use the harbour of Genoa). These factors caused an increase in production costs and a loss of competitiveness (already negatively affected by the relative strength of the Italian currency in the first two years of the 1990s), and eventually brought an end to the joint venture. Such experiences, when considered alongside the Ajinomoto and ARNA failures, are likely to militate against any upsurge in Japanese investment in the south in the foreseeable future.

As for the other peripheral areas in Italy, outside the south, it is interesting to note that two of the regions enjoying stronger autonomy – the Alpine border regions of Trentino and Valle d'Aosta – have been able to attract the attention of a number of Japanese firms. As a result, three important greenfield investments have appeared, including Sony's only Italian plant in Rovereto, the Ebara plant for the production of pumps set up in Trentino near the border with Austria, and the production unit for liquid crystal displays, partially owned by Seiko Instruments and located in Châtillon, close to the border with France.

As in other European countries, in these examples of greenfield investment Japanese firms have preferred to locate themselves in regions – such as Trentino and Valle d'Aosta – lacking strong industrial and labour union traditions. These regions are also well known for the good quality of their labour force which can more easily adapt to Japanese methods and practices. And, last but not least, these are autonomous regions that have adopted and consistently pursued a policy of offering fairly generous incentives to domestic and foreign investors. This policy was an important element in Sony's decision to choose the industrial park of Rovereto as the location for its plant, together with the fact that the town is well connected not only with the rest of the country but also with the northern regions of Europe:[18] two factors explaining Sony's decision in this case, and also providing some insight into the causes behind the more general reluctance of Japanese firms to locate in Italy.

CONCLUSION: LIMITING FACTORS AND FUTURE PROSPECTS

The patterns of establishment examined in previous sections indicates a lack of investment in science-based and scale-intensive sectors, such as consumer electronics and motor vehicles, in which Japanese firms enjoy a strong competitive advantage. Furthermore, the predominant interest in specialised machinery and traditional and scale-intensive sectors like chemicals, is closely related to the high number of co-operative arrangements between Japanese and Italian firms. The search for and the exploitation of complementary skills and resources is, in fact, the driving force behind many joint ventures: a point confirmed by the examination of various cases.

However, the cases outlined above do not definitively tell us why Japanese firms are reluctant to establish wholly-owned greenfield subsidiaries in Italy in those sectors where their presence in other European countries is already well established. This is despite the fact that Italy is an important market, whose size and growth is certainly considerable. We may well ask whether this reluctance is related to the poor state (actual or perceived) of Italian infrastructure, to labour and human resource problems, or to other locational disadvantages such as the policy-making environment.

Probably all these aspects have had, and still have, a significant influence on the Japanese perception of Italy as a manufacturing base, but two further points are also of particular relevance. The first concerns the relatively high cost and difficulty of obtaining access to the detailed and up-to-date information that Japanese managers require when considering an investment abroad. From this point of view the economic distance between Italy and Japan seems to be wider than the distance between Japan and other European countries. In Italy, whilst there are many agencies dedicated to the internationalisation of domestic industry, it is difficult to find one like the IDA in Ireland with the specific mission of attracting foreign investment and, therefore, effective in the task of providing useful and comprehensive information to potential investors.

The second point, which is closely related to the first, concerns the lack of co-ordination between public agencies and the various branches of government: a factor which causes a high degree of uncertainty and misunderstanding regarding the real intentions of policy-makers, as well as the (incorrect) perception that Italy does not welcome foreign investment. Appreciation of these weaknesses is actually quite widespread in Italy, but it may well be that solutions are likely to emerge too late, long after the more significant waves of Japanese direct investment have passed and the advantages they bring have for the most part accrued to other European economies.

NOTES

1. MITI, *Dai 22 kai wagakuni kigyo no kaigai-jigyo katsudo* (22nd Survey on Overseas Business Activities of Japanese Companies) (Tokyo, 1993).
2. JETRO, *The 10th Survey of European Operations of Japanese Companies in the Manufacturing Sector* (Tokyo, 1994).
3. The YKK group in Italy included at the beginning of September 1994 the following companies:

Company Name	Factory Location	Year of Establishment	Capital (million lira)	Employees (Japanese)
Yoshida Italia	Prarolo (Vercelli)	1968	2000	298 (13)
Yoshida Mediterraneo	Ascoli Piceno	1977	3000	102 (5)
YKK Marmi	Verona (headquarters)	1981	320	3 (1)
YKK Fasteners	Colonnella (Terni)	1990	9000	35 (4)
YKK AP Design	Milan	1991	n.a.	2 (1)

4. In December 1994, the ENI group sold to Toray Industries all its shares of the joint venture, which is now entirely controlled by the Japanese firm. The sale occurred as part of the privatisation and rationalisation programme of ENI activities undertaken by the government.
5. Later Toray established manufacturing units in France (1980), the UK (1989) and in the US (1988).
6. In 1993 Alcantara registered a 21 billion lira profit, with a profit to sales ratio of 14.6 per cent (*Mondo Economico*, 31 December 1994).
7. Roger Strange, *Japanese Manufacturing Investment in Europe*, (London: Routledge, 1993), pp. 284–5; JETRO, *Kaigai Shijo Hakusho – Toshihen* (White Paper on Overseas Markets – Investment) (Tokyo, 1981, 1988).
8. Nihon Zaigai Kigyo Kyokai (Association of Japanese Companies Overseas), *Itaria, Berugii, Lukusenburugu no Toshi Kankyo – Kaigai Toshi Kankyo Chosadan Hokokusho* (Investment Environment of Italy, Belgium and Luxembourg – Report of the Overseas Investment Environment Survey Mission) (Tokyo, June 1988), pp. 9, 21.
9. The six investments in the transport equipment industry are as follows:

Italian Company	Japanese Investor	% Shares Owned	Main Product
Alfred Thun	Shimano	50	bicycle parts
Belgarda	Yamaha Motor	40	motorcycles
CIAP	Honda Motor	100	motorcycle parts
Honda Italia Industriale	Honda Motor	100	motorcycles
Motori Minarelli	Yamaha Motor	30	motorcycle engines
P&D	Daihatsu	49	commercial vehicles

10. Italy has the largest market share among the industrialised countries in sectors such as clothing, textiles and shoes, and a high share in machinery and equipment. Its market share is below average in sectors like chemicals and motor vehicles, and it is lowest in high-technology sectors. On the international specialisation of Italy, see B. Tajoli, 'Il modello di specializzazione internazionale dell'Italia', *Congiuntura IRS* (September 1994).

11. See the MITI survey (1993), p. 69. On the pattern of entry in Europe of Japanese multinationals, see also Hideki Yamawaki, 'Japanese Multinationals in U.S. and European Manufacturing Industries: Entry, Strategy and Patterns', paper presented at the *Japanese Direct Investment in an Unifying Europe: Impacts on Japan and the European Community* Conference (Fontainebleau, June 1992).

12. For a detailed analysis of these joint ventures and others, see Corrado Molteni, 'Japanese Joint Ventures in Italy. A Second Best Strategy?', in Nigel Campbell and Fred Burton, eds., *Japanese Multinationals* (London: Routledge, 1994); and ISESAO, *Gli investimenti diretti giapponesi in Italia* (Milan, 1993).

13. This part is based on interview with P&D managers, including Mr Kinji Kanda, former Director General Manager of the joint venture; Maria Paola Garbarino, 'Il caso aziendale della joint venture Piaggio-Daihatsu', in ISESAO, *Gli investimenti diretti giapponesi in Italia*, (1993); and Toshihiro Horiuchi, Hiroshi Tomizawa, *Daihatsu to Piajjio no yonrinjidosha no jointo seisan – keiyaku no jittai to gijutsuiten no genkai no bunseki* (Joint Automobile Production by Daihatsu and Piaggio: an Empirical Analysis of the Contract and the Transfer of Japanese Production Technology), *Keizai-Keiei Ronso* (September 1984).

14. Since the mid-1980s. Daihatsu has examined several options in various European countries, including Germany, Switzerland, the United Kingdom and Spain.

15. Daihatsu's global strategy was and still is basically Asian-centred. Its main exports are (55 per cent of total exports in 1993) towards Asia, where since 1979 it has been operating a knock-down plant in Indonesia and from 1989 another one in Thailand. Europe absorbs only 25 per cent of its exports. As for the United States, in February 1992 the company took the decision to renounce the penetration of this market. See MOF, *Yukashoken Hokokusho Soran – Daihatsu Kogyo Kabushikigaisha* (Report on Securities – Daihatsu Industries Ltd) (Tokyo, June 1994).

16. Following the strong appreciation of the yen, and the depreciation of the lira after September 1992, the joint venture decided to increase the percentage of locally produced parts and components, including the engine.

17. On this point see Horiuchi and Tomizawa (1994) pp. 17–25.

18. See Nihon Zaigai Kigyo Kyokai (1988), p. 122. According to this report, Sony initially considered the option of Valle d'Aosta, but it was eventually abandoned for two reasons: the small population, which might have caused subsequent recruitment problems, and the fear of remaining isolated as the only Japanese undertaking in the area.

9 Italy and Japanese Investment: The Influence of the European Monetary System

Paolo Ramazzotti[1]

INTRODUCTION

1992 referred to the establishment of a unified market, a step in Europe's progress towards an integrated economy. It is still a keyword today, but ironically it also denotes the year of the break-up of the European Monetary System (EMS). In the latter months of 1992, as certain obstacles to fuller economic integration were being removed, exchange-rate barriers were reintroduced.

Research on the economic impact of Japanese multinational enterprises (JMNEs) in Europe was carried out mostly during the 1980s, when particularly high growth rates in Japanese foreign direct investment (JFDI) coincided with the existence of the EMS. It is, however, plausible to argue that the changes which took place in the year 1992 have begun to affect patterns of growth and trade, and that this will in turn influence the strategies of JMNEs. What is more, the phenomenon of JFDI (what it is now as well as what it may become) may be fully assessed only when patterns of growth and foreign trade are properly examined.

The aim of this paper is to examine JFDI in Italy, both in terms of its determinants and its effects, in relation to Italy's position within the European division of labour. It will be stressed that JFDI in Italy has been strongly affected by the economic consequences of the EMS and the abandonment of the fixed exchange-rate regime.

The next section of the paper will outline the main features of Japanese manufacturing FDI and will refer to existing explanations of JFDI in Europe. The third section will introduce the major characteristics of Japanese subsidiaries in Italy and consider the circumstances that have specifically favoured FDI by JMNEs. In the fourth section an attempt

Table 9.1   Stock of JFDI in Italy (all industries): Percentage composition and total

Year	1971	1976	1981	1986	1991	1993
Energy	0	0	0	1	1	1
Manufacturing	79	61	57	45	29	26
Services	21	39	43	54	70	73
Total (Lire billions)	2	14	39	226	1064	1518

Source: Ufficio Italiano Cambi.

will be made to explain why so little JFDI has been undertaken in Italy and what the objectives of Japanese firms may be in this context. In the fifth section the analysis shifts to JFDI in the service sector. Since the share of this sector as a proportion of total global JFDI is very high and is concentrated in the financial sector, the question considered is what links, if any, are maintained with the parallel processes of manufacturing JFDI. It is argued that a link probably exists but that it may not be exclusive. The final section presents a few concluding remarks.

JAPANESE FDI IN ITALY

JFDI in Italy is small not only with respect to JFDI in other European countries but also in relation to Italy's global stock of inward FDI: in 1993 the stock of JFDI was 1518 billion lire or 1.7 per cent of the total stock of FDI in Italy (the US share is 11.1 per cent).[2] To some extent this may render Italy less interesting than other major economies of the European Union with respect to Japan's direct role in influencing the division of labour in Europe. However, this minor role assigned to Italy will, in itself, be shown to be revealing.

Despite its size, the pattern of Japanese multinational involvement in Italy appears on the surface to be quite similar to that of other European countries. Table 9.1 shows the value and sectoral distribution of the stock of JFDI in selected years. In 1993 little more than one quarter of the stock of JFDI was in manufacturing. Since 1971, the first year for which data are available, the stock of both manufacturing and service investment has consistently grown, both in absolute terms and with respect to GDP,[3] but there has been a change in their relative importance. Note also that although the rate of growth of JFDI

Table 9.2 Stock of JFDI in Italy (manufacturing): Percentage composition and total

Year	1971	1976	1981	1986	1991	1993
Transport equipment	0	0	1	36	19	17
Mechanical engineering	0	2	10	27	48	48
Mining & metals	0	0	0	0	0	2
Chemicals	100	41	28	12	10	8
Food	0	0	0	7	0	0
Textiles	0	57	61	13	9	10
Others	0	0	1	6	13	16
Total (Lire billions)	2	9	22	101	306	398

Source: Ufficio Italiano Cambi.

Table 9.3 Stock of JFDI in Italy (services): Percentage composition and total

Year	1971 %	1976 %	1981 %	1986 %	1991 %	1993 %
Transport	0	1	0	0	4	10
Trading	100	75	61	50	34	24
Banks, Insurance	0	22	31	0	21	*
Finance*	0	2	2	45	31	57
Others	0	0	5	4	9	9
Total (Lire billions)	–	6	17	123	744	1111

Note: *For 1993 data on finance and banking/insurance are aggregated.

Source: Ufficio Italiano Cambi.

declined from 1991 to 1993, it remained positive.[4] This contrasts with its recent general downturn in the rest of the world.

Japanese manufacturing in Italy (Table 9.2) is relatively well developed in the engineering and transport equipment sectors.[5] As for services (Table 9.3), the trading sector is also well developed, given the traditionally strong links between Japanese export penetration and JFDI. Its relative weight has declined recently, however, in favour of investment related to banks, insurance and finance, to which we will refer later.

The determining features which Japanese investment patterns in other countries share with those in Italy have already been considered in general studies on JFDI. The establishment of a unified European market has received great attention, although with different emphases. In this regard, Balasubramanyam and Greenaway[6] have identified two possible explanations for the timing and the intensity of JFDI in Europe: the first relating to Japanese penetration and expansion in foreign markets as a form of bridgehead; the second depicting a defensive reaction to the establishment of what is perceived as Fortress Europe.

A different although not necessarily contrasting viewpoint is provided by Ozawa, where not only the timing and intensity of JFDI but also its sectoral composition is considered. His analysis stresses the long-run determinants of JFDI and focuses on Japan's domestic manufacturing agenda, namely the need to reorganise its manufacturing sector and change the domestic composition of output in favour of technologically more sophisticated products.[7]

The above explanations focus upon industrial factors and on FDI in manufacturing, which is not a major share of current JFDI stocks. Other approaches look at the changing role of Japan in the world economy. Japan's balance of payments' surpluses have undoubtedly engendered the threat of trade-related sanctions. FDI may, therefore, represent a way to bypass possible protectionist measures. And aside from the issue of protectionism, Japan's direct investment overseas – as well as portfolio investment – is enhanced by the appreciation of the yen, which is in turn a consequence of Japan's balance of payments surpluses.[8] These issues are important, especially for countries whose currency depreciates with respect to the yen. But they appear to be specific aspects of a more general issue, that of Japan's role as an international creditor country, and the asymmetry between its leadership in trade, which entails significant balance of payment surpluses, and its less developed financial role in the world economy.[9]

Given these general trends, the choice of the location of subsidiaries depends either on efficiency considerations or on strategic aims or, possibly, on a combination of both. The existence of firm- or sector-specific ownership advantages does explain some JFDI. Table 9.4 compares the revealed comparative advantage (RCA)[11] for exports and FDI in the sectors most involved with Japanese multinationalisation.[12] Japan's indicator is positive both for exports and for FDI in the engineering and automobile industries. This rough correlation testifies to the existence of a Japanese competitive advantage in these two industries. It also conforms to Ozawa's explanation of Japanese industrial restructuring, since JFDI in the engineering and automobile sectors is considerable and grew over the 1980s as a result of the completion of what Ozawa named Phase III in Japan's trade-dependent industrialisation.

In the chemicals sector, Japan is a net exporter but Italy is a net

Table 9.4 Japan's revealed comparative advantage in selected industries

	Transport equipment	Mechanical engineering	Chemicals	Textiles
FDI	1.00	0.19	−0.77	0.13
Trade	0.49	0.56	0.27	−0.70

Source: Ufficio Italiano Cambio (FDI figures); ICE (1994) (Trade figures).[10]

foreign investor. Note that the share of JFDI in chemicals has constantly declined (Table 9.2). The domestic development of the chemicals industry in Japan occurred during Phase II (the late 1950s to the early 1970s). Thus, JFDI in Italy in this sector began earlier than for the engineering and auto industries. Furthermore, its growth in the 1980s did not parallel that of the other two sectors, so that its share of total JFDI declined. The two indicators of revealed comparative advantage are apparently inconsistent for the textile industry as well. In this case, Italy is a net exporter while Japan is a net investor. Note that the textile industry developed in Japan during Phase I (1950 to the mid-1960s). Contrary to what would be expected, JFDI was nil in 1971, it grew in the 1970s, and then subsequently declined.

We may conclude this section by noting that examination of the different phases of Japanese industrial development provides useful insights when we focus on ownership advantages as possible determinants of JFDI. However, the data show that consistent results are obtained only when we look at recently developed sectors. As we try to understand the determinants of JFDI in other sectors (i.e. those developed in previous stages) other factors, more specific to Italy, play a significant role. These will be considered more fully below, after the characteristics of the existing cadre of Japanese subsidiaries in Italy have been introduced.

JAPANESE SUBSIDIARIES IN ITALY

As of 1993, 57 Japanese manufacturing subsidiaries in Italy have been identified.[13] In Table 9.5 they are classified according to the same criteria used for JFDI, and the engineering industry is the most prominent sector, with chemicals and textiles more favoured than transport equipment. Table 9.6 classifies projects in terms of their technological characteristics and share of ownership.[14] About 50 per cent of the firms are specialised suppliers or engaged in the production of high-technology

Table 9.5   Japanese manufacturing subsidiaries in Italy: Percentage Composition, 1993

Transport Equipment	Mechanical Engineering	Mining & Metals	Chemicals	Food	Textile	Others	(Total)
9	47	5	23	0	16	0	(57)

Source: Cominotti and Mariotti (1994).[15]

Table 9.6   Japanese manufacturing subsidiaries in Italy: Technological sector and degree of ownership

	Majority-owned	Minority-owned	Shared Equity	Total
Traditional	8	4	0	12
Scale-intensive	9	6	1	16
Specialised	9	7	2	18
High-technology	3	8	0	11
Total	29	25	3	57

Source: Cominotti and Mariotti (1994),[16] and calculations based on author's questionnaire survey data.

goods. Given the relative weakness of Italian manufacturing industry in these sectors, it is fairly easy to believe that these firms came to Italy on the strength of some form of competitive advantage.

Twenty per cent of the subsidiaries, however, are in traditional sectors, where Japanese industry does not have strong comparative advantages. As we shall examine more fully later, there is no reason to believe that productivity and prices in Italy could make FDI based on cost advantages feasible. A rather more convincing explanation is that JFDI in traditional sectors is due to the non-price competitive edge of items such as Italian clothing, leather goods, etc.; that is, due to the specific features of Italy's industrial development.

Firms engaged in sophisticated production (high-tech and specialised producers) tend to be larger (Table 9.7) and minority-owned. The size of the firms in terms of employees is linked to their level of technological sophistication: as we shift from traditional sectors to the scale economy, specialised supplier and hi-tech sectors, the number of workers rises. As for ownership, on average around 50 per cent of the firms are majority-owned by the Japanese investor, but while the proportion of controlled subsidiaries in the traditional sector is 67 per cent, it is less than 30 per cent in the high-technology sector.

Table 9.7 Japanese manufacturing subsidiaries in Italy: Average number of employees and sales, 1993

	Employees	Sales (Lire billions)
Traditional	160	49
Scale-intensive	304	161
Specialised	380	85
High-technology	721	132

Source: See Table 9.6.

Table 9.8 Japanese manufacturing subsidiaries in Italy by technological sector and method of establishment

	New Establishment	Acquisition	Total
Traditional	1	11	12
Scale-intensive	5	11	16
Specialised	2	16	8
High-technology	2	9	11
Total	10	47	57

Source: See Table 9.6.

FDI has occurred largely through acquisition and minority participation (Table 9.8): less than 20 per cent of the subsidiaries were originally established[17] by a JMNE. Also, in five instances, although the JMNE was a founder member of the Italian subsidiary, it holds a minority stake. Note that the highest proportion of subsidiaries that were set up by JMNEs is in the scale-intensive sector. This is due to the fact that the organisation of production is presumably more crucial in scale-intensive sectors, so that the investing Japanese firm is more keen to initiate and to control the establishment of the subsidiary.

The relationships between technological level, ownership, control and firm size are rather interesting. Although it is straightforward to suggest that the acquisition of a majority stake in a small company is easier in financial terms, other factors may also be relevant. Majority ownership should allow a firm to avoid disclosing its firm-specific knowledge and to exploit it in the most efficient way. Since minority shareholdings prevail in the *sophisticated* sectors, one is led to ask what it is that makes Italian firms agree to have a Japanese partner, and what makes the latter confident that a minority shareholding is

Table 9.9   Percentage share of exports on sales by technological sector:
Japanese subsidiaries that sell abroad[20]

Traditional	Scale-intensive	Specialised	High-technology	Total
44	39	49	52	45

Source: See Table 9.6.

worthwhile. A possible explanation is that the Japanese advantage lies
in the organisation of production, an advantage which is more cultural
than technical, thus not easily disclosed. However, this does not explain why JMNEs should avoid setting up new firms. Indeed, financial
reasons may make acquisitions more convenient. None the less, it is
here suggested that Italian firms have advantages of their own, which
JMNEs are interested in.

In the traditional sector majority ownership is likely to be less a
way to manage a firm's ownership advantages efficiently than a means
of gaining access to a sector-specific advantage peculiar to the Italian
productive structure, or what constitutes the essence of *Made in Italy*:
quick adaptation to a continuously changing and highly sophisticated
consumer market. As for other sectors, we shall see in the next section
that although in sophisticated sectors Japan has a comparative advantage Italian manufacturing also has advantages of its own.

Japanese subsidiaries have a significant ratio of exports to sales (Table
9.9). All but one[18] of the subsidiaries for which data were available
(24) are exporters. It is no surprise that traditional industries have a
high share of exports,[19] given that the traditional sector in Italy is typically
export-oriented. The sophisticated sectors, less predictably, also appear
to be characterised by a high share, when considered in terms of Italy's
revealed comparative advantage. This may well be accounted for by
the firm-specific advantages of the investing firm. The scale-intensive
sector is the one with the lowest share. This would appear to be rather
counter-intuitive: scale economies are supposed to determine concentration of production in Europe and subsequent shipping patterns in a
market where transport costs had dropped.[21] However, not all scale-
intensive industries require a market as large as Europe. Indeed, the
overall size of the subsidiaries in this sector is, with exceptions, not
very large.

Exports basically go to Europe (Table 9.10), much in line with Italy's
general orientation.[22] The share of exports to Japan is relatively high
when compared with Italy's overall share of 1.9 per cent in 1992. On

Table 9.10 Destination of exports of Japanese subsidiaries that sell abroad[23]

Europe	Japan	Elsewhere	Total
76	5	19	100

Source: Information obtained through questionnaire-based inquiry.

Table 9.11 Origin of imports by Japanese subsidiaries that buy abroad[27]

Europe	Japan	Elsewhere	Total
55	32	13	100

Source: See Table 9.10.

Table 9.12 Imports of intermediate goods by Japanese subsidiaries as share of purchases by technological sectors[29]

Traditional	Scale-intensive	Specialised	High-technology	Total
98	31	55	75	49

Source: See Table 9.10.

the whole, the export pattern of Japanese subsidiaries is geographically similar to Italy's general pattern; it is more pronounced, and also characterised by a greater technological content.

Import behaviour is less easy to generalise. Only 14 out of 25 firms for which data were available are importers.[24] The share of imports from Europe is much lower (Table 9.11) than the overall Italian total,[25] while the Japanese share is particularly high.[26]

The composition of imports by technological sector (Table 9.12) must be considered with great caution, since very few firms are included. What appears to be the case, however, is that when subsidiaries do import, they are highly dependent on foreign supplies. As far as the sophisticated sectors are concerned,[28] this may suggest that the positive effects of Japanese MNEs on the industrial structure – in terms of technological upgrading – are diluted by a substantially low degree of integration with the local productive environment and, possibly, within the firm.

In sum, Japanese subsidiaries operate in diverse sectors, not all of which are characterised by (Japanese) country-specific comparative advantages. Most firms were established through acquisitions and half of them are minority-owned. The general conclusion seems to be that, although Japanese MNEs have organisational advantages and, possibly, other firm-specific advantages, these are not enough to justify their presence in Italy. Import behaviour is not the same for all subsidiaries, contrary to export performance. Thus, while single firms may be export platforms or part of a regional corporate network in Europe, this does not seem to be the general case. JFDI as a way to disguise Japanese exports and penetrate Fortress Europe does not seem to be a completely satisfying explanation.

Strategies seem to differ. Particularly in the case of traditional sectors the impression gained is that subsidiaries are established to gain access to Italy's country and sector-specific advantages. Minority holdings in sophisticated-sector firms may be evidence that, at least in part, this applies to these subsidiaries as well. Clearly, therefore, if the above considerations are correct, one question to be answered is why the stock of JFDI in Italy is so small, that is to say, what locational disadvantages detract from the industrial advantages of operating in Italy. This is the main concern of the following section.

AN EXPLANATION FOR THE SMALL STOCK OF JFDI IN ITALY

The overall stock of JFDI in Italy, especially manufacturing FDI, is very small. If we assume that the supply-side determinants for Japanese FDI are the same throughout Europe, it is locational factors that we must focus on. It may be worth recalling that, as Yamazawa[30] points out, a distinction has to be made between sub-sectors within a manufacturing industry: the auto sector requires big plants and this necessitates a concentrated geographical distribution within Europe; the engineering sector often requires much smaller plants, so that a greater geographical dispersion is possible. Thus, as far as the automobile (and also the chemicals sector) is concerned, it could be argued that locational advantages were greater elsewhere – due to subsidies, weaker trade unions, etc. – and that FDI in other countries has displaced FDI in Italy. This would not be an appropriate explanation for the lack of FDI in other industries.

In order to understand what may have influenced JFDI, Italy's major features in terms of industrial structure and economic policy must be recalled. During the 1970s, and until the EMS was established, devaluations had fostered competitiveness abroad. This favoured indus-

Table 9.13 The real exchange rate between Italy and the EU/EC

1978	1979	1980	1981	1982	1983	1984	1985
94.2	95.7	100.0	98.0	102.3	106.8	108.2	106.2

1986	1987	1988	1989	1990	1991	1992	1993
106.3	107.0	104.6	107.8	109.8	110.2	106.7	93.8

Source: ICE (1993).[33]

tries whose competitive edge was determined by low prices rather than by the technological and qualitative features of their products. Innovations that would enhance non-price competitiveness were not favoured.

This policy prevented dramatic economic and social consequences when firms were suffering rather large losses.[31] The cost of this policy was rising inflation and growing reliance upon devaluations, but it allowed a more gradual and effective productive and financial reorganisation of large firms during the late 1970s, while the trade unions and their claims on distribution were gradually weakened. The failure of the occupation of Italy's largest plant, FIAT's Mirafiori, in 1980, symbolically represented the completion of a reorganisation of production within large firms and the end of the period of social turmoil that characterised the late 1960s and the 1970s. These circumstances reduced the above-mentioned economic costs of the change in monetary policy.

Following the establishment of the EMS, Italian monetary policy became tight. Some devaluations did occur during the first half of the 1980s but exchange rate policy became stricter during the second half. Given fixed nominal rates, Italy's relatively high inflation rate entailed a constant appreciation of the real exchange rate, especially the rate between the lira and the currencies of its major trading partners, the EU member states (Table 9.13). The underlying aim of the Bank of Italy was to force Italian firms not to rely on devaluations and to pursue competitiveness at the level of the firm.[32] Wage conflicts were reduced but, given the new monetary and exchange rate policy, competitiveness had to be non-price.

Italy specialises in the production of goods in traditional industries and in machinery, basically producer goods. In the former, although competitive advantage is related to the introduction of advanced technologies in productive activities that would otherwise be mature, and despite a peculiar ability to adapt to the nature of a market where fashion and tastes change very rapidly, price competition is still important. During the 1980s a somewhat unexpectedly long period of high in-

Table 9.14   Italian market shares of G7 Imports (percentages) by
technological sectors

	1982	1992
Traditional	76	56
Scale-intensive	27	25
Specialised	37	38
High-technology	16	14

Source: ICE (1993).[35]

ternational growth rates partially substituted for the drop in devaluation induced exports. Table 9.14, however, shows Italian exports by
technological sectors as a proportion of G7 imports[34] in 1982 and 1992.
The pressure that the overvaluation of the lira put on the traditional
industries is fairly easy to see. Italy's relative share grew only in the
specialised producer sector, while it declined in the others. Structural
change was not as rapid as may have been expected, at least as far as
foreign trade is concerned.

Thus, since high exchange rates favour imports – to the detriment
of exports and local production – and since they also make FDI relatively expensive, Italy's persistently high real exchange rate prevented
price competitiveness from being a significant locational determinant
for export-oriented Japanese subsidiaries.

JAPANESE FDI IN THE SERVICE INDUSTRIES

Table 9.3 shows data on JFDI in the services which, it may be worth
recalling, in 1993 accounted for 73 per cent of the overall stock. Two
elements are very clear. The importance of the trading sector declines
while that of banking, insurance and finance rises. Note that finance as
such – as opposed to banking and insurance – accounts for at least
one third of the stock. This reflects a general trend which has been
pointed out[36] but has received less attention than in the case of manufacturing. In view of the limited information available, only a few
observations will be made.

Usually, data on finance are provided together with data on banks,
and FDI is basically attributed to the latter. A strong and twofold link
is assumed to exist between banks and manufacturing industry.[37] First,
banks are believed to become multinationals in order to provide ser-

vices to their clients who operate in foreign markets. Here the link relates to manufacturing activities and banking activities. Second, it is assumed that banks operate much like manufacturing firms, so that the prevailing explanations for multinationalisation are extended to this specific industry.

Since financial services include leasing, factoring and merchant banks, an extension of the above-mentioned approach might be suggested. Although there has always been a strong relationship between Japanese manufacturing firms and Japanese banks[38] and also between manufacturing and finance, the share of FDI in banking and finance relative to FDI in manufacturing (and trade) appears to be particularly high, and can hardly be explained by the provision of banking and financial services to Japanese firms going abroad.

Apart from the statistical data, recent events have tended to reduce the importance of the above-mentioned link, in both of its aspects. Following general trends in other countries, the role of the Japanese financial sector has been changing. Financial asset-holding by manufacturing firms has grown, much as in other countries; deregulation in international financial markets has created new profit opportunities, independent of the activity carried out by Japanese manufacturing subsidiaries and trading companies. The Japanese financial sector does not appear to be fully equipped to cope with these changes, although Japan's bubble economy showed that a first attempt has been made.

Considering these points, an explanation for JFDI in financial services would appear to be that Japanese companies are going abroad to learn from more developed markets, as well as to flee what Dufey names the 'repression of financial market development inside Japan'.[39] Although this explanation may be worth further investigation, it should be kept in mind that there are no such places as London or Frankfurt in Italy. Financial centres may exist, but they do not appear to be significant enough to explain the above phenomenon.

Another element which relates to financial evolution and may be of some interest is the reorganisation of property structures and the increasing presence of holding companies. These may be set up for various reasons. Leaving aside tax-related explanations, there may be organisational and managerial reasons, whereby it is more convenient to manage a large corporation by splitting it up and co-ordinating its productive activities and financial sourcing through the holding company. These circumstances have certainly occurred in Italy. Should they be the underlying explanation of the high level of service JFDI, the conclusions might be that manufacturing FDI is underestimated but that there is nothing specific to finance.[40]

Holding companies, however, have provided not only internal flexibility (i.e. related to management of a corporation) but also external flexibility: mergers and acquisitions have been made easier, with results that have not always led to market efficiency but allowed oligopolistic concentration to increase. Furthermore, as firms formerly specialised in manufacturing increased their awareness of financial market factors, this has sometimes led to the pursuit of merely financial yields rather than profits out of production, thus causing, as well as receiving, benefits out of asset inflation. To some extent, this leads us away from an investigation of JFDI as such. But it suggests that, although industrial features are important, general conclusions cannot disregard more general processes.

CONCLUDING REMARKS

JMNEs are forced to expand internationally as a result of domestic factors. These relate both to specifically industrial aspects and to the more general fact that the persistent balance of payments surplus has transformed Japan into a net international creditor. JFDI in Italian manufacturing reflects competitive advantages held by JMNEs as well as the search for advantages held by Italian firms. As for traditional locational advantages, they have been rather scarce, given Italian exchange rate policy in the 1980s.

Patterns of JFDI seem to adhere to, rather than change, patterns of industrialisation. The existence of specific advantages on both sides – Japanese and Italian – may foster organisational and technological upgrading within Italian firms. Structural change seems to be much more dependent upon other factors. This, however, is not the only possible outcome. In 1992 Italy abandoned the fixed exchange rate regime it had adhered to for 13 years. This was the outcome of a persistent current account deficit. Despite the industrial reorganisation of the late 1970s and early 1980s, the overvaluation of the lira was not paralleled by a new composition of output that would render exports less sensitive to prices.

The devaluation determined a rise in exports which, together with stagnating domestic demand, allowed an (until now) non-inflationary recovery. To some extent a new pattern of growth seems to have substituted itself for the one experienced in the 1980s, a pattern that recalls what occurred in the 1970s. Exports drive growth, and the depreciation of the lira enhances exports. Major differences from the 1970s are that today wage bargaining is not as fraught as it was and the prices of commodities – especially oil – are not as subject to dramatic shocks.

Industrial sectors that are less subject to technological innovation may be favoured by such a growth model. Innovation and technological upgrading, however, would be less enhanced, while competitiveness would presumably be pursued through reductions in labour costs and beggar my neighbour policies. Although in the long run Italy would suffer stronger competition by less developed, and East European, countries, short-sighted policy-makers might well choose to follow this path.

JFDI in Italy, as we know it, was undertaken despite the exchange rate policy of the 1980s. It relied on non-price competitiveness. Should a process similar to that experienced in the 1970s return, different types of JFDI would become acceptable. The constraints on the location of subsidiaries in Italy would be loosened. Japanese FDI in the traditional sectors would be favoured not only because Italian fashion constitutes an advantage to be acquired, but because Italian market shares would rise and because FDI in Italy would be relatively cheap. Export-disguising subsidiaries would be favoured as well. Available evidence seems to corroborate this line of reasoning. While JFDI in the world as a whole has decreased during the past three years, in Italy it has kept on growing.

The third phase in Japanese industrial reorganisation seems to be over. Japan remains a creditor country, however. It is interesting to speculate how, as domestic determinants on industrial foreign investment are reduced, the problems posed by the balance of payments surplus will be dealt with. No possible scenarios will be outlined here. But, should there merely be a shift from foreign investment in manufacturing to foreign investment in finance and/or portfolio investment, the result could be an increasing mobility of capital. In turn, this could increase the difficulty of preventing the exchange rate fluctuations that prevailed in the 1970s, and seem to have returned today.

NOTES

1. The author wishes to thank L. De Benedictis and R. Schiattarellla for their comments on a previous version of this paper. The usual disclaimer applies.

2. Unless otherwise stated, the source of the data on JFDI is Italy's Foreign Exchange Bureau (*Ufficio Italiano Cambi*). Data for 1993 are provisional.
3. With the exception of 1981, when there was a 1.5 per cent drop in manufacturing JFDI/GDP.
4. This is also true when JFDI is measured in terms of US dollars or yen.
5. To be precise, this is mainly motorcycle, bicycle, small commercial vehicle and component investment, rather than car-making.
6. V.N. Balasubramanyam and D. Greenaway, 'Economic Integration and Foreign Direct Investment: Japanese investment in the EC', in *Journal of Common Market Studies*, 2 (1992).
7. T. Ozawa, 'Japanese Multinationals and 1992', in B. Burgenmeier and J.L. Mucchielli, eds., *Multinationals and Europe 1992 – Strategies for the Future* (London: Routledge 1991). Ozawa identifies four phases in Japanese industrialisation, each based on a leading group of industries: (1) labour-intensive, low wage, such as textiles; (2) scale-intensive, such as petrochemicals; (3) assembly-based consumer durables, such as automobiles; and (4) flexible manufacturing and highly differentiated, such as super-computers. Stages in Japanese multinationalisation correspond to the constraints arising within these phases. The crucial constraints for the first three phases are, respectively: (a) shortage of factory workers; (b) air pollution and shortage of industrial space, and (c) foreign reactions to the Japanese export surplus.
8. The evidence on the relation between the yen–US $ exchange rate and JFDI is clearly outlined in UNCTAD *World Investment Report 1994 – Transnational Corporations, Employment and the Workplace* (New York: United Nations 1994), p. 47.
9. See R. Bonavoglia and M. Gresti, *Al Servizio dell'industria. Il ruolo della finanza nello sviluppo economico del Giappone* (Bologna: Il Mulino 1993).
10. See note 2; ICE (Istituto nazionale per il commercio estero) *Rapporto sul commercio estero* (Rome: ICE, 1994).
11. RCA = [(Aj − Ai)/(Aj + Ai)] × 100, where A is FDI or exports and j and i represent Japan and Italy respectively. Data sources for JFDI and trade are different so the comparison is only indicative.
12. Given the small size of the stock of JFDI in Italy, great caution is needed when interpreting the data, since a single operation could greatly affect the overall figures.
13. Data on subsidiaries are drawn from R. Cominotti and S. Mariotti, (eds., *Italia multinazionale 1994. Le nuove frontiere dell'internazionalizzazione produttiva* (Milan: Etaslibri 1994), and from a questionnaire-based survey, carried out by the author.
14. A word of caution is required, given the small number of cases, and the possibility of data for single firms giving rise to misleading overall conclusions.
15. See Cominotti and Mariotti (1994).
16. Ibid.
17. The term *greenfield* may be misleading in that it usually refers to new firms that create new capacity. When new subsidiaries are established through joint ventures, most often the Italian partner provides pre-existing plants.
18. This one exception is interesting in that it imports all its intermediate

products from Japan and assembles them for the Italian market.

19. Since the aim of this analysis is to identify patterns of behaviour or strategies of Japanese subsidiaries, data on exports and imports are applied only to firms that actually sell or buy abroad.

20. Figures refer to 23 firms for which data were available.

21. This view was originally expressed by M. Itaki and M. Waterson, *European Multinationals and 1992*, University of Reading Working Papers in International Investment and Business Studies B, 141 (1991), but it is also consistent with explanations of a European division of labour based on regionally integrated corporate networks. See also J. Cantwell, ed., *Multinational Investment in modern Europe – Strategic interaction in the integrated Community* (Aldershot: Edward Elgar 1992).

22. In 1992, 65.9 per cent of Italian exports went to Europe. For this figure, and for those that outline Italy's trade, see ICE (Istituto nazionale per il commercio estero) *Rapporto sul commercio estero* (Rome: ICE, 1993, 1994).

23. See note 18.

24. The other firms presumably resort to intermediaries rather than having direct links with foreign suppliers.

25. In 1992, 66.6 per cent of Italian imports were from Europe.

26. Italy's share in 1992 was 2.3 per cent.

27. Figures refer to 14 firms for which data were available.

28. The traditional sector is here represented by a single firm that imports raw material from the Far East.

29. See note 25.

30. I. Yamazawa, '*Japan*' in S. Borner and H. Grubel, eds., *The European Community after 1992. Perspectives from the outside* (London: Macmillan, 1992).

31. Large firms, where the trade unions were strong, were characterised by tough wage disputes and dependence upon the banking sector. See F. Giavazzi and L. Spaventa, 'Italy: The Real Effects of Inflation and Disinflation', *Economic Policy* (April 1983).

32. See G. Nardozzi, ed., *Il ruolo della banca centrale nella recente evoluzione dell'economia italiana* (Milan: Angeli 1993) for a detailed analysis of the Bank of Italy's industrial policy during the 1980s.

33. See note 20.

34. The indicator is $(Xi/X)/(Mi/M)$, where X is Italian exports, M is G7 imports, and i represents one of the technological sectors.

35. See note 20.

36. See UNCTC, *Transnational Corporations in World Development: Trends and Prospects* (New York: United Nations, 1988).

37. See J.H. Dunning, 'The Globalisation of Service Activities', in J.H. Dunning, ed., *The Globalisation of Business* (London: Routledge, 1993).

38. This is according to G. Hawawini and M. Schill, 'The Japanese Presence in the European Financial Services Sector', in M. Mason and D. Encarnation, eds., *Does Ownership Matter? Japanese Multinationals in Europe* (Oxford: Oxford University Press (1994), one of the few competitive advantages that Japanese banks do have.

39. G. Dufey 'Comment', in M. Mason and D. Encarnation, eds., *Does Own-*

ership Matter? Japanese Multinationals in Europe (Oxford: Oxford University Press, 1994), p. 289.

40. Although this circumstance cannot be denied, note that the proportion of Japanese manufacturing subsidiaries is roughly the same as the proportion of JFDI over total inward JFDI, and that the size distribution of Japanese manufacturing subsidiaries does not seem to be significantly different from that of others. It is therefore reasonable to believe that Japanese financial subsidiaries are not significantly involved in manufacturing.

10 The Evolution of Japanese Investment in Spain: An Economic Evaluation[1]

Paloma Peláez,
Javier de Quinto,
Santos Ruesga and
Kazuei Tokado[2]

INTRODUCTION

In 1994 the Department of Economic Structure at the Autonomous University of Madrid initiated a research project the aim of which was to evaluate the performance of Japanese investment in Spain. The study was focused upon companies with more than 50 per cent of their capital in the hands of Japanese investors. As part of the study only industrial and service sector projects were to be examined, with portfolio investment by Japanese interests excluded from the analysis.[3]

The conclusions now being presented are provisional only, as the research process has not yet been concluded. Consequently, this paper should be considered as an interim summary of the results obtained in the first phase of the research, as well as an introduction to the later stages of the project.

THE EVOLUTION OF JAPANESE INVESTMENT IN SPAIN

The liberalisation process associated with foreign investment in Spain began in the late 1960s. As this liberalisation process was getting underway, the international economic crisis of the mid-1970s had the effect of retarding a massive influx of foreign capital until the period leading up to the accession of Spain to the European Community (EC) in 1986.

The main objective of investors based in Japan, the United States or countries in the European Free Trade Area (EFTA) was to establish a trading position in Spain which would mitigate the potential replacement of extra-Community imports by products from trading partners within the enlarged EC-12, and by so doing take advantage of the significant growth anticipated for Spain at that time. Japanese investment in Spain in this context, therefore, needs to be understood as a phenomenon that emerged in the specific context of the late 1980s and early 1990s, in the same way as significant American investment appeared in Spain in the period 1965–72, at the end of the post-war era of high growth.

For some other countries in what is now the European Union, Japanese investment became noticeable earlier, in the middle 1970s.[4] Indeed, most Japanese multinational companies opened branches in other European countries, mainly in Germany, the United Kingdom and France, before they established themselves in Spain. Relative to the situation in many larger economies in northern Europe, therefore, the Japanese presence in southern European countries has been unimpressive, and not least in Italy, despite a direct market with nearly 57 million consumers living in that country.

Additionally, it should be pointed out that although significant.[5] Japanese productive investment in Europe does not match the volume of Japanese manufacturing in the US. Hence in Europe there were 728 industrial companies with Japanese participation exceeding 10 per cent of capital in 1994, while in the US (in 1992) there were 1724.

THE TIME PROFILE OF JAPANESE INVESTMENT IN SPAIN

The emergence of Japanese investment projects in Spain has been discontinuous, with a peak year value in 1987 of more than 30 billion pesetas halved in the next 12-month period. Since then, the volume of investment has increased year by year, until it reached a new maximum in 1991. Since 1991, total foreign investment in Spain has started to decline. This reversal, which was very noticeable by 1992, may be linked to the general dullness of the global economy. In 1993, nevertheless, total inward investment kept stable in relation to the previous year; whereas by 1994 the recovery process had apparently begun, with a 26 per cent year-on-year increase.

Inward investment in Spain originates mainly from firms based in other European Union member-states. It is biased sectorally towards manufacturing industry and favours locations close to Madrid and Barcelona. Investment originating in Japan increased constantly until

Figure 10.1 Recent growth of confirmed Japanese investment in Spain

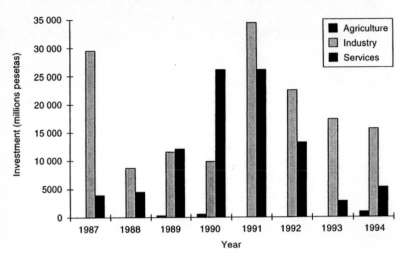

Source: Calculated from Secretary of International Economy and Foreign Transaction, Ministry of Economy and Treasury.[8]

1991 (Figure 10.1), even though the expansive phase of the economic cycle had ended by 1990. Subsequently, since 1991, annual output growth rates have gradually decreased.[6]

As has been noted, a significant influx of foreign capital to Spain became apparent in the middle of the 1980s. But even before then, at the end of the 1970s, many leading general trading companies or *sogo shosha*,[7] such as Marubeni, Mitsubishi, Mitsui, Nissho Iwai, Tomen or Sumitomo had already begun to establish themselves in Spain. At this time the *sogo shosha* started to operate as trading agents, having invested as Spanish companies. This was attributable to the fact that the Spanish economy began to expand rapidly and there were more business opportunities in the Spanish market.

The 1980s witnessed a relative upsurge in the growth of projects involving Japanese capital in Spanish locations.[9] In the first years of the decade, a number of Japanese companies established representational offices in Spain, especially banks and financial intermediaries which later established subsidiaries in many cases. This was shortly followed by a considerable number of industrial investments, which were essentially concentrated in the electronics and automobile sectors, and to a lesser extent, in the chemicals sector. At this time, world-renowned companies in the electronics sector, such as Sony, Sanyo,

Panasonic, Pioneer, Seiko, Sharp and Canon, established themselves in Spain. Contemporaneously, vehicle assemblers also opened factories in Spain, with a Kubota tractor plant in 1987, Suzuki purchases of 32 per cent of Santana Motor in 1985 and 100 per cent of Puch in 1986, the Honda purchase of Montesa in 1986, and continuing investment by Nissan in the Motor Ibérica truck plant near Barcelona. Important vehicle component investments, including the Bridgestone acquisition of Firestone Hispania in 1988, and the NHK spring investments in 1980 and 1992, were also made during this period.

The crisis at the beginning of the 1990s has led to a retrenchment in the pattern of Japanese investment in Spain. In 1994, Suzuki decided to cease production in the Santana Motor plant in Linares, Kubota made a stop payment order and Nissan broke up its Spanish operations into five independent companies. But it seems that from 1995, in keeping with a new trend in the business cycle, the outlook is changing, with some new investment in Motor Ibérica and an agreement to continue production in the Suzuki-Linares plant.

INVESTMENT IN SERVICES

The analysis of Japanese investment by sector shows that investment in the tertiary sector has a cyclical character, and has been deeply affected by the economic expansion of the 1980s, as well as by the progressive liberalisation of the law on banking establishment. The profile of investment in this sector can be interpreted mainly in terms of the growth of investment in financial services. Consequently, neither the public utilities, such as water, gas or electricity, nor the transport and communication service sectors, reveal any important Japanese involvement.[10]

The presence of Japanese banks in Spain, as well as financial services companies, is relatively recent. This apparent hesitation can be explained in part by legal obstacles to the establishment of foreign banks in Spain, which only permitted the opening of a maximum of three branches, and restricted promotional activities.

Investment by the Japanese banking sector in Spain is noticeable only between the years 1986 and 1991. As a consequence, this restricted presence differs significantly from that achieved by Japanese tertiary sector investors in other major financial markets, such as London, Frankfurt, Paris or Milan. Freedom of establishment in the banking sector, effective since 1 January 1993, did not, however, seriously

Table 10.1 Position of Japanese banks in Spain, 1993

Ranking in Spain	Bank	Total Assets	Credit Investment	Branches	Staff
47	Sumitomo Bank	143 396	110 248	2	34
53	Bank of Tokyo	111 434	96 571	2	65
55	Industrial Bank of Japan	116 382	71 111	1	25
58	Mitsubishi Bank	101 899	73 482	1	29
63	Sanwa Bank	90 035	71 582	2	23
64	Dai Ichi Kangyo Bank	85 530	41 667	1	19
66	Sakura Bank	72 335	68 305	2	38
70	Fuji Bank	62 812	52 056	1	20
93	Tokai Bank	36 680	24 900	1	17

Note: The ranking does not include the Saving Banks. Figures in millions of pesetas.

Source: Own elaboration.

influence the pattern of establishment by Japanese banks in Spain, if only because by that time all the larger firms were in place.

The operating system of Japanese banks in relation to attracting funds is based on the inter-bank market. The strategy applied to their lending activities involves the search for low-risk clients, such as local and regional authorities, public utilities, Japanese companies operating in Spain and other multinationals. Of lesser importance, they also participate in import–export trading agreements. The lending operations of Japanese banks in Spain therefore usually have very high unit volumes and very long maturity dates. Borrowing, on the other hand, involves widely diverging expiration dates.

The most common operations are forwards, collars, swaps (now in open decline after the fluctuation band widening of the exchange system in the European Monetary System), caps, floors and exchange insurance. The more adventurous institutions are now introducing in-project financing, leverage leasing and some involvement in corporate equity management, such as mergers and acquisitions, debenture and bond issues, and the launching of share offers.

Japanese banks established in Spain were almost unanimous in their response to survey questions about their prospects and future development plans. Maintaining current business until the current economic climate improves and retaining the existing client basis was emphasised in most cases.

The Japanese banking executives also pointed out, as an important reason for their establishment in Spain, the advantages associated with the liberalisation of the Spanish financial system and full membership of the European Union. Reasons which were disregarded or de-emphasised include limited business opportunities in the Japanese market, liquidity excess, negative experiences of Japanese banks in business links with less developed countries and the specific attractions of the financial sector in Spain, protected by the exchange mechanism of the European Monetary System.

While Japanese investment in Spain in a number of service sector activities, such as insurance, are not recorded,[11] all the leading *sogo shosha* companies are established in Spain. These firms stated in the survey that their initial purpose in coming to Spain was the anticipated growth of the Spanish market, and reduced trading prospects in Japan. The operations of this type of Japanese company began with the performance of financial and trading advisory services, leading on to the diversified general trading of goods to and from Spain and Japan, as well as third countries. In addition, they trade in the commodities market, maintain distribution and wholesale chains, participate in some manufacturing ventures, offer services to business, and generally engage in a variety of other trade-related activities. All the trading companies that were surveyed express optimism, despite the rigidity of the labour market which is widely viewed as a major handicap for the Spanish economy, and believe they are achieving satisfactory results.

A Japanese presence in the Spanish economy can also be detected in the parcel delivery service industry (Nippon Express), air transport (Japan Airlines) and the alcohol and restaurant industry (Suntory). Other Japanese transport services in Spain are also represented by firms such as Hankyu Express International, Kintetsu Express, Nissin Transportes España and OCS.

With regard to manufacturing, Japanese companies operating in Spain are concentrated in the industrial machinery, machine tool, steel, non-ferrous metals, transport equipment (especially cars and motorcycles), medical equipment, solvents, petrochemical products, food, textile products and jewellery sectors. Companies in these sectors, however, although they have been on the point of obtaining some important public contracts in Spain (as in the case of Mitsubishi and the AVE high-speed train project), have not yet achieved any significant public purchasing successes.

Table 10.2 Position of Japanese companies in Spain by sector

Food and beverages	Limited
Mining	Nothing
Equipment goods	Limited
Textile, clothing and footwear	Nothing
Steel, aluminium and metal	Nothing
Wood and cork	Nothing
Energy	Nothing
Transport	Nothing
Public services	Nothing
Tourism and catering	Nothing
Computers and electronics	Important
Automobiles	Important
Aeronautics	Nothing
Naval	Nothing
Chemicals, fertilisers and paper	Almost nothing
Building materials and cement	Almost nothing
Wholesale and retail trades	Some activity
Films, television, books, leisure	Nothing

Source: Own elaboration.

INVESTMENTS IN MANUFACTURING

A comparison of Japanese-owned manufacturing and service sectors firms in Spain shows clearly that the former emerged first, are more diversified and display more microeconomic linkages. The bulk of Japanese manufacturing in Spain is attributable to the electronics and automobile industries, or to be more precise, the transport equipment sector. Although chemicals-related projects have been present since Japanese firms began to invest in Spain, they have been overshadowed by the continuing prominence of these two sectors which are so strongly identified with Japanese manufacturing competitiveness.

The industrial companies that were surveyed were questioned about their own firm's economic situation, as well as the national and international productive environment. They were unanimous in referring to problems related to the labour market in Spain as the most intractable feature of manufacturing in Spain. In this context, three aspects were stressed, with frequent labour disputes, the high cost of dismissing employees in one of the most inflexible labour markets in Europe and relatively high wage costs combining to ensure that only 50–75 per cent of the level of productivity the same firms achieve in Japan could be achieved in Spain.

All the companies surveyed made negative comments on the evolution of the Spanish market during the last few years, especially the automobile companies. Furthermore, the results of these Japanese industrial companies reinforce this negative outlook, with profits in previous years becoming significant losses. Nevertheless, at the beginning of 1995, this negative evaluation begins to weaken.

The specific situation of automobile companies in Spain in some sense parallels that of firms in the same sector in other developed countries, just as the constraints on Japanese car companies resemble those of competitors in other major auto-makers. To illustrate this situation, it is apparent that roughly 40 per cent of the 90 000 workers in the automobile sector in Spain are directly affected by employment regulation (Iveco-Pegaso, Citroën, Peugeot-Talbot, Ford, Seat, Ebro-Kubota, Santana Motor and Nissan), while in 1993 40 000 jobs related to the automobile sector were lost in the European Union as a whole.

In spite of the adverse national and international economic situation in 1992 and 1993, one of the Japanese automobile companies, Nissan Motor Ibérica, continued making large-scale investments in production processes in its factories. This permitted an increase in staff numbers up until 1992 (7000 workers at that time), with the maintenance of production volumes. Although a commitment to production in Spain is very clear in this case, profit figures were transformed into major losses by 1992 (14 billion pesetas in that year and 41 billion in 1993). For Nissan Motor Ibérica, the cost of the crisis in the sector is expected to involve 150 billion pesetas, this figure incorporating the firm's own forecasts that predict losses until 1996. The Suzuki case, however, presents substantial differences when compared with the responses of Nissan. Job cuts had been undertaken previously, investment volume was lower and losses appeared earlier. The scale of commitment to the Spanish economy in this case is less apparent, but is still significant, in view of the fact that 3000 are currently employed in the subsidiary.

In this brief sectoral analysis of the Japanese manufacturing presence in Spain, it is apparent therefore that substantial employment is involved in a limited number of sectors, while there has been very little involvement in some sectors that are well represented in Spain by non-Japanese multinationals, such as oil, petrochemicals, fine chemicals, pharmaceutical products, retailing, food and beverages, insurance and clothing.

Table 10.3 Evolution of confirmed Japanese investment in the Spanish regions as a percentage of the total investment

Regions	1987	1988	1989	1990	1991	1992	1993	1994
Andalucia	0.1	0.8	16.4	7.7	4.0			
Aragon			4.3	0.5				
Asturias			1.8				7.6	
Balearics		0.1		0.5				
Basque country	0.1			4.0	0.3	22.4	0.1	3.0
Canaries			0.1					
Cantabria					0.8	11.2		
Castilla-Leon		5.8	2.1			14.0		
Castilla-La Mancha								
Catalonia	1.9	53.9	34.9	29.6	19.2	11.0	41.0	15.9
Estremadura								
Galicia		0.1						
Madrid	11.1	38.4	27.6	56.6	65.1	37.7	47.1	57.3
Murcia								4.1
Navarra		0.4	10.2	0.2	2.7	0.4	4.2	10.1
La Rioja								
Valencia		0.1	2.6		7.2	2.1		2.7
No region	86.7	0.5		0.9	0.6	1.4		6.9
Total	100.0	100.0	100.0	100.0	100.0	100.0	100.0	100.0

Source: Secretary of International Economy and Foreign Transactions, Ministry of Economy and Treasury, and own elaboration.

SPATIAL IMPACT OF JAPANESE INVESTMENT IN SPAIN

For an analysis of the geographical distribution of Japanese invest-ment in Spain, the only official Spanish source of information on for-eign capital classified by spatial destination has been used. This is the record of foreign investment confirmed by the Secretary of Interna-tional Economy and Foreign Transactions. In previous pages this source has been referred to and its limitations have been mentioned. Never-theless, it is also used to appreciate the nature of the information used in this paper and to reiterate some of its shortcomings.[12]

The available data are presented in Table 10.3, where it is possible to see that more than two-thirds of the Japanese registered investment in the period of analysis was received by Madrid and Catalonia, the two most developed regions of Spain. The other autonomous commu-nities did not register considerable investment inflows, although totals for Andalucia and the Basque country (the third industrial area in the country), were respectable.

It would be easy, therefore, to conclude from this initial view of investment flows that there are two very clear poles of attraction in Spain for Japanese investors, which are clearly identical with the more industrially developed and populous regions of the country. Indeed, the initial interest of Japanese investors was particularly centred on the highly industrialised region of Catalonia. The progressive consolidation of economic growth since 1985 has meant that the investment flow in that region has unambiguously increased in absolute terms, although the attraction exerted by other areas in Spain has entailed a relative decline in Catalonian pre-eminence during 1991 and 1992.

The influence of economic cycles and the traditional behaviour of Japanese capital in its initial pattern of foreign establishment can partly explain these developments. The high growth rates in the second half of the 1980s and the excellent growth expectations after accession to the European Community are the main reasons for the choice of Spain as an investment destination. Moreover, the productive nature of the manufacturing projects determined that Catalonia was the most favoured location in Spain. Its consolidated industrial infrastructure, traditional manufacturing sectors, excellent access to proximate European markets, and a skilled labour force, all make it a likely choice for initial establishment.

These first investments in manufacturing emerged alongside other Japanese projects which sought to provide business services. In this way, a number of the Japanese operations in Madrid were assisted by the establishment of companies such as banks and trading services.

Other investments, located outside the Madrid and Catalonia regions, are characterised by sectoral diversity, but with automobile and electronics projects prominent in Andalucia. This can be seen by comparing Tables 10.3 and 10.4, where it is clear that the scale of Japanese investment in Andalucia is largely attributable to the establishment of Suzuki and Fujitsu, as well as some investment in the hotel business and services.

CONCLUSIONS

Under normal conditions, Japanese investment in Spain ought to increase markedly in the next few years. The scale of the Japanese presence in Spain is small and appears inconsistent with the actual size of both economies. Japanese investment represents about 2 per cent of foreign direct investment in Spain, and this figure placed Japan in 1991

Table 10.4 Location of leading Japanese manufacturers in Spain

Company	Location	Activity
Suzuki	Gijón (Asturias): Puch-Suzuki	Motorcycles
	Linares (Jaen/Andalucia): Santana	Automobiles
	La Carolina (Jaen/Andalucia): Santana	
	Manzanares (Ciudad Real/Castilla-La Mancha):	
	Santana	
Sony	Viladecavals (Barcelona/Catalonia)	Electronics
Suntory	Ciudad Real (Castilla-La Mancha)	Distillery
NHK	Navarra	Automobiles
Nissan	Zona Franca de Barcelona (Catalonia)	Automobiles
	Moncada-Reixach (Barcelona/Catalonia)	Printing
	Cuatro Vientos (Madrid)	Motors
	Avila (Castilla-Leon)	Lorries
	Anoain (Navarra)	Trolleys
Honda	Cornellà d'Llobregat (Barcelona/Catalonia)	Motocycles
Kubota	Cuatro Vientos (Madrid)	Tractors
Yamaha	Palau de Plegamans (Barcelona/Catalonia)	Motocycles
Sanyo	Barberà de Vallès (Barcelona/Catalonia)	Electrical
Kao	Mollet (Barcelona/Catalonia)	Chemicals
	Barberà de Vallès (Barcelona/Catalonia)	
Fujitsu	Málaga (Andalucia)	Electronics

Source: Own elaboration.

in tenth position as a national source of foreign investment in Spain. In many of the cases studied, nevertheless, the presence of the Japanese firms in Spain would seem inevitable if the market ambitions of leading Japanese firms were considered against the size and growth expectations of the Spanish market.

Japanese investment in Spain is a typical phenomenon of the 1980s, after an earlier introduction into other European countries. We can conclude that its manufacturing side is essentially concentrated in the automobile and electronics sectors. It is also relevant to point out the absence or minimum presence of Japanese industrial investment in sectors that have been attractive in other cases for investors from other countries.

A large share of investment volume has gone to assembly, distribution, advertisement, promotion and consumer services, and this has not been typical for Japanese investment elsewhere. Nevertheless, it is possible to point out the commitment of many well-known Japanese investors in producing in Spain, with Nissan, Suzuki, Fujitsu, Sony, Panasonic, Honda, Yamaha and others heading the list. Since 1993, however, problems of disinvestment by Japanese firms have been noticeable.

Table 10.5 Japanese firms in the rank order of the largest non-financial companies in Spain, 1991

Ranking in Spain	Company	Revenue (millions of pesetas)	Staff
32	Nissan Motor Ibérica	162 756	7974
65	Sony	88 019	1077
112	Firestone Hispania	49 000	4480
134	Santana Motor	43 129	3311
163	Canon	36 200	430
184	Mitsubishi	32 000	30
224	Fujitsu	26 835	2200
225	Panasonic	26 500	605
237	Sanyo	25 000	844
–	Sharp	24 309	615
–	Montesa-Honda	15 300	290
–	Marubeni	14 800	26

Source: Own elaboration.

Regarding the financial sector, two observations can be made. First, the very recent establishment of the main firms; and second, the appeal of Japanese expansion in other European cities may have declined relative to the perceived attractions of locations in Spain.

Spain is no longer a country with an abundant, cheap and relatively skilled labour force and is no longer a country of highly protected sectors. Other countries have appeared in the global economy with similar economic profiles and, moreover, they have cheaper, more docile and less organised labour. The stability of foreign direct investment in manufacturing industry, and the maintenance of short- and medium-term investment flows will only be achieved if the factors that ensure that a location is attractive to investors are maintained and developed. Less timid reforms in the labour market, expansion of recent initiatives in continuous training, upgrading of the educational system and the modernisation of infrastructure can all increase the appeal of Spain as a destination for foreign investment. In the long term, therefore, it is clear that infrastructure endowments and human capital will be the centrepiece of any plans by Spanish economic policy-makers to attract higher quality inward investment from Japan or elsewhere.

NOTES

1. For the preparation of this study we have had the unselfish collaboration of a number of Japanese firms, which have generously given their time. We also want to acknowledge a group of third-year business students at the Autonomous University of Madrid, who have helped in the collection of data during the 1993-4 academic year.

2. Paloma Peláez, Javier de Quinto and Santos M. Ruesga work as professors in the Department of Economic Structure and Development Economics in the Autonomous University of Madrid. Kazuei Tokado is professor in the Kanda University of Tokyo.

3. The study is based on information supplied by a very broad sample of companies. They were sent an open survey with the objective of understanding the nature of their establishment in Spain, their growth (or in some cases decline and extinction), their present-day situation and their plans for future development. We have also used the available data on foreign investment in Spain from the Secretary of International Economy and Foreign Transaction in the Ministry of Economy and Treasury.

4. In January 1983 there were 157 Japanese industrial companies (with more than 10 per cent Japanese capital) in Europe. In January 1993 there were 713, and in January 1994, 728.

5. It is estimated that Japanese firms have created 200 000 direct jobs in Europe since 1983.

6. A rise occurred at the beginning of 1991, followed by a sharp and absolute decline at the end of 1991, in the last two quarters of 1992, and in the second quarter of 1993.

7. The *sogo shosha* are very diversified corporations with widespread international trading activity. The products they deal in include raw materials, textile products, food, business equipment, electronic products and all kinds of technology.

8. The use of data from the Secretary of Foreign Transaction as a source of information of the evolution of foreign investment in Spain presents noteworthy problems, given that there have been some significant gaps in the series. This has been due to modifications in the law on investments. Nevertheless, trends and movements can be accurately detected in so far as the investments that require confirmation are all large scale.

9. The first large investment by a Japanese firm in Spain was the acquisition of Secoinsa by Fujitsu in 1975; this action can be understood as an attempt to create a big Spanish–Japanese computer firm. The second major investment was the purchase of Motor Ibérica by Nissan in 1980.

10. Most industrial companies manage their own distribution, and therefore these capital movements are assigned to industrial activity.

11. However, there are some insurance activities from Japanese companies in Spain through their British subsidiaries.

12. All foreign direct investment in Spain is recorded by the Ministry of the Economy and Treasury, and these figures have been used for this analysis. However, Spanish legislation on foreign investment has changed a great deal recently. This has had the result that data have become discontinuous, but can still be usefully applied in comparisons.

11 Nissan Motor Ibérica in Spain and Japanese Production Systems

Montserrat Pallares-Barbera

INTRODUCTION

Globalisation of production processes in the automobile industry has increased competitiveness among firms. Some firms have responded by moving from the Mass Production System (MPS) to the Lean Production System (LPS), characterised by flexible manufacturing and Just-in-Time (JIT) inventory. This paper will focus upon the structural changes brought about by the shift from MPS to LPS in the automobile industry in Spain, examining in particular Nissan's Motor Ibérica (NMI) subsidiary. Analysis of trends in total production, exports, industrial structure and employment in NMI between 1975 and 1990 suggests that the subsidiary has transformed its production system, with LPS gradually replacing MPS since 1986, although the transition is still far from complete.

The objective of this paper is to show how examining one Japanese investment project in Spain can illustrate the global automobile producer's strategy of utilising the comparative advantages offered by particular countries. Changing production systems in the motor industry require new locational advantages in order to achieve the goal of cost minimisation (locational strategies), and these are intrinsically linked to productivity and efficiency. Furthermore, changing technologies are accompanied by the need to alter organisational and management systems. The Lean Production System (LPS) is only the latest example of manufacturing processes that adjust themselves to internal and external pressure for cost reduction and quality enhancement. This paper analyses the structural changes associated with this transition in the motor industry in Spain, which is emerging as one of the most important industries in terms of employment, value-added, productivity, export share and the balance of payments.

PRODUCTION SYSTEMS IN AUTOMOBILE MANUFACTURING

Changes in production systems do not appear suddenly. A new manufacturing system is the result of multiple changes in existing production methods. Technological improvements may be the basic factor, but other factors also influence shifts from one production system to another, such as cost reduction, production differentiation and changing demand. The development of LPS in Japan was the result of multiple changes in MPS, in order to adapt the latter to domestic productive conditions and conditions of demand.[1]

Manufacturing is a complex system which works at different levels. The structure of the automobile manufacturing industry consists of several firms linked in a hierarchical manner, with the output of one type of firm constituting an intermediate input to the next level of the hierarchy. This division of function also has geographical consequences. In the system of production developed in the American automobile industry at the beginning of the twentieth century, following innovations by Ford, Taylor and Sloan, a majority of high value-added tasks such as management, design and distribution were retained by home country manufacturers. Production of parts and components were performed at geographically diverse locations and assembly was usually done close to final markets. Until the mid-1970s, this system (MPS),[2] was also the norm for most other leading industries.

The invention of a new and more flexible system in Japan by the Toyota Company allowed the automobile industry to respond to increased fragmentation of demand while maintaining scale economies.[3] The Japanese system is called, among other things,[4] the Lean Production System (LPS) in so far as it uses a minimum amount of resources and factory space. In the LPS, firms are becoming more and more dependent upon the resources of other firms to reach their level of output because an increasing share of the resources needed for production – intermediate outputs and knowledge (R&D and design of the car) – is provided by the joint effort of a network of firms.

Furthermore, in the LPS, the development of JIT[5] deliveries further underlines the interdependence of firms, which require changes to be made by managers to organise relations with supply firms. Assemblers now require more efficient delivery systems, and there is increased demand for out-sourcing alternatives in an attempt to reduce vertical integration. This new arrangement demands specific investments from a subgroup of firms in the network and therefore presupposes longer-term commitment by the parties involved. Automobile firms find themselves integrated into long production chains where coordination between firms within the chain becomes a requirement for more effective performance.

THE GROWTH OF THE SPANISH AUTOMOBILE INDUSTRY

In the 1980s, Japanese and European firms achieved the economies of scale required to challenge the competitive position that had been held by US companies in the world market since the first quarter of the century. The motor industry in Spain was at that time a relatively new industry, with production, value-added, employment, export shares and productivity in an expansive phase. In addition, the number of vehicles per person in Spain suggested that room for rapid growth existed, being considerably inferior to the average for the EC.[6]

By 1990, Spain occupied fourth position among European car producer countries behind Germany, France and Italy. This position clearly differed from the situation in 1950, when Spain produced only 0.02 per cent of European car output. By 1980 the proportion had reached almost 10 per cent, and in 1990 Spanish production was 12.5 per cent of European production. Similar trends were present in Spanish car exports, which were mainly destined for other European countries. While in 1970 Spain's car exports represented 8.2 per cent of domestic car production, in 1980 this figure went up to 47.8 per cent, and by 1989 it had reached 56.4 per cent.[7]

In the expansion period, Spain received new and important automobile investments, as joint ventures or greenfield firms, from countries like Germany, Japan and the US, which benefited from the comparative advantages offered by the country. These included strong domestic demand, a good strategic position with respect to Central European and Mediterranean countries, a well-established network of suppliers and an educated labour force familiar with automobile production. The advantage provided by Spain in the 1970s as a cheap labour force country disappeared at the beginning of the 1980s, and was taken up by other countries in Europe, as well as emerging industrial economies.[8]

The introduction of LPS in Spanish automobile firms began in 1986 in Nissan Motor Ibérica and, much later on, in 1990 and 1991, in SEAT-Volkswagen and General Motors España. One of the first changes introduced in the old production practices of the firms was the JIT inventory system. In addition, other developments in the system of production included an increase in group approaches to task work, in-

Table 11.1 Japanese investment in the Spanish automobile industry, 1987–93

Year	Pesetas (millions)	%
1987	28 877.51	70.45
1988	56.25	0.14
1989	1 337.29	3.26
1990	1 206.80	2.94
1991	2 007.20	4.90
1992	869.47	2.12
1993	6 637.40	16.19
Total	40 991.92	100.00

Source: Ministerio de Industria Dirección General de Transacciones Exteriores.

creasing workforce skills and academic qualifications, larger investments in flexible manufacturing systems and increasing efforts to monitor the quality of both intermediate and final products.

However, while important features of the LPS were introduced in Spanish automobile manufacturing firms, there were some established features of the Spanish economy and its motor manufacturing sector, which modified the introduction of the LPS in Spain.[9] These mainly involved levels of unionisation and the size of the foreign-owned sector. The level of unionisation in Spain is not very high – 18 per cent of the working population in 1987 – compared to 44 per cent in Italy and 53 per cent in the UK and Portugal in the same year. Nevertheless, the number of days lost through strikes is much higher than in these other countries, and a longer process of discussion before labour will adapt to any new job practices seems to be needed. Additionally, many competitive assembly firms located in Spain are the subsidiaries of foreign multinational firms, where innovations such as LPS may be slower to emerge due to a lack of scope for local initiatives.

NISSAN MOTOR IBÉRICA

Even though Spain received a relatively small share of Japanese investment between 1982 and 1991 compared with some other European countries, data show a clearly increasing trend throughout the period. It was in the mid-1980s that Spain opened its doors wide to Japanese investment, particularly in the motor manufacturing sector, which received the highest proportion of inward investment (Table 11.1).

Table 11.2   Japanese passenger car import penetration levels: Selected
countries

Year	Spain %	France %	W. Germany %	Greece %	Italy %	Portugal %	Switzerland %	UK %	USA %
1975	n.a.	1.5	1.7	10.8	n.a.	20.5	8.4	9.0	9.4
1980	n.a.	2.9	10.4	49.2	0.1	7.5	23.2	11.9	21.3
1981	1.3	2.6	10.0	48.2	0.1	11.9	27.2	11.0	21.8
1982	1.4	2.9	9.8	45.8	0.1	8.5	26.7	11.0	22.6
1983	1.2	2.7	10.6	39.9	0.2	8.1	27.4	10.7	20.9
1984	0.6	3.0	12.0	30.9	0.2	8.5	24.5	11.1	18.3

Source: World Motor Vehicle Data (1986, 1991).

On the demand side, although Spain imposed a limitation of 1200
direct car imports from Japan in 1992, there was a high demand for
Japanese cars. Indeed, in January 1992, the demand for Japanese cars
reached 36 600 vehicles. Japanese indirect car imports to Spain – Japanese
cars assembled in the EU[10] – equalled 12 860 units for the same year,[11]
further indicating that there is a clear imbalance in the Japanese car
market in Spain. High demand coincided with the 1987–91 period of
economic expansion in Spain, but before this, data on Japanese car
import penetration show quite low figures for Spain, reaching only 0.6
per cent in 1984, while Switzerland and Greece had reached totals of
24.5 per cent and 30.9 per cent respectively (Table 11.2).

Restructuring was the main theme at the Nissan plant in Barcelona
during the 1980s. The goal of the management was to adapt the plant
to the requirements of a new product and a new method of production.[12] In 1980 Nissan Motor Company, the second largest Japanese
motor manufacturer, bought a share of a Spanish automobile firm called
Motor Ibérica, renaming it Nissan Motor Ibérica.[13]

The Japanese company increased its share of NMI equity later in
the decade, as restructuring continued. This was done in two ways,
changing both the type of product and the system of production. First,
until 1984, production was devoted to commercial and industrial vehicles, such as trucks and tractors. Then from 1984, NMI produced sta-
tion wagons (the Nissan Patrol and Nissan Vanette, and more recently
the Nissan Serena). Parallel to this product change, NMI also pioneered
the introduction of LPS in Spain. In 1986, one of the main features of
LPS – JIT distribution – was introduced at the NMI plant in Barcelona. With this new distribution system, NMI wanted to achieve two
objectives: to diminish the amount of stock in the assembly plant and

Table 11.3   Nissan Motor Ibérica: R&D activities

	1975 %	1980 %	1985 %	1990 %
Assembly R&D is done:				
By the assembly firm	95.0	90.0	75.0	40.0
By other firms	5.0	10.0	25.0	60.0
Parts and components R&D is done:				
By the assembly firm	60.0	60.0	50.0	20.0
By the component firm	40.0	40.0	40.0	50.0
By other firms	–	–	10.0	30.0
Other type of arrangement	–	–	–	–

Source: Interviews conducted by M. Pallares-Barbera in 1992.

to introduce rigorous sequential order into component delivery to the assembly line.

The new supply system also initiated a completely new relationship between the suppliers and NMI, which was clearly reflected in a number of developments. The first of these was the diminishing number of suppliers (down from 1000 in 1983 to 290 in 1992), with the eventual goal of reaching 250 suppliers. The second was the establishment of a quality control filter for suppliers, which meant that the intermediate product goes through a process of quality control in the production plant before arriving at the NMI plant, and suppliers that do not reach required NMI quality levels have their contracts discontinued. Thirdly, supplier firms are to be responsible for new technology improvements and the new R&D demanded by NMI.

Consequences of this policy may be detected in the increased participation of other firms in vehicle design between 1975 and 1990, since 95 per cent of car innovations were made by the assembly firm in 1975, and only 40 per cent were made in 1990 (Table 11.3). This trend partly illustrates the change from MPS to LPS, in which R&D design under MPS is strictly the responsibility of the assembly firm, while in the LPS these functions may be undertaken jointly by the assembler and its suppliers.

As a consequence of this fundamental restructuring, internal characteristics of the firm, such as employment and capital investment, have changed, and production has increased. The rate of growth in production between 1984 and 1990 was 22.66 per cent; and while in 1984 productivity was 2.3 vehicles per worker, in 1990 it had risen to 12

Table 11.4 Nissan Motor Ibérica: vehicle production and employment totals

Year	Output (1000 Units)	Employment (1000s)	Productivity
1975	–	8.8	–
1976	–	10.3	–
1977	–	11.3	–
1978	–	11.9	–
1979	27.3	11.8	2.3
1980	27.1	11.4	2.4
1981	20.2	10.8	1.9
1982	18.2	10.1	1.8
1983	20.3	9.0	2.6
1984	19.5	8.6	2.3
1985	27.7	8.0	3.5
1986	42.7	6.5	6.6
1987	53.5	6.0	8.9
1988	76.1	6.8	11.2
1989	86.4	6.6	13.0
1990	81.3	6.8	12.0

Source: Nissan Motor Ibérica Annual Reports 1975–90; Chambre Syndicale des Constructeurs d'Automobiles, *Répertoire Mondial* (1983, 1985).

Table 11.5 Nissan Motor Ibérica: worker training levels

	1980	1990	1991
Number of courses per year	406	778	816
Number of hours per year		170 218	241 975
Number of participants	4 300	4 701	5 472

Source: Interviews conducted by M. Pallares-Barbera in 1992.

(Table 11.4). This increase was reflected in the declining number of workers, which suffered a negative growth rate of 1.57 per cent between 1975 and 1990. Otherwise, there was a noticeable increase in the skills of the labour force, a product of the continuous educational strategy of NMI between 1980 and 1991, which is evident from the data shown in Tables 11.5 and 11.6.

This process of restructuring also engendered some unexpected consequences for the study of NMI's production function. Due to massive investment by the parent firm in the plant, the elasticity of output with respect to capital was negative over this period.[14] This result suggests

Table 11.6 Nissan Motor Ibérica: labour force skills and qualifications

Academic qualification	No. of Workers (1990)	% of Labour Force	No. of Workers (1991)	% of Labour Force
A. *Higher education*:				
Engineering graduates	136	2.0	150	2.2
Other graduates (Masters)	–	–	58	0.8
Technical engineers	225	3.3	223	3.2
Bachelors degree	155	2.3	126	1.8
B. *Secondary education*:				
Formación Profesional 1st year	701	10.4	751	10.9
Formación Profesional 2nd year	801	11.8	901	13.1
C. *Primary education*:	4744	70.2	2241	32.5
D. *Other*	–	–	2437	35.4
Total	6762	100.0	6887	100.0
Average seniority	12.9		13.9	
Average age	38.6		39.1	

Source: Interviews conducted by M. Pallares-Barbera in 1992.

that the expected returns to capital were not attained in the 1980s, and seems to be a manifestation of the Japanese business policy of looking for longer-term returns to capital and pursuing higher market share, rather than short-term profits.

Most NMI production has serviced domestic demand, with around 70 per cent of production in the period up to 1990 sold in Spain (Table 11.7). The cost structure of NMI's operation shows that the cost of materials was around 70 per cent of the total at the beginning and end of the 1975–90 period, with a value of around 60 per cent recorded between 1980 and 1985. The trend in labour costs moved in the opposite direction, however, rising from 22.7 per cent in 1975 to 30.2 per cent in 1981, before falling consistently to a figure of 15.9 per cent of total costs in 1990 (Table 11.8).

The picture given by these NMI figures suggests that, even though the firm was located in Spain in the middle of the economic expansion period of the 1980s, the main locational determinant was not the prospect of an immediate increase of a market share. The position of Spain was important relative to Mediterranean markets, and its place in Europe after accession to the EC in 1986 reduced problems of potential

Table 11.7   Nissan Motor Ibérica: domestic sales and exports
(thousands of units)

Year	Domestic Sales	Exports	Total Sales	% Domestic Sales	% Exports
1975	34.3	15.0	49.3	69.5	30.5
1976	33.8	14.3	48.1	70.3	29.7
1977	41.7	12.9	54.6	76.3	23.7
1978	43.0	13.9	57.0	75.6	24.4
1979	37.8	8.7	46.5	81.2	18.8
1980	34.3	6.2	40.5	84.6	15.4
1981	23.8	6.9	30.8	77.5	22.5
1982	25.5	8.6	34.1	74.7	25.3
1983	23.4	6.4	29.8	78.7	21.3
1984	20.5	8.1	28.6	71.7	28.3
1985	26.6	12.0	38.5	69.0	31.0
1986	31.9	14.8	46.7	68.3	31.7
1987	40.9	20.1	61.1	67.0	33.0
1988	53.1	24.7	77.9	68.2	31.8
1989	64.6	26.0	90.6	71.3	28.7
1990	60.4	31.3	91.7	65.8	34.2

Source: Nissan Motor Ibérica (1975–90).

market access. Furthermore, Barcelona's well-established component suppliers network was a major attraction, given that in 1992 Barcelona contained around 40 per cent of the Spanish car component industry, ensuring that NMI would continue to operate close to its suppliers, 42.9 per cent of which are located in Barcelona, over twice the number (19.3 per cent) of those located in Madrid.

Once the decision to locate in Spain was made, there nevertheless remain some questions concerning the decision of Nissan to acquire a company that required considerable restructuring. The most important factor may have been that Nissan wanted to locate in Barcelona close to the commercial port where shipments of finished products could be exported promptly to Europe and beyond. Given the shortage of industrial land in the city the good location of the old Motor Ibérica (in Barcelona's Zona Franca) was a determining factor in making the locational decision. In additional, Nissan may have wished to pre-empt any competing firms (Japanese or otherwise) from acquiring Motor Ibérica and establishing themselves in Spain first.

Table 11.8   Nissan Motor Ibérica cost trends: percentage breakdown, 1975–90

Year	Labour Cost	Material Cost	External Services	Capital Depreciation	Total
1975	22.7	69.7	4.1	3.5	100.0
1976	23.4	67.9	5.0	3.7	100.0
1977	24.7	67.5	5.0	2.8	100.0
1978	23.4	69.1	5.5	2.0	100.0
1979	26.5	68.3	3.5	1.7	100.0
1980	28.4	62.9	6.5	2.2	100.0
1981	30.2	57.8	9.1	2.9	100.0
1982	27.2	60.4	8.9	3.5	100.0
1983	24.3	59.2	12.3	4.2	100.0
1984	22.3	59.5	13.0	5.2	100.0
1985	19.0	60.5	12.6	7.9	100.0
1986	19.0	64.2	9.0	7.8	100.0
1987	16.9	65.6	8.9	8.6	100.0
1988	14.8	68.8	9.5	6.9	100.0
1989	14.6	69.0	9.3	7.1	100.0
1990	15.9	72.9	10.3	0.9	100.0

Source: Nissan Motor Ibérica (1975–90).

CONCLUSION

From a spatial perspective, changes in industry breed changes in the wealth and prosperity of regional economies. Changing technologies of production are an important means of effecting these regional changes. The health and survival of regional economies depend upon the ability of enterprises to adjust to changing production technologies and changing consumer preferences. Supply adjustments to the fluctuations of market demand are crucial to the well-being of firms and the regions in which they are located.

The introduction of flexible specialisation and the initial stages of the lean production system have been necessitated by changes in demand. Automobile assemblers found that they could no longer compete successfully by offering a standard product, but had to adjust to new demand characteristics. Changing the manner of production in an effort to maintain scale economies and adapt to global competition seem to be the only mechanisms available to a firm wishing to survive in the changing international division of labour. The drastic restructuring of NMI illustrates this process of adaptation and demonstrates how inward investment, in this case involving a major Japanese motor manufacturer, can effect structural changes in regional economies in Europe.

NOTES

1. 'U.S Auto Makers Reshape for World Competition', *Business Week* (1982), pp. 58–63; D. Hounshell, *From the American System to Mass Production 1800–1932. The Development of Manufacturing Technology in the US.* (Baltimore: Johns Hopkins University Press, 1975).
2. Other terms found in the literature are Fordism, Taylorism,and Standard Production System.
3. P. Bianchi, 'Nivells de Politica i Naturalesa de la Competencia Post-Fordista', *Revista Econòmica de Catalunya* 14 (1990), pp. 94–102; E. Toyoda, *Toyota: Fifty Years in Motion* (Tokyo: Kodansha International, 1987); P. Wells and M. Rawlinson, 'New Procurement Regimes and the Spatial Distribution of Suppliers: the Case of Ford in Europe' *Area*, 24, 4 (1992) pp. 380–90.
4. Just-In-Time, Toyotism or Flexible system.
5. Just-in-Time systems involve a sequential, frequent and timely delivery of parts and components in order to satisfy the immediate demand of each step of the production process. This also implies a reduction of inventory, and a change in the ways of delivering intermediate goods.
6. Spain's average car density in 1988 was 263 vehicles per 1000 inhabitants, while the EC's average was 359 (Econ. Commission for Europe, *Annual Bulletin of Transport Statistics for Europe* (1994); EUROSTAT 1994).
7. M. Pallares-Barbera, *The Structural and Spatial Adjustments of the Automobile Industry in Spain: 1975–1990*, Ph D thesis (Boston University, 1993).
8. R.B. Cohen, 'The New Spatial Organisation of the European and American Automotive Industries', in Noulart and Wilson Salinas, eds., *Regional Analysis and the New International Division of Labour* 1983) pp. 135–43.
9. SEAT-Volkswagen (Martorell, Barcelona), opened in 1991, and Nissan Motor Ibérica opened a warehouse logistic centre 15 minutes away from its factory in the Zona Franca (Barcelona) See 'Nissan Motor Parts España S.A.', *La Vanguardia* (27 January 1995).
10. There is doubt as to whether cars made in the EU and cars made by the Japanese transplants in Europe are exactly the same product. The Certificate of Origin of Goods concept states that 'goods will originate from a country when they are produced entirely in this country or when the last justified transformation or substantial elaboration is done in this country' (*Diario Oficial de las Comunidades Europeas* 1968).

11. Interbask S.A. (1992).
12. Nissan Motor Ibérica, *Annual Reports* (1975–90).
13. This is a factory with a long history. What started in 1920 as a Ford Motor Company plant in 1933 changed its name to Ford Motor Ibérica; and in 1959 it became Motor Ibérica.
14. Output elasticity with respect to labour was also negative. Moreover, labour costs, consisting of wages and social security benefits per worker, increased rapidly in this period.

12 Japan and Sweden: Two Countries Far Apart

Bert Edström

INTRODUCTION

Neither the scope nor the volume of relations between Sweden and Japan changed to any significant degree for several decades after the turn of the century. After the Second World War, however, the scope of Swedish–Japanese relations started gradually to expand. Exchanges increased, not only in trade, but in other fields as well: foreign direct investment, tourism, student exchange, missionary activities in Japan by Swedish churches and cultural contacts.

The image of Japan as a modern, advanced country, first broadcast at the time of the 1964 Olympic Games, achieved a breakthrough with the publication of Håkan Hedberg's *Den japanska utmaningen* (The Japanese Challenge) in 1969, an instant bestseller not only in Sweden but in many other countries as well.[1] Hedberg extrapolated current trends and concluded that Japan was destined to become a future economic superpower, more powerful than the Soviet Union and richer than the United States.

The evolution in the image of Japan that began at the end of the 1960s gained speed in the 1970s. A perusal of Swedish journals after 1945 reveals that the number of articles dealing with Japan, particularly articles on economics, increased noticeably beginning in the mid-1960s.[2] After 1970, the interest in Japanese industrial efficiency and management methods stimulated by Hedberg's book continued to grow. And like the rest of the West in the 1980s, Sweden was to experience a surge of interest in books on Japanese management and industrial organisation.

Notwithstanding the Japan boom of the 1980s, mutual exchange remained rather lacklustre and has continued to be so. Whatever indicator is used, figures for Swedish–Japanese bilateral relations and exchange are seldom impressive:

- High-level visits are a recent phenomenon. The first visit to Japan by a Swedish Minister for Foreign Affairs, for instance, took place as late as 1964. The first prime ministerial visit did not take place until 1991. Ministerial visits have subsequently become much more common, but only ministers responsible for economic affairs visit Japan regularly.

- Swedish business has never been lured by the mirage of the Japanese market: the total number of established Swedish companies in Japan was fewer than 90 at the end of 1994 – a grouping comprising giants such as ABB and Volvo down to small one-man establishments.[3]
- The Swedish colony in Japan consists of only a few hundred. Also, very few Japanese citizens live in Sweden: the Japanese colony consists of only about 1200 residents, including the children of Japanese married to Swedes.[4]

TRADE AND FOREIGN DIRECT INVESTMENTS

As a small open economy, Sweden is very internationalised. The share of total production which is exported (often called trade dependence) is high: in 1989, the figure for Sweden was 27.1 per cent, compared to 18.3 for the UK, 13 for Australia, 7 for the United States and 9.4 for Japan.[5] The Japanese share of Sweden's total exports and imports is modest, as can be seen from Tables 12.1 and 12.2, in which the 1992 figures for Swedish trade are presented. Imports from Japan comprised 5.1 per cent of total imports, while exports to Japan amounted to 2 per cent of total exports.

Japan ranks as the 7th largest supplier of Swedish import goods and the country's 13th largest export market.[6] The low level of total imports and exports conceals the fact that trade with Japan is important for some of Sweden's industrial sectors. Products of manufacturing were important both for imports and exports, comprising 87 per cent of total Swedish imports from Japan (51 per cent being machinery and various types of apparatus), and 52 per cent of the country's exports to Japan.[7] The most remarkable feature of Tables 12.1 and 12.2 is the gap between total imports from, and exports to, Japan. Imports were 2.2 times larger than exports. This trade surplus in Japan's favour has continued for a number of years, but there has been little interest on the Swedish side in closing the gap. The strong trade imbalance in Japan's favour (1:3) has not generally been seen as a problem, as long as the total Swedish balance of trade remains positive.[8]

The lack of effort at the national level is indicated by a laconic comment from a well-known economist in April 1994, speaking about

Table 12.1   Swedish imports, 1992 ($US millions)

SITC	Imports (A)	From Japan (B)	B as Share of A (%)
0, 1, 2.2, 4 (Foods, etc.)	3 695	3	0.1
2, excluding 2.2, 3 (Raw materials and fuel)	6 102	14	0.2
5–9 (Manufactured and semi-manufactured goods)	40 053	2 504	6.3
0–9 Total	49 850	2 521	5.1

Source: Kommerskollegium [National Board of Trade], *Handelspolitiska relationer mellan EU, USA och Japan: Konsekvenser för Sverige som EU-medlem* [Trade policy relations between the EU, the United States and Japan: consequences for Sweden as a member of the EU]. Rapport 1994:3. (Stockholm, 1994), p. 72.

Table 12.2   Swedish exports, 1992 ($US millions)

SITC	Exports (A)	To Japan (B)	B as share of A (%)
0, 1, 2.2, 4 (Foods, etc.)	1 109	14	1.2
2, excluding 2.2, 3 (Raw materials and fuel)	6 309	34	0.5
5–9 (Manuactured and semi-manufactured goods)	48 515	1 089	2.2
0–9 Total	55 933	1 137	2.0

Source: As for Table 12.1, p. 7.

the widespread view that part of the solution to the economic problems with which Sweden was struggling lay in increased exports. 'The United States, Canada, Australia and Japan', the economist revealed, 'no longer figure in discussions of export-promoting activities'.[9] If Japan's share of Swedish trade is small, Sweden's share of Japanese trade is minuscule. Overall figures show that Sweden barely counts as far as gross figures for Japanese trade are concerned. As can be seen from Tables 12.3 and 12.4, Sweden accounted for a mere 0.5 per cent of Japanese imports, as well as exports, in 1992. Nor did many Swedish prime export commodities count for much on the Japanese market. In fact, only five commodity groups on the SITC double-digit level accounted for 2.5 per cent or more for imports; none for exports.[10]

Table 12.3   Japanese imports, 1992 ($US millions)

SITC	Imports (A)	From Sweden (B)	B as Share of A (%)
0, 1, 2.2, 4 (Foods, etc.)	39 718	12	0.0
2, excluding 2.2, 3 (Raw materials and fuel)	78 224	36	0.0
5–9 (Manufactured and semi-manufactured goods)	113 034	1 158	1.0
0–9 Total	230 976	1 206	0.5

Source: As for Table 12.1, p. 78.

Table 12.4   Japanese exports, 1992 ($US millions)

SITC	Exports (A)	To Sweden (B)	B as share of A (%)
0, 1, 2.2, 4 (Foods, etc.)	1 952	2	0.1
2, excluding 2.2, 3 (Raw materials and fuel)	3 833	10	0.2
5–9 (Manufactured and semi-manufactured goods)	333 706	1 689	0.5
0–9 Total	339 490	1 700	0.5

Source: As for Table 12.1, p. 79.

To a certain extent, the gross figures mask reality. Even if the two countries are not important trading partners for each other in terms of total trade, the Japanese share of the Swedish market is sizeable for some specific commodities. Japanese brands are as well known in Sweden as anywhere else in the world: Toshiba, Sony, Honda, Mitsubishi, Canon, Minolta are all household names in Sweden.

For Swedish export goods on the Japanese market, the situation is different. Very few Swedish brands are known to Japanese consumers apart from Volvo, SAAB and Absolut Vodka.[11] Market gains for Swedish companies on the Japanese market in recent years may improve the situation, however. With regard to total exports to Japan, Sweden now ranks fifth among suppliers of pharmaceuticals, fourth among suppliers of passenger motor cars, and second among suppliers of telecommunications equipment.[12]

According to Japanese statistics, the overall trade balance switched to Sweden's favour in 1993.[13] One important factor behind the overall change in the trade balance was the change in car sales, primarily the shrinking number of Japanese cars sold in Sweden. While 90 562 Japanese vehicles were sold in Sweden in 1989, the figure had declined to 17 962 by 1993; sales of Swedish vehicles in Japan increased from 9753 to 13 116 in the same period.[14] In 1994, Volvo sales increased sharply to 17 500.[15] While the Swedish automobile market expanded in 1994 and early 1995, sales of Japanese cars continued to be sluggish and their share of the Swedish car market was 10 per cent,[16] a significant decrease from previous years, in which they sustained a 25 per cent share of the market.

A similar pattern of development for trade and foreign direct investment can also be perceived. Despite the fact that both Japan and Sweden have made substantial investments abroad, neither has been a heavy investor in the other country. Between 1951 and 1992, the total figure for Swedish investments in Japan was $US59 million (according to Japanese statistics) – according to Swedish statistics, the figure was $US119.6 million from 1981 to 1992.[17] Japanese investments in Sweden have been even fewer and more modest than Swedish investments in Japan. Between 1951 and 1993, Japanese companies invested in Sweden in only 77 instances for a total of only $US106 million. This corresponds to 0.16 per cent of Japanese investments in Great Britain, 0.07 per cent of Japanese investments in the EU, and less than Japan's investments in Portugal, Greece, and Denmark. In addition, only seven cases involved manufacturing.[18]

A comprehensive report commissioned by the Swedish government, published in 1991, cited similarly gloomy figures for Japanese investments in Sweden between 1985 and 1990, which led the author of the report to lament that 'direct investments have so far been insignificant in both directions', and to characterise them as 'marginal'.[19] A survey published in 1994 by JETRO lists ten Japanese investments in the manufacturing sector in Sweden,[20] while another report from 1993 mentions only two Japanese companies even considering investing in Sweden.[21] The total number of Japanese-owned companies in Sweden was 55 in 1993, with an employment total of 3756, compared to 53 companies employing 4056 in 1992.[22] Against such a background it is not surprising that Swedish officials have expressed an interest in attracting Japanese investments to Sweden, and it is no exaggeration to say that, in recent years, Swedish policy-makers have been preoccupied with the problem of how to bring about an increase in Japanese investments.

The promotion of Japanese investments was cited as one of the reasons for the visit to Japan by the prime minister, Ingvar Carlsson, the first ever by an acting Swedish prime minister.[23] One of the main tasks for the members of the high-level delegation was to convey to Japanese counterparts the Swedish interest in attracting Japanese investments.[24] Carlsson told a reporter: 'we are above all interested in Japanese investments. So far no important Japanese investments have been made, but Sweden is one of the most advanced industrial countries in Europe and I think Japanese companies have a self-interest in investing in Sweden'.[25] Rune Molin, the minister of industry and a member of the prime minister's delegation, indicated that learning from Japan was another reason: 'we believe that it would be fruitful for Swedish business to experience how the Japanese work, both in organising labour and motivating personnel.'[26]

The visibly keen interest in Japanese investment continued with the Conservative-led coalition government that took over in 1992, and was enhanced in March 1993 with a high-profile delegation to Japan,[27] headed by the prime minister, Carl Bildt, accompanied by his foreign secretary, Margareta of Ugglas, and finance minister, Bo Lundgren.

The main reasons for Japanese investments having been limited in Sweden are often said to have to do with the small domestic market, high wage levels and high social security costs.[28] In a survey of Japanese companies conducted by Dentsu in 1994, the impact of such factors is confirmed: the chief reported image of Sweden was that of a welfare but high tax state with an expensive health care system, high personal taxation, a small domestic market and a modest market growth potential.[29] 'In economic terms', the report concludes, 'Japanese companies rate Sweden a "low-risk, low-return investment, a nation whose market is fully matured" [30]

Against this background of limited Japanese investment in Sweden, a proposal for remedying the situation was advanced in 1992 by the Japanese Businessmen's Club in Stockholm, in a memorandum sent to the Swedish government. Among the organisation's suggestions were reform of the paid vacation system, in the redundancy scheme, in public services, and in the exemption of foreigners from high VAT on hotels and restaurants, as well as in tax incentives (reduction of income taxes, VAT, corporate taxes, road taxes, social insurance premium), tax exemptions for housing rents and education fees, investment incentives (a subsidiary system for investing companies, preferential banking rates, etc.), improvement of the environment for investment (including publicity policy and reform of welfare policy, especially concerning working hours, the vacation system and provisions for job security), maintenance of public order and the provision of longer-term working and resident permits.[31] The impression gained from all of this cannot be other than that the Japanese Businessmen's Club dislikes the Swedish welfare system and sees fundamental changes in it as a precondition for increased Japanese investments in Sweden.

On the other hand, according to the Dentsu report referred to above, Sweden was not only seen by Japanese companies as a welfare but high tax state but also as a country with a clean and safe environment, boasting a well-educated workforce, a stable political environment and high quality infrastructure.[32] Thus, the Japanese businessmen's image of Sweden held both positive and negative elements. The strategy outlined to counter factors seen as having a negative impact on potential Japanese investors was to establish an Investment in Sweden Office in Tokyo, the funding of which was a direct result of Prime Minister Carlsson's visit to Japan. As the office has only been functioning a few years, it is still too early to evaluate the results of its activities, but it seems not unreasonable to expect that there might be an increase in Japanese investment if only basic facts about Sweden became more widely known in Japan.[33]

SWEDEN AS A MEMBER OF THE EUROPEAN UNION

As noted above, one of the main purposes of the prime minister visit to Japan in 1991 was to promote Japanese investments. He was eager to bring Sweden's plan for membership in the European Community to the attention of the Japanese as a way of attracting such investments.[34] This has been a main theme of Swedish foreign policy and the foreign policy debate in recent years and has, consequently, had an impact on discussions pertaining to Sweden's relations with Japan. The main argument has been that Swedish membership in the EU would make Sweden a part of the large intra-European market by eliminating the disincentive towards investments caused by the small size of the Swedish market; it was argued that if Sweden rejected membership of the EU it would make it hard for Sweden to attract foreign capital for advanced industrial projects.[35] EU membership would put Sweden on the map for Japanese investors.[36] Before the referendum, it was claimed that a number of Japanese companies had advanced plans for investing in Sweden but were waiting for the result of the Swedish referendum as 'the Japanese tend to look at Europe as more or less one market'.[37]

In the study of the attitudes among Japanese companies towards investing in Sweden referred to above, the views of Japanese companies of the effect of Swedish membership in the EU were investigated. Of the companies polled, 54 per cent responded that it would be better for Sweden to participate in the EU, 3 per cent thought the opposite, and 43 per cent claimed to have no views on the subject. The reasons given for the positive answers were either that the EU would have 'a beneficial impact on Sweden's domestic market and economy' (32 per cent), or that entry into the EU 'will give foreign companies easier access to, or make it easier for them to invest in, Europe' (24 per cent). Almost 7 per cent agreed with an argument commonly heard in Sweden, that 'Sweden will be isolated unless it participates in the EU'.[38] From this it is hard to discern any particular enthusiasm or even interest among Japanese companies in Swedish EU membership as a factor promoting investments in Sweden. A similarly cautious attitude was revealed by a MITI representative in June 1994.[39]

CONCLUDING REMARKS

There seems to be a lingering misunderstanding or misconception about the scope and volume of Sweden's relations with Japan. At the rhetorical level, Japanese relations are often described as important to Sweden. However, exchange and contacts between Sweden and Japan are fairly limited: shares of exports and imports are small, foreign direct investments are limited, and personal and cultural exchanges are not particularly intensive. As the figures demonstrate, relations with Japan are not very important to Sweden, nor in practice have they been given any priority, whether at the national or (with a few exceptions) at the company level.

In recent years efforts have been made to rectify the situation at the level of national policy. Two initiatives are worthy of note. The first entailed the decision of the prime minister, Ingvar Carlsson, to allot time to a week-long visit to Japan in 1991, the need for which had apparently never been felt by his predecessors.[40] This was a serious attempt to promote a Swedish–Japanese political dialogue. By giving the impression that his focus was on Japanese investments, Carlsson's success in achieving his objective was limited.

Another attempt to further relations with Japan was made by Carlsson's successor Carl Bildt, who launched a new Swedish East Asian policy in 1993. Bildt declared that improving relations with the countries of East Asia was a task that was almost as important as that of furthering relations with Europe, and he stated: 'we attach special importance to our relations with Japan'.[41] According to Bildt, East Asia had been assigned too low a priority for too long.[42] In 1994, he reiterated that developments in East Asia constituted both a great opportunity and a decisive challenge to Sweden.[43] Furthermore, the priority he gave to East Asia was demonstrated by the fact that he made a round-tour of the region in both 1993 and 1994. Unfortunately, Bildt's declaration of an East Asian policy has not yet been followed by much in the way of concrete measures.

The scope of Swedish–Japanese relations at the company level is similar to relations at the national level. The activities of Swedish companies in Japan were the object of a study published in 1993 by a leading authority on international management in the Stockholm School of Economics, Gunnar Hedlund. Based on an empirical investigation of all Swedish companies working in Japan, Hedlund concluded: 'the overall impression is still that Japan has not been given a priority commensurate with its potential'.[44] He found that Swedish firms had been modestly successful in Japan. His conclusion was straightforward:

> complaints about 'structural impediments' in general, and difficult or complex access to distribution channels in particular, are exaggerated ... [this] study suggests that effective penetration of the Japanese market is primarily a question of commitment and basic competitiveness'.[45]

Since Hedlund conducted his inquiry, some of the largest Swedish companies have started to make inroads in the Japanese market. As noted above, spectacular results have been reported in recent years for cars, pharmaceuticals and telecommunications. And – a notable event in 1994 – Swedish exports to the Far East became greater than trade with North America.[46]

At the root of Swedish problems in dealing with Japanese relations seems to be a misunderstanding of the significance that Sweden has for Japan. Prime Minister Carlsson inadvertently demonstrated Sweden's high self-esteem when he argued that Japanese companies had 'a self-interest' in investing in Sweden. But Japan is a country solidly anchored in the Pacific Asian region, albeit nowadays with a global reach, whose relations with Europe have never had any real priority – least of all relations with a small, sparsely populated country in the sub-Arctic region. On the other hand, Swedish attention and interest are primarily directed towards Europe. Sweden is a European country, and the lion's share of its trade and international exchange is with the countries of Western Europe. This, however, is also the case with the other Nordic countries and Germany, which reflects the fact that neighbours tend to trade with each other.[47] Thus, the limited scope and volume of Swedish–Japanese trade can, in part, be seen as natural – as the result of the workings of economic laws.

Another misconception concerns the state of contemporary Swedish–Japanese relations. The official Swedish assessment is that relations are excellent; the Swedish ambassador to Japan writing in his annual report in 1991, for instance, wrote: 'relations between Sweden and Japan are harmonious and mainly free from disturbances'.[48] As a semi-official organisation dealing with Swedish–Japanese co-operation in research and development noted in a report in 1994: 'in general the relations between Japan and Sweden are excellent. There are few, if any, real trade frictions'.[49] What is overlooked, however, is the fact that relations between Sweden and Japan being excellent or harmonious is, in reality, merely a token of their limited extent. Taking into account the figures for Swedish–Japanese contacts and exchanges, the harmonious state of the relations will not be a surprise to anyone, if only because relations and exchanges which are so limited do not leave much room for misunderstanding, friction or problems.

NOTES

1. Håkan Hedberg, *Den japanska utmaningen* (The Japanese challenge) (Stockholm: Bonniers, 1969). Hedberg's book was translated into at least 12 languages.
2. See Torsten Burgman, *Japanbilden i Sverige 1667–1984* (The Swedish image of Japan, 1667–1984) (Stockholm: Almqvist & Wiksell International, 1986), pp. 81–108, in which lists of articles in Swedish journals are produced, based on the annual *Svenskt tidskriftsindex* (Index of articles in Swedish journals).
3. Based on *Swedish Companies in Tokyo/Yokohama and Swedish Companies in Other Districts*, a list prepared by the Swedish Trade Council, a governmental–private organisation in charge of trade promotion activities. The total number of employees working in Swedish companies in Japan was 4038 in 1993, while the total number of employees in Swedish companies abroad was 436 196. See Statistiska Centralbyrån (National Statistics Office of Sweden), 'Anställda utomlands i svenska industri- och tjänstekoncerner 1990–1993' (Employees abroad in Swedish-owned manufacturing and service groups 1990–1993), *Statistiska meddelanden*, F 20 SM 9501 (Stockholm 1995), p. 5.

4. Sweden–Japan Foundation, *Relations between Sweden and Japan 1994* (Stockholm: Sweden–Japan Foundation, 1994), pp. 1f.

5. *Suji de miru Nihon no 100 nen* (100 years of Japan seen in figures), ed. Zaidan hojin Yano Tsuneta Kinenkai. 3rd rev. and enlarged edn (Tokyo: Kokuseisha, 1991), p. 350.

6. Figures for 1991. See Utrikesdepartementet Handelsavdelningen Enhet 5 (Ministry for Foreign Affairs Trade Section Unit 5), *Något om de svensk–japanska ekonomiska förbindelserna m.m.* (A short presentation of Swedish–Japanese economic relations, etc.), Promemoria 1991-10-11, pp. 1, 2.

·7. Kommerskollegium (National Board of Trade), *Handelspolitiska relationer mellan EU, USA och Japan: Konsekvenser för Sverige som EU-medlem* (Trade policy relations between the EU, the United States and Japan: Consequences for Sweden as a member of the EU). Rapport 1994:3 (Stockholm, 1994), pp. 72–3.

8. Sveriges ambassad (Embassy of Sweden, Tokyo), *Förbindelserna Sverige–Japan* (Swedish–Japanese relations), 62 A 1990-12-18. 1991-02-26, Nr 29, p. 2.

9. Hubert Fromlet, 'I-länder viktig exportmarknad: Låt inte spektakulär asiatisk tillväxt skymma sikten mot "mogna" länder' (Industrial countries important export market: spectacular Asian growth should not obscure the view of 'mature' countries), *Svenska Dagbladet* (27 April 1994).

10. Kommerskollegium, *Handelspolitiska relationer mellan EU, USA och Japan*, pp. 78–9.

11. The situation has improved markedly in recent decades, however. In an investigation of the Swedish image of Japan in 1974, only one company – SAS – was known by around 10 per cent of the respondents. See 'Nihonjin no suedenkan' (The Japanese image of Sweden), *Hoku-O*, no. 6 (April 1974), p. 129.

12. Sweden–Japan Foundation, *Relations between Sweden and Japan 1994*, p. 3.

13. Gaimusho Kokusai keizai Dai 1-ka (Ministry of Foreign Affairs International Economics First section), *Nichi-Sueden keizai kankei to Sueden keizai* (Japanese–Swedish relations and the Swedish economy). Keizai-shiryo 93C1-W03T (December 1994), p. 12.

14. Ibid., p. 6.

15. Volvo is one of the Swedish companies with a long-term Japan strategy. According to press reports in 1989, Volvo's target for the Japanese market was 25 000 cars. See Christer Lövkvist, 'Volvo siktar högt i Japan: på väg mot 25 000 bilar' (Volvo aims high in Japan: on its way to 25·000 cars), *Göteborgs-Posten* (21 May 1989).

16. 'Nya bilar säljer i rasande takt' (New cars selling at a frantic rate), *Dagens Nyheter* (2 March 1995).

17. Gaimusho, *Nichi-Sueden keizai kankei to Sueden keizai*, p. 6.

18. Ibid., pp. 3f. According to a list prepared by the 'Invest in Sweden' office in Tokyo in 1994, 18 cases of Japanese direct investments in Sweden had resulted in manufacturing activities (as of August 1994). According to this list, five cases started in the 1980s, while two began in 1991, five in 1992, two in 1993, and four in 1994.

19. Anne-Christine Strandell, *Kan japanska investeringar öka i Sverige?* (Can

Japanese investments increase in Sweden?). SIND 1991:7 (Stockholm: Statens industriverk, 1991), p. 64.

20. JETRO, *The 10th Survey of European Operations of Japanese Companies in the Manufacturing Sector* (Tokyo: Japan External Trade Organization (JETRO), October 1994), p. 164.
21. JETRO, *Potential Investors from Japan* (Tokyo: JETRO, 1993), pp. 38, 203.
22. Statistiska Centralbyrån (National Statistics Office of Sweden), *Utlandsägda företag 1993* (Foreign-owned enterprises 1993). *Statistiska meddelanden*, F 18 SM 9301 (Stockholm 1994), p. 5.
23. It is a remarkable fact that such a visit did not materialise until 1991, *after* the period in which the foreign policy horizon of Sweden had been widened by the internationalist Olof Palme. Japan simply did not seem to have been included among countries considered important enough to be visited by Swedish prime ministers: indeed, Prime Minister Carlsson did not pay *an official* visit to Japan, but rather *an official working-level visit*. For additional comments on Carlsson's visit, see Bert Edström, *Inledning* (Introduction), in Bert Edström, ed., *Japans globala roll: Implikationer för Sverige* (Japan's global role: Implications for Sweden) (Stockholm: Carlssons, 1994), pp. 8f.
24. Cecilia Axelsson, 'Teceremoni och industribesök under statsministervisit i Japan' (Tea ceremony and industrial visits during the prime minister's visit to Japan), *TT:s nyhetstelegram*, 368 (13 March 1991); Gerd Larsson, 'Molin vill öppna yen-väg till Sverige' (Molin wants to open a yen route to Sweden), *Dagens Industri* (19 March 1991).
25. Cecilia Axelsson, 'Carlsson framme i Tokyo' (Carlsson arrives in Tokyo), *TT:s nyhetstelegram*, 136 (16 March 1991).
26. Rune Molin in a statement to the Swedish press, quoted in Edström, *Inledning*, p. 8. See also Jan Magnus Fahlström, 'Recept för arbetsmarknaden: Sverige måste lära av Japan' (A recipe for the labour market: Sweden has to learn from Japan), *Dagens Nyheter* (30 June 1984).
27. Gaimusho, *Nichi-Sueden keizai kankei to Sueden keizai*, p. 7.
28. Ibid., p. 7. In an interview in 1993, the two first-mentioned factors were pointed to as obstacles to Japanese investments in Sweden by Koyano Toshio, chief economist of Dai-Ichi Kangyo Bank. See Sten Gustafsson, 'Riskfyllt att stå utanför EG' (Dangerous to be outside the EC), *Dagens Nyheter* (22 February 1993).
29. Dentsu PR Centre Ltd, *Report on Market Research Conducted for the Invest in Sweden Office among Japanese Companies*. Prepared for Invest in Sweden Office (Embassy of Sweden, Tokyo, 26 August 1994), p. 21.
30. Ibid., p. 45.
31. Japanese Businessmen's Club in Stockholm (JBC), *Proposal to Promote the Investment from Japan to Sweden*, section 2, pp. 2–3.
32. Dentsu PR Centre Ltd, *Report on Market Research Conducted for the Invest in Sweden Office among Japanese Companies*, p. 21.
33. A report in 1994 indicated that the lingering view of Sweden as a country with high wages was disappearing. See 'Låga löner lockar japaner till Sverige: Tokyobörsnoterade Jeco det senaste i raden av företag som flyttar tillverkning hit' (Low wages lure Japanese to Sweden; Jeco, listed on the

Tokyo stock exchange, the latest company to move to Sweden), *Svenska Dagbladet* (8 April 1994).

34. Axelsson (1991); Larsson (1991).

35. See e.g. Lars Gårdö, 'Utanför EG får vi nobben av Japan' (Outside of the EC, Sweden will be brushed off by Japan), *Dagens Industri* (27 January 1989); 'EU-nej ger fortsatt utflöde: Medlemskap avgörande för utländska investeringar enligt forskarstudie' (No to the EU will result in continued outflow: membership decisive to foreign investments according to research report), *Svenska Dagbladet* (6 December 1993).

36. Hans Ekdahl, 'Japans ekonomiska förbindelser med EG' (Japan's economic relations with the EC), *Center for Pacific Asia Studies at Stockholm University Occasional Paper 18* (September 1993), p. 11.

37. Thomas Andersson and Hans Karlander, 'Vad betyder utvecklingen i Ostasien?' (What does the development in East Asia mean?), *Aktuellt om Näringspolitik och Ekonomi*, 3 (1994), p. 23.

38. Dentsu PR Centre Ltd, *Report on Market Research Conducted for the Invest in Sweden Office among Japanese Companies*, p. 37.

39. Anders Karlsland, *Sammanfattning av Japanbesök 7–10 juni, 1994* (Summary of a visit to Japan, 7–10 June 1994), Kommerskollegium Första utrikeshandelsbyrån (National Board of Trade First Foreign Trade Bureau), PM 1994-08-16, p. 4.

40. The fact that he was the first Swedish premier to visit Japan was embarrassing to Carlsson. He assured jounalists that the reason was not Swedish self-conceit or unwillingness to learn from Japan. See the TT news dispatch *Carlsson framme i Tokyo* (16 March 1991).

41. Prime Minister's Office, *Remarks by Prime Minister Carl Bildt at the Japan National Press Club, Tokyo, 8 April 1993.*

42. Carl Bildt, '"Tyst produktivitetsrevolution" i ekonomin' (Silent productivity revolution in the economy), *Svenska Dagbladet* (15 May 1993).

43. Carl Bildt, 'Svensk ekonomi bör lära av Sydöstasien' (Swedish economy should learn from South-East Asia), *Svenska Dagbladet* (3 April 1994).

44. Gunnar Hedlund, 'Barriers to Market Penetration through Foreign Direct Investment in Japan: An Empirical Analysis of Swedish Firms' Experience 1982–91', in Thomas Andersson, ed., *Japan: A European Perspective* (New York: St Martin's Press and London: Macmillan, 1993), p. 90.

45. Ibid., p. 92.

46. 'Ljust i öster för svensk export' (Bright prospects in the East for Swedish exports), *Affärsvärlden* (26 October 1994).

47. For a penetrating discussion, see Nils Lundgren, 'Ekonomin över gränserna' (Transborder economy), in *Utsikt mot Europa* (Perspective on Europe) (Höganäs: Bokförlaget Bra Böcker, 1991), pp. 61–76.

48. Sveriges ambassad, *Förbindelserna Sverige–Japan*, p. 2.

49. Sweden–Japan Foundation, *Relations between Sweden and Japan 1994*, p. 1.

13 Japanese–Nordic Trade and Japanese Manufacturing in the Nordic Countries
Claes Alvstam
and
Inge Ivarsson

INTRODUCTION

This paper will describe and explain the pattern of Japanese manufacturing investment in the Nordic countries (Denmark, Finland, Norway and Sweden). In particular, it seeks to investigate whether the limited market size of these countries in Northern Europe gives rise to a different type of Japanese FDI from that establishing itself in other parts of Western Europe. Special attention will be paid to the issue of direct, as opposed to indirect, economic relations between Japan and the Nordic countries, in trade as well as in investment. It is assumed that the Nordic countries, when seen from the Japanese perspective, are not a priority area in the process of developing direct trade and investment relations within a single internal European market. Accordingly, indirect trade via larger countries in Western Europe is expected to grow at the expense of direct bilateral trade. On the other hand, the Japanese view of Europe as a single economic unit may also give rise to investment in the Nordic countries within special production niches, serving the entire European Union. Another objective of this paper will therefore be to establish the difference between trade and investment serving solely domestic Nordic markets, and those investments aiming at production for export to other European countries as well as to Japan.

The bilateral imbalance between exports and imports in Japanese–European trade also applies to Japan's trade with the Nordic countries. It has often been suggested that the Japanese state has stimulated the growth of outward FDI as a means of reducing the embarrassingly large and growing visible trade surplus which first appeared during the 1970s and early 1980s, and in so doing to avoid further trade friction by replacing exports with local production. A similar assumption can be made in the case of Sweden, Norway and Finland, which all sustain a huge trade deficit with Japan, although in recent years this deficit has diminished. Denmark, however, is a different case, as it is one of the few industrial countries in Europe having a surplus in bilateral trade with Japan. In the case of the Nordic countries it is also assumed that the volume of FDI up to now has been marginal in relation to the trade volume, and accordingly, that the direct substitution effect – if any – may be marginal. On the other hand, the indirect substitution effect via the countries of the former EC-12 is assumed to be more worthy of detailed scrutiny.

The paper will first present some methodological comments on the survey. This will be followed by a description of the structure and dynamics of foreign trade between Japan and the Nordic countries. The major part of the paper will then be devoted to a presentation of some empirical findings on the size and structure of Japanese manufacturing subsidiaries located in the Nordic countries at the beginning of 1995, including an analysis of the extent of host-market production, exports, local sourcing and intra-firm trade. The findings concerning the operations of Nordic-based subsidiaries will then, as far as the data allow, be compared to the general characteristics of Japanese manufacturing in Europe. The paper will conclude with a summary which highlights the main empirical findings.

METHOD

The structure and characteristics of Japanese manufacturing operations in the Nordic countries have been investigated through a firm-level survey of all manufacturing firms with a Japanese interest exceeding 10 per cent ownership at the beginning of 1995. The survey was conducted during January and February 1995, when information from individual subsidiaries was collected by telephone interviews with local executives. The subsidiaries were identified from the most recent JETRO survey of Japanese manufacturing operations in Europe.[1] The information was complemented with information from the Japanese embassies, Central Banks and Ministries of Industry in Denmark, Finland, Norway and Sweden.

Combining the information from the above sources produced a database of 18 manufacturing subsidiaries with a direct or indirect Japanese interest exceeding 10 per cent of ownership. Compared to the JETRO survey of 1994, this is almost the same number of firms. However, the individual subsidiaries are somewhat different, since the JETRO survey included four subsidiaries which cannot be characterised as manufacturing firms as they only acted as sales companies. In addition, we identified three Japanese manufacturing firms which were not included in the JETRO survey, amounting to 18 Japanese manufacturing subsidiaries operating in the Nordic countries at the beginning of 1995. Figures on investment have then been compared to the development of bilateral trade relations between Japan and each of the Nordic countries, as compiled in national trade statistics, and reported at the international level by the IMF.

JAPANESE–NORDIC TRADE

The most striking feature of bilateral trade relations between Japan and the Nordic countries during the past 20 years, as seen from the Japanese perspective, has been a gradual decline in the role of the Nordic countries as a market for Japanese exports, from 2.5 per cent of total exports by value in 1976, to 1.2 per cent in 1994. At the same time, the countries of what was until the beginning of 1995 the EC-12 have shown a continuously increasing share of Japanese exports – from 11 per cent in 1975 to a peak of around 19 per cent during the years 1990–2. Subsequently, in 1994, a steep fall to 14.5 per cent was recorded, mainly due to the strength of *endaka* or the rising yen. Looking at the same trade flows, as recorded in European trade statistics, Japan's exports grew continuously for the EC-12 – from 1.8 per cent of total import value in 1974 to 4.8 per cent in 1993, but declined to 4.2 per cent in 1994. On the other hand, Japan's imports to the Nordic countries, as a proportion of total imports, only increased until 1986, after which they exhibited a significant decline, indicating a possibly growing role for indirect imports to the Nordic countries from Japan via other European countries, or a substitution effect between trade and local production. In actual fact, Japan's share of total imports into the EC-12 since 1993 has been larger than its share of imports directed to the four Nordic countries.

Sweden, being the largest of the Nordic countries, has been investigated in greater detail with regard to the commodity composition of imports. Japan's share of imports into Sweden is fairly similar to its

Table 13.1	Commodity composition of Sweden's imports from Japan, 1984, 1989 and 1994

SITC		1984	1989	1994
0–4	Raw materials	1.0	0.5	0.6
5–6 (excl. 69)	Semi-manufactures	6.8	5.7	8.6
69–75	Metals, general machinery	27.1	27.9	30.9
76–77	Electrical machinery	26.9	23.8	33.5
78–79	Transport equipment	25.7	32.0	14.8
8–9	Miscellaneous manufactures	12.4	10.2	11.6
Total		100.0*	100.0*	100.0*

Note: *Aggregated totals may not total 100 per cent exactly.

Source: Statistics Sweden (1984–94).[2]

share of total Nordic imports, although time-lagged by about one year. At their highest level in 1988, imports to Sweden from Japan accounted for 6.4 per cent of total Swedish imports by value, after which they tumbled to 4.7 per cent in 1994. For Sweden, a huge trade deficit with Japan during the last three decades has been recorded, although this deficit has rapidly diminished since 1988.

It is also important to take into account the huge shifts in the bilateral exchange rates between the two countries. The steep decline of the Swedish krona – from around 70 yen per krona during the pre-1972 Bretton Woods System to the present exchange rate of little more than 12 yen per krona in early 1995 – has indeed stimulated purchases of Swedish companies by Japanese interests. The Swedish krona has tumbled further than the Danish, Norwegian and Finnish currencies throughout the period, although all have more or less depreciated against the yen.

Disaggregating Swedish–Japanese bilateral trade into commodity categories, industrial imports accounted for 48 per cent of total imports to Sweden from Japan in 1994, followed by capital goods within the machinery and apparatus sector, which amounted to 30 per cent. When broken down according to SITC groups, a major part of Sweden's imports from Japan originate in the machinery, apparatus and transport equipment sectors. A notable decline in the importance of passenger cars can also be observed, accounting for the major part of the general decrease of imports from Japan between 1988 and 1994. As Japanese cars continued to become more popular in the Swedish market up to 1993, this seems to be indicative of the growth of imports of Japanese commodities assembled in other European countries.

Table 13.2   Japanese manufacturing subsidiaries in the Nordic countries, 1983–94

Nordic Host Country	1983	1987	1990	1993	1994
Denmark	1	2	3	3	2
Finland	1	2	4	5	4
Norway	1	2	1	1	1
Sweden	0	3	6	10	11
Total	3	9	14	19	18
% of European total	2.5	3.1	2.7	2.6	n.a.
Total subsidiaries in Europe	117	283	516	728	n.a.

Source: JETRO (1993, 1994) and survey data compiled by the authors, February 1995.

FOREIGN DIRECT INVESTMENT AND JAPANESE MANUFACTURING IN THE NORDIC COUNTRIES

Introduction

Generally, compared to other OECD countries, inward FDI in the Nordic countries is relatively scarce. However, if inward FDI is measured instead as a proportion of GDP, the Nordic countries occupy a middle position. According to official balance of payment statistics, Japanese investment is marginal in all Nordic countries, responsible for less than 1 per cent of total inward investment stock in all countries except in Norway, where Japanese investments in the oil industry have contributed to Japanese investment accounting for almost 5 per cent of the Norwegian total.

While Japanese investment in the Nordic countries is generally marginal, this is especially true for the manufacturing sector. According to JETRO,[3] only 19 firms with Japanese interests exceeding 10 per cent of equity capital operated in the Nordic countries at the end of 1993. Although the total number of Japanese manufacturers in the Nordic countries is therefore relatively small, and most are located in Sweden, we can note an increase from three in 1983 to 18 in 1994, representing a stable share of around 2.5 per cent of all Japanese manufacturing subsidiaries in Europe (Table 13.2).

The geographical location pattern of Japanese manufacturing subsidiaries in the Nordic countries is probably not an outcome of any strategic decision, since all subsidiaries have been established through

Table 13.3 Japanese manufacturing affiliates in the Nordic countries in 1994 and in Europe in 1993, by industry

Industry	DN	FN	NO	SW	Total	Employees	Total Europe	
General machinery	1	0	0	3	4	215	83	(11%)
Transport equipment & parts	0	0	1	3	4	670	39	(9%)
Electrical/electronic products	1	1	0	1	3	1109	183	(25%)
Chemicals	0	1	0	1	2	1187	124	(17%)
Pulp and paper	0	2	0	0	2	89	5	(<1%)
Wood products	0	0	0	1	1	39		n.a.
Metal products	0	0	0	1	1	175	35	(5%)
Precision instruments	0	0	0	1	1	135	39	(5%)
Total number of subsidiaries	2	4	1	11	18		728	(100%)
Total number of employees	180	2141	200	1098		3619		

Source: Survey data compiled by the authors, February 1995.

takeover or minority capital partnership, and therefore location choice is most often an effect of the historical legacy of investment by domestic firms. Half of the subsidiaries are located in the big city areas of Denmark, Finland and Sweden, while the others show a dispersed locational pattern. In Sweden, a number of Japanese manufacturing plants are located in the traditional central Swedish industrial area of Bergslagen, to the north-west of Stockholm.

Japanese Manufacturing in the Nordic Countries and Western Europe: Some Comparisons

Industry structure

The major industry sectors in which all European-based Japanese manufacturing subsidiaries operate are shown in Table 13.3, together with the disaggregated profile of the Nordic-based subsidiaries. Most of the latter operate in the general machinery sector and in the transport equipment and parts industries, although firms operating in the electronics, chemicals, wood products, pulp and paper, metal products and precision instrument industries can also be found.

By analysing the industry patterns of Japanese manufacturers in the Nordic countries in more detail, it is evident, as shown in Table 13.4,

Table 13.4 Nordic locational advantages (NLA) of locally-based Japanese manufacturers

Industry	Products	Industry Cluster with NLA
General machinery	Diamond tools; industrial robots; feeding devices for packaging machines; high-frequency motor generator and thermal refining facilities	Transport equipment, rock tools, food
Transport equipment & parts	Truck steering parts; shock absorbers; radiator strips; dump trucks	Transport equipment
Electrical/electronic products	Position-finding electronic components; projection television screens; PCs	
Chemicals	Printing ink; tyres	
Pulp and paper	Thermosensible paper; paper plant pots.	Paper
Wood products	Custom-ordered semi-constructed houses	Wood products
Metal products	Sheet-iron pressing	Transport equipment
Precision instruments	Spectacle lenses	

Source: Survey data compiled by the authors, February 1995.

that a substantial number operate in industry clusters where Nordic firms possess comparative advantages.[4] In Sweden, for example, besides those three Japanese subsidiaries operating in the transport equipment industry, in which Swedish firms are internationally competitive, another three Japanese subsidiaries are found in the machinery and metals sectors, manufacturing products related to the transport equipment industry (e.g. robotics and metals). The only subsidiary in Norway also belongs to the transport equipment industry and, moreover, is related to Swedish partners within the same sector through substantial material purchases such as vehicle motors. In addition, another Japanese subsidiary is operating in the Swedish machinery industry, manufacturing products with major applications in the highly competitive Swedish rock tool industry. Other examples of Japanese firms operating in strong Nordic industries can be found in the wood products and paper industries, in which Swedish and Finnish firms have location-specific advantages. In Denmark, the Japanese subsidiary operating in the machine industry manufactures industrial goods related to the food-processing industry, in which Danish companies are internationally competitive. Taken as a whole, therefore, two-thirds of Japanese manufacturing firms in the Nordic countries operate in industries characterised by internationally competitive domestic firms.

Size of subsidiaries

In Europe, Japanese subsidiaries seem to be smaller compared to their US counterparts. For example, in 1989, Japanese affiliates in Europe employed on average 108 persons, compared to 344 in US subsidiaries.[5] This can partly be explained by national governments in Europe exerting political pressure on Japanese firms to produce and source inputs locally, forcing Japanese firms to establish (smaller) subsidiaries in many countries. In 1993, according to the 1994 JETRO survey,[6] the average number of employees in Japanese manufacturing firms in Europe had increased to 275. Compared to these figures the size of Japanese manufacturing subsidiaries in the Nordic countries is on average substantially smaller. Only two out of 18 firms, both located in Finland, have more than 300 employees, while 11 firms employ fewer than 100 people. The average number of employees is 201, but if we exclude the two biggest firms, which employ around 1000 people each, it is only 73.

Moreover, we find that the average gross annual sales of all Japanese manufacturing subsidiaries located in Europe in 1993 was estimated at $US116 million, with 13 per cent of subsidiaries having sales exceeding $US100 million.[7] In 1994 the average sales in Nordic-based subsidiaries was around half of this figure, or $US55 million. Excluding the two biggest subsidiaries, which were the only firms with more than $US100 million in annual sales, average sales were around $US20 million, or less than one fifth of the average annual sales of all European-based subsidiaries. Overall, therefore, Nordic-based subsidiaries are substantially smaller than their counterparts in the rest of Europe, both in terms of employment and total sales.

Age of subsidiaries

Most Japanese manufacturing operations in Europe have been established recently, with approximately one third of the manufacturing subsidiaries operating in 1993 being established before 1986, while one third have begun operating after 1990.[8] Japanese firms located in the Nordic countries are even more recent than their European counterparts, since only 10 per cent arrived before 1986, and as many as two-thirds have been established during the 1990s.

Mode of establishment

It is generally acknowledged[9] that Japanese firms prefer to establish European subsidiaries by means of greenfield investments, a form of establishment which most efficiently facilitates the internal transfer of firm-specific advantages from parent firms in Japan to their European subsidiaries. In 1993, it was estimated that approximately two-thirds of all Japanese manufacturing subsidiaries in Europe were greenfield, while one fifth entered by means of acquisitions and one tenth were in the form of capital participation.[10] At the same time, Japanese multinational enterprises (MNEs), like their US and European counterparts, are penetrating foreign markets increasingly through techniques such as mergers and acquisitions (M&A). For example, in total FDI inflows by Japanese firms into the EC in 1989 and 1990, as much as 40 per cent were by means of M&A.[11]

Expansion through acquisitions or capital participation is most common in sectors where Japanese companies do not possess competitive advantages compared to US and European MNEs, e.g. in the food-processing and chemicals industries, and when they are expanding horizontally into Europe, that is, when the European subsidiary does not operate in the same industry as the parent firm in Japan.[12] The way the Japanese firms have established manufacturing operations in the Nordic countries is somewhat different compared to other European subsidiaries, since none of the Nordic subsidiaries operating in 1995 was established through greenfield investment. Instead, almost 60 per cent entered through acquisitions and around 40 per cent through minority capital participation in existing companies.

Japanese corporations expanding into Europe in the 1980s were also known to prefer majority control of their foreign subsidiaries rather than minority partnerships. Indeed, as many as 90 per cent of Japanese subsidiaries in Europe in 1990 were wholly-owned. However, a slight tendency towards increasing minority partnership has been identified since the 1980s.[13] Minority partnership is especially used by Japanese firms operating in the European food and chemical industries, where half of the subsidiaries are minority-owned.[14] The latest available figures for the degree of ownership indicate that 70 per cent of all Japanese manufacturing subsidiaries operating in Europe in 1993 were wholly-owned.[15] Compared to these figures, the degree of Japanese control among the Nordic-based subsidiaries at the beginning of 1995 seems to be substantially lower, since less than one third are wholly owned.

Table 13.5   Business relations with local Nordic firms prior to investment

Status of Japanese Firms before Takeover or Joint Venture	No. of Cases	Industries
Customer	4	Electronics, transport (2), wood
Supplier	2	Instruments, machinery
Technological co-operation	2	Chemicals, machinery
Licence (donor)	2	Paper, transport
Licence (recipient)	1	Transport
Supplier to common customer	1	Metals
Competitor	2	Chemicals, electronics
No business relation prior to link	2	Electronics, paper

Source: Survey data compiled by the authors, February 1995.

Previous business relations between Japanese and Nordic firms
It is also noteworthy that almost all the Japanese firms located in the Nordic countries had already established some kind of business relationship with a local firm before investment. In 12 of the 16 firms where information was supplied to us, business relations were established prior to takeover or minority participation, as shown in Table 13.5.

The most common form of business relationship was one where the Japanese firm was a customer of the Nordic firm. Other relationships included those situations where the Japanese firms were suppliers, licence givers or partners in technological co-operation with the Nordic firms. Moreover, in at least four of the cases, the Japanese firm was invited to become a partner of the local firm through capital participation. These invitations all resulted in 50/50 joint ventures or Japanese minority ownership.

Main reasons for establishment
Up to and including the early 1980s, Japanese FDI strategies seem to fall into two broad categories.[16] The most common was a defensive market-oriented strategy devised to protect existing export markets in industries where Japanese firms already possessed a comparative advantage vis-à-vis European and US firms, e.g. the car, electronics and electrical equipment industries. These were often greenfield investments, performing relatively low value-added activities, often of the screwdriver type. The second type of strategy, which became more important after the mid-1980s, was offensive and supply-oriented in order to gain access to the information and technology needed to upgrade and rationalise domestic operations and to advance a global competitive strategy. This strategy involved investments in industries where Japan-

Table 13.6 Main motives for the establishment of Japanese manufacturing subsidiaries in the Nordic countries

Motives	No. of Firms	Industries
Acquiring new technologies	7	Chemicals, electronics (3), transport (2), wood
Establishing a European production base	6	Machinery (3), metals, paper, transport
Host market production	2	Chemicals, instruments
Other	1	Paper

Source: Survey data compiled by the authors, February 1995.

ese competitive advantages were inferior to local ones (e.g. processed foods, pharmaceuticals and chemicals in Europe, and household products, biotechnology and computers in the US).[17] In this situation, the purpose of foreign establishment is to contribute to the continuous upgrading and rationalisation of the parent company's operations, by feeding it information about new markets, products and technologies.

Accordingly, a gradual shift occurred in the late 1980s, from the traditional Japanese post-war system of *exporting–domestic upgrading–exporting* to a system whereby FDI gradually replaced trade as the driving mechanism.[18] As a result, the importance of acquisition as a means of expanding overseas increased significantly, and by the late 1980s about 40 per cent of the value of new Japanese FDI in the EC was by way of acquisitions and mergers.[19]

As indicated in Table 13.6, the main motives for Japanese investment in manufacturing subsidiaries in the Nordic countries, according to the opinion of local managers in 16 of the 18 subsidiaries, relate mainly to two types of factors. These are the acquisition of new technologies held by local firms in the Nordic countries, and the establishment of production bases in Europe. It should be observed that the motive for establishment in all Japanese firms in the electronics sector seems to be related to the acquisition of new technologies, while Japanese firms in the machinery industry are more concerned to establish a production base in Europe.

Stand-alone operations or part of a European network
Most Japanese manufacturing subsidiaries in Europe are stand-alone operations. According to the 1994 JETRO survey,[20] 90 per cent of all Japanese manufacturers in Europe had only one plant located in Europe in 1993. Among the Nordic-based subsidiaries, however, more than

Table 13.7 Percentage of total sales in different markets by Japanese manufacturing subsidiaries in the Nordic countries, 1994

	Local[a]	Nordic[b]	W. Europe[c]	C/E Europe	N. America	Japan	ROW	N[d]
Nordic-based subsidiaries	20	15	49	0	6	2	7	17
All except the two largest	31	5	39	1	16	8	1	15

Notes:
(a) Local sales are sales in the host country.
(b) Sales to all Nordic countries, except the host country.
(c) Western Europe does not include the four Nordic countries.
(d) N=number of cases.

Source: Survey data compiled by the authors, February 1995.

half of the subsidiaries had European sister firms, although not necessarily manufacturing the same or similar products. At the same time, 40 per cent also had sister manufacturing subsidiaries in the US, besides those in Japan. Almost a quarter of the Nordic-based subsidiaries can be considered as specialised manufacturers, in so far as no other firm in the Japanese parent or partner corporation is manufacturing the same product as the Nordic subsidiary.

Export or host market production
Although exports from the home base in Japan are still the major method of supplying European markets, Japanese manufacturing investments in Europe increased significantly at the end of the 1980s, to the extent that, by 1990, around 20 per cent of total European sales of products manufactured by Japanese firms were produced by their subsidiaries in Europe. Nevertheless, even though this proportion of European production is twice as large as in the early 1980s, it is still substantially lower compared to US firms operating in Europe.[21]

Japanese investments in the EU are generally viewed as market-oriented, seeking to exploit the whole European market through regionally integrated product and location strategies. Unlike many American firms, Japanese firms have typically pursued a rationalised European strategy from the very start, especially in industries characterised by surplus capacity.[22] Although many Japanese firms in Europe operate with a rationalised strategy in order to supply a number of European national markets through centralised production, empirical evidence still suggests that most output is sold within the subsidiaries' host or local market.

The final customer markets for Nordic-based Japanese subsidiaries are shown in Table 13.7. Because the size of two firms is substantially

Table 13.8 Sales markets for Japanese manufacturing subsidiaries located in the Nordic countries, by industry, 1994

	Local	Nordic	W. Europe	C/E Europe	N. America	Japan	ROW	N
Chemicals	37	27	18	1	9	0	9	2
Electrical & electronics	10	14	63	0	3	1	9	3
Machinery	34	13	45	0	7	0	0	4
Transport equipment	15	2	56	0	18	7	3	3
Wood and paper products	3	8	52	0	15	21	0	3
Others	93	0	7	0	0	0	0	2
Total	20	15	49	0	6	2	7	17

Note: See notes to Table 13.7.

Source: Survey data compiled by the authors, February 1995.

larger than the others, the table shows the percentage of sales going to different markets in two groups of firms, the first including all investigated firms, and the second excluding the two largest firms in order to discern whether the geographical markets of the larger firms are significantly different from the others. As can be seen, local sales account for one-fifth of total sales, and almost one-third excluding the two biggest firms. Even if we consider all Nordic countries as the 'local' market, around two-thirds of output is exported elsewhere. Western Europe is the main market, responsible for almost 50 per cent (40 per cent excluding the two largest firms) of sales. We can also see that there are significant sales in North America, especially if the two largest firms are excluded. In total, exports back to Japan amount to only 2 per cent. However, if the two largest firms are excluded, almost 10 per cent of sales are shipped back to Japan.

Table 13.8 shows sales in different markets from an industry perspective. High total export figures are most apparent in the wood and paper, transport equipment and electronics industries, where most output is shipped to Western Europe. It should also be noted that there are relatively high shares of non-European sales in firms operating in the transport and wood and paper industries, above all to North America and Japan. Table 13.9, on the other hand, compares the exports of Nordic-based subsidiaries with corresponding totals for all Japanese manufacturers in Europe, and shows the destination of sales generated by sector in each group of firms. Japanese subsidiaries based in the Nordic countries in 1995 seem on the whole to be more export-oriented when compared to the entire cadre of Japanese manufacturers operating

Table 13.9 Destination of sales by EC subsidiaries of Japanese firms in 1989 and Nordic subsidiaries of Japanese firms in 1994, by industry (%)

Industry	EC Subsidiaries 1989			Nordic Subsidiaries 1994		
	Local[a]	Japan	Other[b]	Local[a]	Japan	Other[b]
Total manufacturing	66.4	1.6	32.0	20	2	78
Chemicals	51.8	0.8	48.1	37	0	63
Electrical & electronic	73.4	0.8	25.8	10	1	89
Transport	50.9	0.8	48.3	15	7	78
Machinery	59.2	3.4	40.5	34	0	66

Notes:
(a) Local sales are sales in the host country.
(b) *Other* is mainly other EC countries in the case of EC subsidiaries, and for Nordic subsidiaries it includes sales to Western Europe, North America, and the rest of the world.

Source: Gittleman and Graham (1994, p. 133),[23] and survey data compiled by the authors, February 1995.

in Europe, at least when compared to those operating in 1989, which is the latest year for which figures are available.

A higher degree of export activity among subsidiaries in the Nordic countries, compared to their European counterparts, is also indicated by the fact that while almost all Japanese subsidiaries based in the Nordic countries – as well as in rest of Europe – seem to export at least some output from their host countries, a substantially higher proportion of the Nordic-based subsidiaries can be characterised as export-intensive. This is evident from the data given in Table 13.10, which show clearly that they export more of their output. For example, the share of Nordic-based subsidiaries exporting more than half of their output in 1994 was almost 70 per cent, compared to 53 per cent among all European subsidiaries in 1991. Corresponding figures for those exporting more than three-quarters of output were 52 and 36 per cent, respectively. It was also found that around 90 per cent of all Japanese manufacturing subsidiaries located in Europe, as well as in the Nordic countries, export to other European markets. A substantially higher share of the Nordic subsidiaries' output, however, was exported to the US and Japan.

Although we may conclude that, on the whole, Japanese subsidiaries in the Nordic countries seem to be more export-oriented than their European counterparts, some differences exist. Subsidiaries located in Sweden seem to be more host market-oriented compared to those lo-

Table 13.10 Export performance by Japanese manufacturing subsidiaries located in the Nordic countries, 1994, and in the whole of Europe, 1991

	Nordic-based Subsidiaries %	All European Subsidiaries %
Share of subsidiaries with exports	95	92
Share of subsidiaries with >50% exports	70	53
Share of subsidiaries with >75% exports	52	36
Share of subsidiaries exporting to:		
EC	n.a.	88
EFTA	n.a.	33
EC+EFTA	95	n.a.
USA	58	18
Former USSR and Central Europe	5	12
Japan	35	17

Source: JETRO (1992, pp. 39–40);[24] and survey data compiled by the authors, February 1995.

cated in other Nordic countries. On the whole, Japanese subsidiaries located in Sweden exported only 41 per cent of their total output in 1994, compared to 86 per cent among subsidiaries located in the other Nordic countries. If we exclude the two biggest firms in the sample, the export share of subsidiaries located in the Nordic countries, with the exception of Sweden, is almost 100 per cent. The focus on the local host market among subsidiaries located in Sweden is also indicated by the fact that while five out of ten subsidiaries in Sweden sell two-thirds of their output in the local market and two sell around 50 per cent, only two firms export all or most of their manufactured output. Among the subsidiaries located in the other Nordic countries, all subsidiaries export half or more of total output.

Comparative assessment may also reveal whether or not Japanese manufacturing subsidiaries perform differently from those of other foreign-owned affiliates in the Nordic countries. Using data from a survey on the export performance of 148 small foreign majority-owned manu-facturing affiliates in Sweden in 1993,[26] Japanese subsidiaries in Swe-den seem to have similar proportions of sales going to different markets, except that Japanese subsidiaries are less focused on the Nordic mar-ket outside Sweden, and more on exports back to Japan, as revealed in Table 13.11. The share of export-intensive firms, which export most of their output, seems however to be lower compared to all of the smaller manufacturing affiliates.

Table 13.11 Sales markets for Swedish-based Japanese manufacturing affiliates (1994) and all small, foreign-owned manufacturing affiliates (1993)

	Local	Nordic	W. Europe	C/E Europe	N. America	Japan	ROW
All smaller affiliates	60	12	17	2	4	3	3
Japanese affiliates	60	5	17	1	3	13	0

Source: Ivarsson 1994,[25] Table A1; and survey data compiled by the authors, February 1995.

Intra-firm sales

Few indications on the degree of intra-firm exports by Japanese firms in Europe are available. Those existing seem to suggest that most intra-European exports by Japanese firms are intra-firm. However, the extent of intra-European exports is small, especially compared to those of US firms.[27] Overall, forward linkages of Japanese subsidiaries in Europe seem to be relatively weak, since most of their output is shipped directly to distributors not belonging to the parent corporation. Exceptions to this are found in the relatively high ratios of intra-firm sales by Japanese subsidiaries in the European electrical and electronics industry, where, in 1987, one third of sales were intra-firm.[28] Sales back to Japan also seem to be organised largely through intra-firm arrangements. Figures relating to 1989 indicate that around 40 per cent of the exports to Japan by Japanese subsidiaries were intra-firm.[29]

In the Nordic-based subsidiaries, intra-firm exports seem to be of somewhat greater importance. Around half of the Nordic-based subsidiaries' exports are sold on an intra-firm basis to other parts of the parent corporation, as indicated in Table 13.12. In total, around half of the Japanese subsidiaries use intra-firm exports as a means of supplying foreign markets, at least to some degree. Of those subsidiaries which export on an intra-firm basis, around 50 per cent sell most of their output to other parts of their parent corporation. Out of the nine subsidiaries exporting by means of intra-firm trade, Western Europe is the main market for six, while another two subsidiaries have Japan as their major market for intra-firm exports, and for one it is the United States.

Japanese manufacturing subsidiaries in the Nordic countries also seem to internalise a greater proportion of exports compared to other foreign-owned affiliates. Previous research[30] indicates that this amounts to around one half of exports, compared to only one third among other smaller foreign-owned affiliates.

Table 13.12 Intra-firm exports from Japanese manufacturers in the Nordic
countries, 1994

Intra-firm exports out of total exports	54%
Firms with intra-firm exports	53% (9)
of which intra-firm exports exceed 50%	55% (5)
Main markets for intra-firm exports	
Western Europe	6 firms
Japan	2 firms
USA	1 firm

Source: Survey data compiled by the authors, February 1995.

Procurement of material inputs

In response to political pressure to increase the local content of manufactured output, Japanese firms seem to have fostered locally-based
subcontractors, rather than create their own internal capacity.[31] Survey
data from 1987 show that, on average, some 50 per cent of total purchases of inputs by Japanese affiliates in Europe were still imported
from Japan, while third country imports represented only 3 per cent of
total purchases, and local sources 46 per cent.[32]

Although it is clear that Japanese firms in Europe have begun to
establish backward linkages to the local economy, local content rates
vary substantially between industries. According to JETRO,[33] around
half the Japanese manufacturing subsidiaries in Europe in 1993 procure over 70 per cent of materials and parts inside the EU, while 74
per cent procure more than half their inputs from the same source. It
should be noted that the methodology applied in this and earlier JETRO
surveys measures local content as the ratio of the value of locally
made parts against the total product price. This way of measuring local content is problematic, since it is affected by differences in the
proportion of value-added in individual firms. Moreover, the term *local* refers to the EU market as a whole, rather than to individual host
countries.[34] However, accepting this way of estimating local content,
we find that the ratio of Japanese manufacturing firms in Europe which
procure more than 70 per cent locally is especially high in the iron
and steel, pulp and paper, and food industries, while proportionately
few firms in the rubber, general machinery, furniture, pharmaceuticals
and electronic component industries procure most of their materials
and parts locally.[35] It can also be seen that among acquired firms and
in firms with Japanese capital participation, a much higher proportion

Table 13.13 Origin of material procurements by Japanese manufacturing subsidiaries in Nordic countries by selected sector, 1994

	Local	Nordic*	W. Europe	C/E Europe	N. America	Japan	ROW	N
Subsidiaries located in:								
Nordic countries	37	9	34	0	2	14	6	12
(Sweden)	45	2	24	0	2	18	9	10
Industries:								
Transport equipment/parts	33	16	43	0	3	5	1	3
Metals	95	0	5	0	0	1	0	1
Machinery	21	0	10	0	0	70	0	4

Note: *Nordic countries, except the host country; See notes for Table 13.7.

Source: Survey data compiled by the authors, February 1995.

(between 60 and 77 per cent) purchase over 70 per cent locally, compared to the equivalent for greenfield subsidiaries (44 per cent).

Among the Nordic-based subsidiaries, none of which is a greenfield investment, 8 out of 16 subsidiaries procure at least 70 per cent of inputs in Europe, while all except four subsidiaries procure more than half their inputs in Europe. In the transport industry, all subsidiaries procure more than 70 per cent of inputs in Europe. Significant purchases in the local host market are associated with the metals industry, while in the chemicals industry none of the subsidiaries procures more than 50 per cent (in fact not more than 25 per cent) from the local market. Disaggregated to separate countries, four out of ten subsidiaries located in Sweden procure at least 70 per cent from suppliers within the country, while all of the subsidiaries in Norway and Denmark procure less than half their materials and supplies on the local market.

As regards the average value of procurement in different markets among Japanese subsidiaries in the Nordic countries, we have been able to collect information on the total value of procurements and purchases in different markets from 12 out of 17 subsidiaries, including all ten subsidiaries in Sweden, as shown in Table 13.13. The information on procurement patterns among these 12 subsidiaries seems to suggest that Japanese subsidiaries procure around one third from suppliers located in the host country, and a similar fraction from the rest of Western Europe. Another 10 per cent is procured in the Nordic countries, excluding the host country, which means that, in total, around 80 per cent of the procurement value originates from European sup-

Table 13.14 Local content* in all Japanese manufacturing subsidiaries in Europe in 1990 and in the Nordic countries in 1994

	Nordic-based Subsidiaries 1994 % Purchases of Materials & Parts			All European-based Subsidiaries % Procurement/ Total Sales		
	Local	Japan	Other	Local	Japan	Other
General machinery	30	70	0	76	23	1
Transport equipment/ parts	95	5	3			
Transport equipment				67	32	1
Transport equipment parts				78	22	0
Raw materials	98	2	0	75	15	10
All manufacturing subsidiaries	80	14	6	69	26	5

Note: *For Nordic-based subsidiaries *local* is the average proportion of locally (EC + EFTA) purchased materials and parts (procurement), out of total purchases of materials and parts; for European-based subsidiaries *local* is the average proportion of locally (EC + EFTA) purchased materials and parts (procurement), out of total sales.

Source: JETRO (1991, p. 46)[37] and survey data compiled by the authors, February 1995.

pliers. Procurement from Japan represents 14 per cent of the total, while procurement from the US remains insignificant.

From an industry perspective, great variations in the degree of local procurement exist. The highest shares of local purchases (93 per cent) are found in the metals industry, while almost two-thirds of material inputs in the machinery industry were imported from Japan. Over 40 per cent of inputs in the transport equipment industry were supplied from Western Europe.

Comparisons in sourcing performances between Nordic- and European-based subsidiaries are problematic due to the differences in methodology used when measuring the degree of local sourcing. As noted above, JETRO measures local content as the ratio of local procurement against total sales, while we have chosen to estimate the value of local procurement against total procurement. Given the different ways of estimating the degree of local procurement, Table 13.14 presents some comparisons between Japanese subsidiaries located in the Nordic countries and Europe with regard to sourcing behaviour. Estimates

Table 13.15 Origins of total procurement by all smaller, foreign-owned manufacturing subsidiaries (1993) and Japanese subsidiaries (1994) operating in Sweden (%)

	Local	Nordic*	W. Europe	C/E Europe	N. America	Japan	ROW	N
All smaller subsidiaries	39	14	38	1	2	1	6	148
Japanese subsidiaries	45	2	24	0	2	18	9	10

Note: *Procurement in the Nordic countries, except the host country; See notes for Table 13.7.

Source: Ivarsson (1994, Table A3),[38] and Survey data compiled by the authors.

of the average local content (EU + EFTA countries) of European-based subsidiaries indicate that in 1990 around 70 per cent was procured locally, which was found to be an increase from around 55 per cent in the first years of operations in Europe.[36] From the data given in Table 13.14, it may be suggested that Nordic-based subsidiaries to a greater extent procure material inputs in Europe, and less in Japan. However, the Nordic-based subsidiaries in the machinery industry are mainly dependent upon materials from Japan.

It is also possible to compare the procurement patterns of Japanese subsidiaries located in Sweden with general procurement patterns among smaller foreign-owned manufacturing affiliates in Sweden. Based on a survey conducted in Sweden in 1993 it is evident from Table 13.15 that Japanese subsidiaries procure a substantially lower proportion of total inputs in the Nordic market (outside Sweden) and in Western Europe, and at the same time proportionally more in Japan. Domestic purchases by Japanese subsidiaries in Sweden are roughly of the same magnitude as those among all other small foreign-owned manufacturing affiliates.

Intra-firm procurements
Measurements from 1987 show that some 50 per cent of purchases of total inputs by Japanese manufacturing affiliates in Europe were still being imported from Japan, of which almost 90 per cent were intra-firm transfers.[39] Third country imports represented only 3 per cent of total purchases, of which one third was intra-firm. Out of local purchases representing 46 per cent of the total, some 40 per cent were intra-firm. In 1987, altogether, some 65 per cent of materials was procured through intra-firm transactions. An especially high proportion of

intra-firm transactions was found in the electronics sector where around two-thirds were internalised, while in the transport industry the figures were substantially lower, at around 20 per cent.

Based on information from 12 out of 16 Japanese manufacturing subsidiaries located in the Nordic countries (including all 10 subsidiaries in Sweden), the average share of intra-firm imports as a proportion of total imports is only 13 per cent (14 per cent in subsidiaries located in Sweden only). Among those subsidiaries which import on an intra-firm basis, Japan is the main import market for seven, while the US, Western Europe or South East Asia are, respectively, the main markets for intra-firm imports to the other three.

CONCLUSIONS

Although the total number of Japanese manufacturing subsidiaries in the Nordic countries is too limited to make any categorical statements concerning their characteristics, or to what extent they differ from other Japanese manufacturers located in Europe, a number of conclusions may yet be drawn. First, in relation to foreign trade relations, Japan's role as country of origin in direct imports to the Nordic countries has declined markedly during recent years, suggesting a shift towards indirect Nordic imports from Japan via Western Europe. Also, the commodity composition of imports has shifted to an even more marked concentration on industrial inputs and capital goods within the machinery and equipment sectors.

In terms of the volume of FDI, Japanese investment in the Nordic countries is marginal. The total number of subsidiaries is small, although it has increased from three in 1987 to 18 in 1994, representing around 2.6 per cent of all Japanese manufacturing firms in Europe. Most Nordic subsidiaries are found in Sweden and Finland. Half of the subsidiaries are found in big city areas, whereas the others are dispersed in more peripheral locations. This location pattern is probably not a result of any specific locational strategy, but rather of the result of the prior location patterns of domestic firms which have attracted Japanese capital. In terms of industrial sectors, most Japanese subsidiaries are concentrated in the general machinery, transport equipment and electronic equipment industries. Most of these Japanese subsidiaries seem to operate in industry clusters where Nordic firms traditionally have locational advantages (e.g. transport equipment, wood products, paper and rock tool production).

In general, the Nordic-based Japanese subsidiaries are small compared to those based in Western Europe and have entered the market later than those in the rest of Europe. No subsidiary in the Nordic countries has been established through greenfield investment, which has been the most common method adopted by Japanese firms when establishing themselves in other parts of Europe. It is also evident that around two-thirds of the Nordic-based subsidiaries had already established business relations with local firms prior to the investment. The Nordic-based subsidiaries are also to a much greater extent minority-owned, when compared to those in the rest of Western Europe, where most subsidiaries are wholly-owned. The main motives for the Japanese investor seem, on the one hand, to be either related to the acquisition of new technologies held by local firms, or the desire to establish a production base in Europe.

Furthermore, the Nordic-based subsidiaries seem, more so than their European counterparts, to be part of an international manufacturing network, with sister firms in Europe as well as in the US and Japan. At the same time, one quarter of the Nordic-based subsidiaries were found to be specialised manufacturers within their parent corporations. It may be remarked also that Nordic-based subsidiaries are generally more export-oriented, with more widely dispersed markets, than Japanese manufacturing firms in the rest of Europe. These export sales are also, to a greater degree, shipped as intra-firm sales to other companies within their parent corporation.

Finally, in terms of procurement, the Nordic-based subsidiaries are notable in so far as a substantially larger proportion of material inputs is purchased on the European market, especially from suppliers within the local or domestic market. The dependence on intra-firm procurement among the Nordic subsidiaries is also substantially lower than what has been found among Japanese manufacturers in the rest of Western Europe.

Japanese manufacturing in the Nordic countries can be said, therefore, to display some singular features which set it apart from similar investment activity in the rest of Western Europe. It is less extensive and has emerged later, although it can be said that it has emerged more as a response to the strengths of the industrial environment in the Nordic countries, rather than as a by-product of the export-led strategies of the most prominent Japanese sectors, such as automobiles and electronics, which have more frequently invested in Europe's less competitive national markets. Japanese manufacturing in the Nordic countries has, therefore, been peripheral to these main strategies, with all the advantages and disadvantages that this entails, and its future prospects must be judged accordingly.

NOTES

1. JETRO, *10th Survey of European Operations of Japanese Companies in the Manufacturing Sector* (Tokyo: Japan External Trade Organisation, October 1994).
2. Statistics Sweden, *Foreign Trade, Imports and Exports Distribution by Country/SITC*(Stockholm: annual).
3. JETRO (1994).
4. M.E. Porter, *The Competitive Advantage of Nations* (London: Macmillan, 1990).
5. M. Gittelman and E. Graham, 'The Performance and Structure of Japanese Affiliates in the European Community', in M. Mason and D. Encarnation, (eds.), *Does Ownership Matter?* (Oxford: Oxford University Press, 1994), p. 130.
6. JETRO (1994).
7. Ibid., p. 8.
8. Ibid., pp. 12–13.
9. See, for example, Y. Tsurumi, *The Japanese are Coming* (Cambridge, Mass.: Ballinger, 1976); H. Yamawaki, 'Entry Patterns of Japanese Multinationals in US and European Manufacturing', in Mason and Encarnation (1994).
10. JETRO (1994), p. 10.
11. J.H. Dunning, *The Globalisation of Business* (London: Routledge, 1994), p. 294.
12. Yamawaki (1994).
13. D. Encarnation, 'Investment and Trade by American, European, and Japanese Multinationals across the Triad', in Mason and Encarnation (1994).
14. Yamawaki (1994).
15. JETRO (1994), p. 10.
16. Dunning (1994), p. 141.
17. Ibid., p. 165.
18. Ibid., p. 149.
19. R.I. Kirkland, 'The Big Japanese Push into Europe,' *Fortune* (2 July 1990).
20. JETRO (1994), p. 8.
21. Dunning (1994) p. 140; J.H. Dunning, 'The Strategy of Japanese and US Manufacturing Investment in Europe', in Mason and Encarnation (1994), p. 65.
22. Ibid.
23. Gittelman and Graham (1994).
24. JETRO, *8th Survey of European Operations of Japanese Companies in the Manufacturing Sector* (Tokyo: Japan External Trade Organisation, 1992).
25. I. Ivarsson, 'Small Foreign-Owned Affiliates in Sweden. An Empirical Survey

of Export and Import Performance', *Choros* (Dept. of Human and Economic Geography, Gothenburg University, No. 5, 1994).
26. Ibid., pp. 44–52.
27. Dunning, in Mason and Encarnation (1994), p. 77.
28. Ibid., p. 157.
29. Ibid., p. 221.
30. Ivarsson (1994), p. 95.
31. Dunning (1994), p. 156.
32. Ibid., p. 157.
33. JETRO (1994), p. 60.
34. JETRO (1992).
35. JETRO (1994), p. 62.
36. JETRO, *7th Survey of European Operations of Japanese Companies in the Manufacturing Sector* (Tokyo: Japan External Trade Organisation, 1991), p. 45.
37. JETRO (1991).
38. Ivarsson (1994).
39. Dunning (1994), p. 157.

14 The Role of Japan in Central Europe in an Emerging Multipolar World

Judit Berényi

INTRODUCTION: JAPAN AND CENTRAL EUROPE AFTER THE COLD WAR[1]

This paper will focus on economic aspects of the growth of Japanese influence and will adopt a pragmatic approach. Clearly, as economic relations evolve in a political environment, reference to the international political framework will need to be made. And as a pragmatic essay, directed at least in part towards a policy-making audience, the paper will try to depict a realistic and critical picture of Japan's developing presence in Central Europe.[2]

Without going into a detailed analysis of the main characteristics of the bipolar world order which came to an end in 1990, the system essentially involved a struggle between military superpowers intent on extending their ideological, political and economic influence. The policy of Japan towards the superpowers, as well as their policy towards Japan, derived from this hostile alignment, precluding any autonomous policy stance.

The collapse of the Soviet Union and its abandonment of superpower rivalry was a clear political victory for the United States. Since then, discussion has focused on whether the new world order will be multipolar or unipolar, and on the basic principles that will underly new power structures. A possible new *Pax Americana* resulting from this political victory has nevertheless coincided with the decline of the US domestic economy, questioning the scope of future American influence, particularly in the economic sphere.

Against such a background the future course of Japan's continuing economic and political internationalisation appears uncertain or problematic. Indeed, a few scholars and politicians in the US have expressed the view that the main new source of hegemonic challenge will come from Japan in its role of economic superpower. They also acknowledge an integrated (Western) Europe as a second potential challenger. A number of scholars in Europe have also suspected that in the emerging post-cold war régime Japan might strive – if not for a global political role, then at least for some chance to exploit the vacuum created in the former socialist world.

There remains an expectation in the smaller countries of Central Europe – which emerged from the cold war era politically triumphant but economically perplexed – that after years of one-sided linkages the region could begin to enjoy a multifaceted engagement with Western Europe, the United States and Japan. At the same time the countries of Central Europe could and should develop a new type of relationship with the republics of the former Soviet Union and China, based on something other than ideological considerations.

Available studies, as well as recent interviews with experts in Japan, suggest, however, that the stance of Japanese interests and policy-makers are at variance with this interpretation. In this new era, even after the political collapse of its most important potential enemy, Japan has remained far more cautious about moving in a deliberately internationalist direction. Indeed, it has maintained a low profile and a passive approach to major international issues. Japan still appears to be accepting US political and economic conceptions, as they underpin the political and economic world order. As will be seen later, this might nevertheless be beneficial for the countries of Central Europe, in so far as financial and economic co-operation between the US and Japan might counter-balance the rapid growth of trade and investment relations into the region from Western Europe, and in particular Germany.

There is considerable evidence that in the 1990s Japan is primarily pursuing the role of regional leader, with interests more than ever focused on the emerging *New Asia*. Indeed, during a recent conference on assisting the republics of the Commonwealth of Independent States (CIS), Japanese foreign ministry officials stressed that 'as an Asian nation we would like to lend greater support to the former states in the Asian region. Japan will give priority in its grant aid and other assistance to the five central Asian republics – Uzbekistan, Kyrgyzstan, Turkmenistan, Tajikistan and Kazakhstan – and the Russian Far East region'.[3] This is a realistic and pragmatic approach, and not a kind of isolationism, and should be understood as such within Central Europe in order to avoid misunderstandings with regard to Japanese initiatives. Although there is a more positive attitude towards Central European countries among

Japanese policy-makers, it will be seen that this goodwill and fund of moral capital should not be overestimated.

CURRENT JAPANESE TRADE AND INVESTMENT IN CENTRAL EUROPE

Traditionally, Japan has not enjoyed a significant presence in either Eastern Europe (the former Soviet Union west of the Urals), or in Central Europe. However, for a short time during the early Meiji period at the beginning of the 1880s, Japan looked to the Habsburg and Russian empires as appropriate development models.[4] Only in the latter part of the nineteenth century did Japan turn to the examples of Germany and England to adapt legal, military and postal systems, and others, to the circumstances prevailing in Japan. In subsequent years, due to geographical distance, religious and cultural differences, and a general lack of mutual knowledge, there were to be very few ties between Japan and Central Europe.

The cold war era resulted in an artificial separation of the countries of the two blocs, with Japan and the Central European countries belonging to different alliances which had very low levels of political contact. The highly complex nature of Soviet–Japanese relations exercised a diversionary influence upon political relations, with economic relations mostly determined by political and security priorities. Indeed, both in Japan and Eastern Europe, a kind of inward-looking economic autarky prevailed, although in the case of Japan this was tempered by a successful obsession with export-led growth.

Recent Trends in Economic Relations

After the 1960s, in line with détente, the first economic, cultural and scientific agreements between Japan and Central European countries were established. This paralleled the accession of Japan to a position of strength among the leading free market economies. Japan had concluded agreements on trade and payments with most Central European countries in the early 1960s, with the result that bilateral trade began to grow, although it did not exceed $10 million per annum until the next decade. The beginning of the 1970s was characterised by the efforts of the five small CMEA countries to open their economies to the West. To promote development they applied for and received foreign credits from, among others, Japanese banks. For political reasons priority was given in the 1960s and 1970s to Romania in offering loans, although later Poland and Hungary became important recipients of Japanese credit.

As a consequence of the second oil shock, which made Soviet crude expensive for the energy-dependent industries of Central Europe, economic stagnation led Poland and Romania to ask for a rescheduling of debts. This coincided with serious political unrest in Afghanistan and Poland, which led in some cases to stricter regulation of trade between America's allies and the countries of Eastern and Central Europe. Nevertheless, increasing trade turnover (with Hungary, Poland and to some extent to Czechoslovakia[5]) led to growing Japanese export surpluses, which, together with an unfortunately static product structure for Central European exports, have been the main features of bilateral economic relations. This was the case during both main phases of the developing relationship, the 1960s and 1970–89. In effect, the trade pattern continues to reflect disparities in levels of development. 80 per cent of Japan's exports to Central Europe are general machinery, electrical and electronics products, and cars, while imports are dominated by chemicals, agricultural products and ferrous/non-ferrous metal semi-products.

In 1990, Japan's exports to the five small CMEA countries totalled $888 million, with imports of $654 million. The combined total represented only 0.3 per cent of Japan's foreign trade, which reflects its marginal importance. Correspondingly, in the foreign trade of Central Europe, Japan is a less important partner than many other countries, although this is slightly less true in the case of Hungary (Tables 14.1 and 14.2).

Finance and Direct Investment

Financial contacts between Japan and Central Europe appeared as early as the 1970s, but they began to expand after the mid-1980s. Japanese credits became more widely available in the latter half of the decade, and this was especially true for Hungary, where the National Bank used these resources in its debt policy strategy to switch to long-term credits. As a result, Japan came to account for approximately one third of total Hungarian debt, around $7.5 billion.

It is important to note that the behaviour of individual countries in this region with regard to debt repayment has become the decisive factor in Japan's evaluation of these countries' economies. The Japanese standpoint on this issue is far more uncompromising than equivalent positions in the US and Western Europe. Indeed, in the case of Poland, which was a favoured target for Japanese engagement in the region,

Table 14.1 Japan's foreign trade with Central Europe*

| | Exports | | Imports | | Balance |
	$US (millions)	Previous Year %	$US (millions)	Previous Year %	$US (millions)
1986	634.6	–	316.2	–	318.4
1987	592.1	93.0	446.7	141.3	145.4
1988	743.3	125.5	761.6	170.5	18.3
1989	691.1	93.0	725.6	95.3	34.5
1990	889.2	128.7	664.8	91.6	224.4
1991	927.5	103.6	688.2	103.5	233.3

Note: *Hungary, Czechoslovakia, Poland, Romania, Bulgaria, Yugoslavia and Albania.

Source: *Wagakuni to Tô Shokoku to no Boeki Kankei* (Japan's Foreign Trade with Eastern European Countries), JETRO (15 April 1992).

Table 14.2 Japan's trade with Central European countries in 1990 ($US millions)

	Imports	%	Exports	%
Bulgaria	34.8	0.01	54.0	0.02
Czechoslovakia	128.4	0.05	50.4	0.02
Hungary	146.4	0.06	142.8	0.05
Poland	184.8	0.08	308.4	0.11
Romania	98.4	0.04	81.6	0.03
Yugoslavia	61.2	0.03	250.8	0.09
Total	654.0	0.28	888.0	0.31

Source: Foreign Trade by Commodities Vol. 4 (Paris: OECD, 1990).

the rescheduling of Polish debt has caused Japanese interests to rethink their earlier enthusiasm.

As far as foreign direct investment (FDI) is concerned, Central Europe's contacts with Japan are less well developed than trade links. In 1990, Japanese FDI was $52.7 billion, of which 48 per cent was invested in North America, 25 per cent in Europe and 12 per cent in Asia. By the end of September 1991, the cumulative value of Japanese FDI in Central Europe was $65 million, which was 0.5 per cent or 1/200th of Japan's investment in Europe in that year (see Tables 14.3 and 14.4).

According to JETRO, in September 1991 there were 39 Japanese investments in six Central European countries. FDI is concentrated in three countries: Hungary with 16 investments, Poland with eight, and

Table 14.3 Japanese foreign direct investment projects in 1990

	$US (millions)	%	Number of Projects	%
North America	27 192	47.78	2 246	39.52
Asia	7 054	12.39	1 499	26.38
Europe	14 294	25.12	956	16.82
(Central Europe)	(65)	(0.11)	(39)	(0.69)
Oceania	4 166	7.32	572	10.07
South America	3 628	6.37	339	5.97
Middle East	27	0.05	1	0.02
Africa	551	0.97	70	1.23
Total	56 912	100.0	5 683	100.0

Source: *Zaiseikinyu Tokei Geppo* (Financial Report) (Tokyo: Ministry of Finance, 1991).

Table 14.4 Japanese direct investment projects in Central Europe, September 1991

	Manufacturing	Finance	Services	Total
Bulgaria	1	0	3	4
Czechoslovakia	0	0	1	1
Hungary	5	4	7	16
Poland	0	0	8	8
Romania	0	0	7	7
Yugoslavia	2	0	1	3
Total	8	4	27	39

Source: JETRO.

Romania with seven. The sectoral breakdown shows that investors have favoured services and manufacturing. Regarding the volume of invested capital, manufacturing ranks first and the finance sector second. These figures and shares, however, are somewhat skewed by the sizeable investment by Suzuki in Hungary's fledgling automotive sector. This major investment, both in its volume of capital outlay and as a greenfield investment in manufacturing, remains of unique interest.

CENTRAL EUROPE AND JAPAN'S ECONOMIC STRATEGY IN THE 1990S

Japan's relationship with Europe as a whole remains relatively distant. Relations have been treated marginally by Tokyo due to differing development strategies and the special character of Japanese relations with Washington, which has meant that Japan has sometimes been perceived in Western Europe as 'too much a surrogate of the United States'.[6] Western Europe has been mainly preoccupied with involvement in multilateral treaty organisations such as NATO and the EC/EU, and content to leave Tokyo in relative political isolation. It was not until the early 1980s that there was a movement in Japan towards greater participation in world politics, and consequently more dialogue with European partners. This was demonstrated by Prime Minister Noboru Takeshita's statement in 1988 which described Japan–European relations as the 'third pillar of international co-operation'.

When considering relations between Japan and Central Europe, it is necessary to distinguish different dimensions, spheres of interests and channels of communication. First of all, in a fairly commonplace classification, there is an official or governmental approach, involving a certain way of thinking and acting. This is exemplified by the Japanese Ministries of Foreign Affairs and International Trade and Industry, as well as MITI's agencies, such as JETRO. Then there is the private sector, which considers official guidance but values above all the short- and longer-term interests of the enterprise. To understand the growth of Japan's relations with Central Europe both of these perspectives must be considered in turn.

The Japanese Administration's Policy Towards Central Europe

As far as the position of the Japanese government is concerned, there is an important new element: the disappearance of the former *bloc treatment*. Distinctions between the Central European countries and the successor republics of the Soviet Union are being made. Regarding concrete assistance, it is also significant that the three most advanced countries in the region are receiving the most attention. This new form of attention is based on unspectacular but painstaking research carried out by Japanese experts who are assisting policy-makers to formulate their strategies toward individual countries. And, needless to say, it also involves studying the strategies and initiatives of the United States and Western Europe in the same region.

Japan's official involvement in Central Europe has two main elements: financial assistance, using various channels, and the transfer of Japanese know-how to economic policy-makers; in other words, teaching the Japanese lesson. As evidence of one aspect of the special US–Japan relationship, what might be called a division of labour, Japan seems unwilling to take on independently the responsibility and risk involved in offering official loans. It is said that because of the lack of up-to-date and detailed information on the region Japan prefers taking part in multilateral or even bilateral financing. A good example of this trait is the establishment of the *Japanese Enterprise Facility*, part of the *Global Partnership Plan of Action* between Japan and the United States. The facility was created to support private sector development in Central Europe in co-operation, as appropriate, with the American Enterprise Funds, on the same conditions. For this purpose, a scheme for co-ordination has been set up between the two facilities, with the Japanese Embassy serving as a contact point in each recipient country.

The sources of funding for the facility are the Japan Export–Import Bank *JEXIM* for loans, and the Japan International Development Organisation *JAIDO*[7] for equity investments. Plans call for increasing the amount of *JEXIM* loans to approximately $300 million for the whole region. Of these funds, up to $100 million are to be allocated to Hungary, up to $100 million to the Czech and Slovak republics, and up to $100 million to 'other Central and Eastern European countries, the allocation of which will be determined at a later date'.[8] The loans are made available in the form of an untied two-step loan. This means that *JEXIM* is extending untied loans to the central bank or appropriate government-backed development finance institution of the recipient country so that it can provide loans to individual enterprises. *JAIDO*'s equity investments are made directly to individual enterprises. The *Overseas Economic Co-operation Fund (OECF)* has provided $10 million in capital to *JAIDO* and the authorised share of capital recently was raised to 9 billion yen. *JAIDO* has made a further capital injection in 1993, with the money increasingly coming from the private sector.

The other element of official assistance is more and indirect and intangible: the Japanese government sponsors missions, workshops and studies to assist policy-makers to formulate new methods to develop the market economy. Studying Japanese know-how in industrial policy-making is considered by many economists in Central Europe to be crucial in this transition period.[9] There were many elements of industrial policy pursued by Japan in the 1950s and 1960s which Central European countries with similar ambitions can reasonably attempt to adopt, even though economic and political circumstances are now, of course, quite different. In this context, some recent indications have suggested that the advice of Japanese experts is getting through, not only to independent economists in Central Europe, but also to policy-makers.

The Japanese Private Sector's View of Central Europe

This dimension of the Japan-Central Europe relationship is the most interesting, and at the same time the most delicate. With regard to short-and long-term considerations it is also quite clear that Central European countries are eager to seek a long-term engagement from the Japanese side, principally through attracting capital investments. This does not mean that there is little interest in enlarging trade relations as well. Japanese products, both industrial and consumer goods, are necessary and welcome, but the likely increase in imports will need to be monitored in terms of the growth of prospective exports to Japan.

In the present transition period Central Europe is characterised by a lack of domestic capital, a very low technological level of industry, an outdated industrial structure and the collapse of the most important former market, the Soviet Union. Foreign capital from any country is therefore urgently required. It is expected that this foreign capital will bring new technology, as well as more efficient management and work practices, while simultaneously opening up new marketing channels. As Japanese goods have high prestige in all industrial economies, capital investment from the same source, however tentatively it emerges, will be welcome. Moreover, it is hoped that Japanese participation might preserve economic sovereignty through a greater diversity of foreign investors, dominated up to now by German companies.

These expectations have not yet been fully realised, however. Although the last two years have witnessed a certain increase in new investments, Japan's share of total FDI has remained rather low. Indeed in Hungary, the country with the greatest share of Japanese direct investment among the countries of Central Europe (about $80 million), the share of Japanese FDI in the total from all countries has remained under 5 per cent. It is apparent also that the recent establishment of South Korean companies in this region has provided an interesting basis for comparison, reflecting perhaps a different approach to the realisation of investment opportunities between these two Asian countries (see Table 14.5).

One of the arguments used by Central European countries to attract inward investors is that the region has a central location in the heart of Europe. A further argument is that, despite the shortcomings of the present economic situation and quality of infrastructure, there are many long-run advantages associated with the region. Foreign companies generally decide to invest in this region to get an early foothold in a market that has enormous future potential. The quality of human capital is also important, given the high level of education and experience of

Table 14.5   Foreign direct investments by South Korea in Central Europe,
1991

	Number of Projects	$US millions
Hungary	5	74.4
Czechoslovakia	1	10.8
Poland	3	0.7
Romania	1	0.5
Total	10	86.4

Source: *Figyelô*, no. 14 (1992).

much of the local labour force. Stressing cheap labour and production costs is becoming less important than a focus on the quality of the workforce, especially as the majority of investors are seeking longer-term profits as local purchasing power increases.

Despite the low level of direct investment in Central Europe by Japanese firms it should not be forgotten[10] that none of the Japanese investments are speculative, something that could not be said with regard to all the German, Austrian and American projects in the same region. As far as the manufacturing sector is concerned, companies receiving Japanese capital benefit from high-technology inputs and produce high quality and internationally-competitive outputs. Particularly in the case of the *Magyar Suzuki* project, one of the most important long-term gains has been technology transfer into the Hungarian economy. Furthermore, Suzuki's assembly plant is not insulated from the local economy, having developed links through its establishment of a network of sub-contractors. Indeed, the short-term advantages stemming from Japanese direct investment in Hungary derive from this substitution of local inputs for costly imports, together with the parallel generation of foreign currency inflows arising from increased exports.

Japanese Responses

Japanese businessmen have spoken frankly about the advantages and disadvantages of operating in Central Europe. Many opinion polls and surveys, initiated by organisations such as JETRO and ROTOBO, have outlined the Japanese firms' evaluation of market and investment opportunities. To summarise their thoughts about operating in Central Europe, a number of points are evident.

First, the starting point is always the present situation of the Japanese economy, and against this background, the situation of private firms.

Because of the current recession in Japan and elsewhere, Japanese companies are continuously reviewing their overseas operations. In concrete terms this means that they are postponing investments even in such important markets as the United States. Thus, they are in no mood to expand activity in new, and potentially more risky, markets; the current priority being to protect present positions. The recent dramatic appreciation of the yen is nevertheless changing the investment strategy of Japanese companies, making the establishment of foreign production bases more profitable. A surge of Japanese investment in 1993 may have been a consequence of this.

Second, Japanese people, and in particular businesspeople, greeted the political and economic changes of 1989–90 sympathetically, and with some interest in the possible implications for international business. This perhaps encouraged a short-term boom in exports to the more developed fringes of the region around 1990, but this has been followed by a slump since 1991.

A third point to consider is the traditional strategy of Japanese companies wishing to expand overseas. This begins with some export of goods, followed shortly after by the establishment of marketing and service networks which test a local market and gather market information. A decision concerning direct investment usually follows only after a significant lapse of time, even if general business conditions are favourable. Many Japanese companies, among them branches of the *sogo shosha* or general trading companies, have established offices in Central European capitals and have continued to maintain them *even in years when local business activity has been slight*. This would seem to reflect the long-term approach of many Japanese companies.

Fourth, the traditional linkages of Japanese companies need to be recognised as principal factors in determining where, when, why and how much capital is invested. Much has been spoken and written about this subject, and in the view of one Japanese executive Japanese foreign direct investment is essentially *protective investment* with the aim of keeping traditional export markets. This characterises Japanese multi-national strategy in East Asia, where lower labour costs permit the establishment of subcontracting investments. In the US and Western Europe, however, the trade policy of host economies has forced Japanese companies to invest if they wished to retain or expand markets. At the same time, towards Latin America, the former Soviet Union and Central Europe, a kind of wait and see attitude can be detected. The reason for this is the conflict between Japanese companies' natural preference for longer-term relations and what is perceived as an *unstable business environment* often subject to excessive local regulation and administrative interference. In Hungary there has been some evidence of these negative factors, and the change of regime, although welcomed, was to introduce a new factor of uncertainty, especially when it became necessary to establish contact with new decision-makers. Objective obstacles such as changes in the legal framework, the tax system, property rights and infrastructure have added to these difficulties.

As a fifth factor, we should note that there is at present little interest in joint ventures with Central European companies. Significantly also, Japanese companies are keeping their distance from privatisation, being unwilling to buy shares of Central European companies.

Sixth, the liberalisation of trade, now almost complete in Hungary, has created unprecedented competition for locally-owned firms and foreign investors alike. Indeed, some recent investors from countries which stress the importance of introducing a market economy into Central Europe have requested local protection from imports.

It is accepted that Japanese firms would prefer greenfield investment, rather than taking control of existing plant facilities. This is the seventh point to consider. As a consequence of this the only major investment to date has been Suzuki's car assembly plant in Esztergom, on the Hungarian border close to Slovakia. This project is something of a test case for the future of Japanese manufacturing investment in Central Europe, and is perceived as such by Japanese business circles, as well as local interests concerned with industrial development. There is, therefore, a *joint vested interest* in ensuring the success of the project. It is as well to remember, however, that the Suzuki project is the product of former circumstances, conceived in a period of increasing consumer demand and limited opportunities in Central Europe to purchase high-quality sub-compact cars. These circumstances have become less valid in the mid-1990s.

Another consideration, the eighth, is that Japanese investors making cost/benefit calculations naturally assess the size of markets and market access for products produced in foreign locations. With this in mind not only the Hungarian market, but also the whole Central European market may seem rather limited. In Hungary, and also in some neighbouring states, there is a widespread image of the country as a bridge between East and West. This is reinforced by the associate member status, and anticipated full-member status, that Hungary, Poland, the Czech Republic and Slovakia enjoy in their relations with the European Union. Significantly, this enables these countries to channel goods to Western Europe under favourable conditions. Moreover, the collective

experience of these four nations in doing business with the former
Soviet republics, and continuing contacts, mean that production for a
huge market in the easternmost part of Europe may one day make
Central Europe a particularly attractive production base for foreign
investors. Nevertheless, many Japanese businessmen express profound
doubts concerning the foreseeable future prospects, both political and
economic, of the former Soviet republics. The existence or lack of a
market economy, rather than the population size, was recognised as
crucial.

This is well understood in Japan. Japanese companies rapidly increased
investment in EC countries (above all in the UK and Germany) after
the mid-1980s to establish bases within a potential Fortress Europe.
Hungary (and Poland, the Czech Republic and Slovakia) have therefore
to compete not only with each other in attracting Japanese investors,
but with better developed West European economies. Among these,
Spain and Portugal have low operating costs, as well as greater political
stability and much better infrastructure. Understandably, the issue of
bad infrastructure in Central Europe, whether in transport, communications
or the financial sector, has been a major concern of Japanese companies.

As a final point, and perhaps the most striking with regard to the
prospects of Japanese engagement in Central Europe, several Japanese
businessmen have indicated to the present author *that Japan is unwilling
to create a new field of confrontation with its Western partners in this
region.* Experience of confrontation in other regions, leading to trade
friction, has led Japan to be wary, especially given the uncertain prospects
and unfamiliarity of the territory involved. For this reason Japanese
companies may well prefer to co-operate rather than compete with
American and West European firms, and try to develop a joint or indirect
approach to investment in Central European countries, once they have
developed their presence beyond a certain point.

To summarise, therefore, it would seem that a tangible gap exists
between the expectations of Central European countries and the likely
degree of Japanese support for processes leading to required political
and economic reforms. This is to some extent understandable, being in
part a result of unrealistically inflated expectations in Central European
countries, as well as a cautious approach on the part of Japanese interests
that would generally prefer to wait and see how the situation is likely
to develop in the region. This being so, Central Europe is unlikely to
become a major arena for confrontation involving Japan–West European
or Japan–US rivalry, but is more likely to emerge as a region of
understated co-operation aimed at ensuring the success of democratic

and market reforms. Such a situation would offer Japanese interests a chance to develop a higher profile in the region and buttress its presence in a more integrated European Union which is likely to include, before too long, Central European countries as full members.

CONCLUDING REMARKS

The most important lessons to be drawn from the interviews and studies carried out in preparation for this essay are threefold. First, this decade will be a period when Japan is striving to strengthen its regional leadership in East Asia in both economic and political spheres. In accordance with its *Global Partnership Plan*, Japan will defer to the United States with regard to its future presence in Central Europe. This bilateral co-operation – even though of considerable importance for the region – will not, however, counterbalance the scale of involvement of West European countries, especially Germany, in the backyard of these advanced market economies. One reason for this resides with the attitude of many Central European countries, which despite having had decades of unhappy unilateral linkages followed by a professed wish for *a balanced participation of powers in the region,* still find it more comfortable to give preference to European interests and contacts. This aspect should not be overlooked, notwithstanding the desire for more Japanese engagement in its own right.

Second, there is an active circle of academics, bureaucrats and businessmen in Japan at present working to enlarge and deepen relations with Central Europe. They have the intellectual and financial resources, in universities and in powerful ministries such as the Ministry of Foreign Affairs and MITI, to promote increased Japanese investment in Central European *human capital*. These influential people believe that this investment is among the most important types of assistance in the long run. Scholarships, fellowships and reciprocal missions of Central European policy-makers and Japanese economists with industrial policy-making backgrounds help the development of this human resource. The experience of Japanese businessmen and managers working in foreign operations is also recognised as a valuable source of knowledge transfer. Moreover, agencies of the Japanese government carefully observe how these initiatives are received, and consider them an important criterion for deciding where and when to allocate official financial assistance.

Finally, the main lesson to be learnt from the tentative growth of Japanese involvement in Central Europe is that the wait and see approach may be an affordable luxury for Japanese international business, but Central European countries are not in a position to hesitate or relax. They have to make considerable efforts to create a domestic environment for the inward investor which is stable, welcoming and profitable, and to do this at the same time for locally-owned enterprises. In short, the investment climate which is required to attract foreign capital clearly requires an economy and society which is agreeable both to live in and to work in.

NOTES

1. Central Europe is here intended to mean the smaller Council for Mutual Economic Assistance (CMEA) countries, such as Poland, Hungary, the Czech Republic, Slovakia, Romania Bulgaria, and, for some purposes, former Yugoslavia.
2. This paper relies upon interviews with Japanese and Hungarian experts on politics and economics. I am indebted to the Japan Institute of International Affairs for the opportunity to conduct research in Japan. I also acknowledge the guidance of Professor Nishimura, and the assistance of numerous other persons in public agencies, universities and business companies in both Japan and Hungary.
3. *Japan Times*, 29 October 1992.
4. Kumiko Haba, associate professor at Hosei University, has helped with this historical background.
5. In the early 1990s these three (now four) countries, accounted for a 70 per cent share of Japan's total trade with Central Europe.
6. R. Murata, 'Political Relations between the United States and Western Europe: Their Implications for Japan', *International Affairs*, No. 1 (1987/8).
7. JAIDO was set up jointly by the government and Keidanren to provide industrial assistance to developing countries.
8. Source: Ministry of Foreign Affairs.
9. In the framework of a project recently sponsored by Japan Foundation and organised by the Japan – East and Southeast Asia Research Centre in Budapest the present author prepared a study under the title *Japan's Industrial and Investment Policy – Lessons to be Drawn for Hungary*.
10. Early in 1990, in a study prepared on behalf of the Institute of the World Economy of the Hungarian Academy of Sciences, the present author had already expressed this view.

15 Magyar Suzuki and the Emergence of Japanese Direct Investment in Central Europe

Gabor Bakos

INTRODUCTION

Japan's presence in Central Europe was insignificant before the 1970s and was confined to commercial exchanges. After 1970, the Japanese general trading companies, the *sogo shosha*, established branches in the region, and were closely followed in the period up to 1989 by the lending activities of Japanese banks and the first direct investments by Japanese multinational investors. Since 1989 a third phase of involvement has witnessed the growth of direct investment in both services and manufacturing.

Japanese direct investment in Central Europe totalled $US342 million by 1992, with most directed towards Hungary, and especially the Magyar Suzuki project, located north of Budapest. Only $US10 million had been invested outside Hungary by that year, and the bulk of projects by number were also concentrated in the same country (23), with only five in Poland and three in Bulgaria. As a share of total Japanese investment, however, Central Europe accounts globally for less than 1/2 per cent of total outward investment, which is also insignificant compared with the 20 per cent of investment flow received by Europe as a whole from Japanese sources in the early 1990s. Despite the small scale of investment stock, however, Central European countries have recently attracted a growing share of Japanese investment, with new projects emerging every year.

Japanese direct investment took place in Hungary before other Central European countries, and Hungary has received a larger volume of investment and a greater number of investment projects. In Poland approximately 20 companies have Japanese investors, but most of these are concerned with car sales and the distribution or assembly of electrical

Table 15.1 Newly established Japanese projects in Central Europe, 1990–2 ($US millions)

| | 1990 | | 1991 | | 1992 | | 1951–92 | |
	No.	Value	No.	Value	No.	Value	No.	Value
Hungary	4	29	5	181	4	4	23	224*
Bulgaria	–	–	–	–	–	–	3	1
Poland	2	3	2	2	1	0	5	5
Czechoslovakia	–	–	–	–	1	4	1	4

Note: *Adding $72 million in 1993 and $36 million in 1994, investment in Hungary totals $332 million.

Source: Zaisei Kinyu Tokei Geppo (Financial Statistics, Monthly Report, Tokyo: Ministry of Finance (1993) No. 12).

Table 15.2 Sectoral pattern of Japanese projects in Central Europe, 1993

	Manufacturing	Commerce	Finance, Insurance	Services
Poland	–	8	–	1
Czech Republic	1	7	–	–
Hungary	5	11	2	1
Slovakia	–	1	–	–

Source: Kaigai Shinshutsu Kigyo Soran (Tokyo: Toyo Keizai Shinposha, 1994).

components and appliances. In addition to the $US5 million invested in Poland in these projects, Matsushita and Marubeni have announced plans to proceed with joint ventures to manufacture, respectively, batteries and industrial boilers in association with European Union companies. At present, however, sales and servicing of cars and electrical products, rather than manufacturing, is the main activity of Japanese-invested companies in Poland. In the former Czechoslovakia a similar situation prevails, with a joint venture underway to produce ferrovanadium in Bohemia (Nihon Jukagaku Kogyo, JAIDO, and the *sogo shosha* Nissho Iwai), and plans for polypropylene and wire harness production in Slovakia.

JAPANESE INVESTMENT IN HUNGARY

Among the 54 cases of direct investment by Japanese firms in Hungary recorded at the beginning of 1995,[1] services, trade and banking projects

Table 15.3 Reasons for investing in Hungary given by Japanese investors

Reason	Hungary Number	%	World Number	%
Using, extracting local resources and materials			696	3.3
Labour force			1628	7.7
Preferences granted by the host country	3	12.0	908	4.3
International production and distribution	4	16.0	2961	14.0
Acquiring local markets	9	36.0	6757	32.0
Export to third countries	1	4.0	861	4.1
Re-import to Japan			789	3.7
Following expansion of competitors			407	1.9
Capital injection, exchange rate risk			551	2.6
Royalty, collecting information	6	24.0	3001	14.2
R&D, commercialisation	1	4.0	773	3.7
Expanding into new activities			470	2.2
Integrating regional activity			283	1.3
Avoiding trade frictions	1	4.0	290	1.4

Source: *Kaigai Shinshutsu Kigyo Soran* (Tokyo: Toyo Keizai Shinposha, 1994).

remain prominent. In 1993 five manufacturing projects had been established in Hungary, with the Magyar Suzuki car assembly joint venture accounting for approximately two-thirds of all Japanese manufacturing investment in Central Europe, by value. As well as manufacturing and service sector projects, Hungary has also benefited from a \$1 million investment by Furukawa Denki Kogyo and the *sogo shosha* C. Itoh, which acquired a research institute for chemistry, where research on the development of new materials is now conducted by Hungarian researchers in the renamed Furukawa Electric Institute of Technology.

Japanese research institutes and investment in R&D facilities have emerged in Europe, particularly in the UK and Germany, where access to high quality research staff has prompted Japanese firms to invest directly. Cost considerations have led Japanese firms to invest in manufacturing ventures also, and the relative cost of investing in Western Europe, or choosing sites in Central or Eastern Europe, has been an important determining factor. Wage costs are an important factor, in many cases *the* determining factor, and an examination of relative wage costs in Hungary and other parts of Central Europe can serve to clarify the factors underlying the current pattern of establishment, as well as its prospects for future development.

Spain is sometimes mentioned as a possible alternative for Japanese

Table 15.4   Manufacturing wages in selected countries, 1990–2
($US monthly)

	1990	1991	1992
Japan[a]	2627	2944	3005
Germany	2133	2240	2250
Spain	1488	1639	1503
Hungary[b]	183 (320)	184 (322)	213 (373)
Czechoslovakia	105	124	
Poland	105	148	

Notes:
(a) Including bonus.
(b) Net earnings after deduction of income taxes; totals in brackets for Hungary are before taxation and include social insurance.

Source: Authors calculations using *Yearbook of Labour Statistics* (ILO, 1993) and exchange rate figures from *International Financial Statistics* (IMF, 1994).

firms considering investment locations in Central Europe, while German wage rates are closer to the high wage cost environment of manufacturers in Japan. A brief comparison of Spanish and Japanese wage rates reveals that Japanese domestic producers face an average manufacturing wage which is twice that found in Spanish plants. More significantly however, a much greater discrepancy exists between estimates for Spain and Hungary, which nevertheless has the highest wage costs in Central Europe. Taken together with other factors, this goes a long way towards explaining the desire of Suzuki to scale down production at its facilities in Spain and increase its productive involvement in Hungary. This is understandable when it is recognised that cars in Hungary are sold at approximately the same price as in Western Europe and Japan, while productivity in the Hungarian Suzuki plant is 70 per cent of that achieved in Suzuki's domestic plants in Japan.

INVESTING IN THE HUNGARIAN AUTOMOBILE INDUSTRY

Economic liberalisation in Central European countries after 1980 began to attract Western car manufacturers. In the mid-1980s two Japanese companies, Daihatsu and Suzuki, began negotiations with domestic interests in Poland and Hungary. The strongly established position of the major Italian auto-maker, Fiat, led to Daihatsu's eventual failure to secure an agreement in Poland,[2] but after protracted negotiations

Table 15.5   Monthly wages in the Japanese and Hungarian automobile industries, 1994 (yen)

	Japan*	Hungary
Toyota	300 200	
Nissan	290 920	
Honda	296 437	
Mitsubishi Motors	259 279	
Mazda	280 359	
Suzuki	259 584	40 000

Note: *Base wage, bonus excluded.

Source: Jidosha Soren (1995); Magyar Suzuki (1995).

Suzuki successfully established a joint venture to produce small cars near Esztergom, 50 km north of Budapest.

With a relatively small population of 10 million the Hungarian domestic market seems small, but there is an obvious need to replace existing car stocks, which are ageing and environmentally unattractive. One third of the 3 million Hungarian cars now in use are over 10 years old, often with highly polluting two-stroke engines, such as those in the Trabants and Wartburgs made in the former GDR. In 1989 Hungary imported just over 200 000 cars, a third of which were brought in by private individuals, and the rest by state trading companies. In 1992 36 000 new cars were sold in Hungary, rising in the next year to 45 000, although earlier estimates of a national market of 120 000 to 140 000 new car sales may now appear optimistic. Nevertheless, Suzuki intends to boost production in Esztergom from 40 000 in 1994 to 50 000 in 1995, selling 30 000 cars in the local Hungarian market in both years, and most of the rest in Western Europe.[3]

The world market strategy of Suzuki is to establish regional manufacturing and marketing centres for its various products. Three categories of car are involved, with the minicar *Maruti* assembled in India, the subcompact *Swift* and a larger sedan version to be made in Hungary, and an off-road vehicle produced by Suzuki–Santana in Spain. Until 1994 Suzuki intended to supply markets in Central and Eastern Europe from the Magyar Suzuki plant, with exports from Japan and Spanish output satisfying demand in Western Europe. Since then, output from the company's Hungarian operations has been sold increasingly in all the sub-regions of Europe, starting from a base of total Suzuki sales of 60 000 in Europe in 1993.[4]

Table 15.6 Capital contributed to the Magyar Suzuki project, 1991 and 1993

	1991	1993
Capital invested (cumulative)	$US70 million	$US160 million
Suzuki	40%	49.9%
C. Itoh	11%	15.6%
Autokonszern	40%	30.2%
International Finance Corporation	9%	4.3%
Total	100%	100%

Source: Magyar Suzuki.

FINANCE AND COMPONENT SUPPLY

After almost ten years of negotiation an agreement was signed in 1990 to commence production of a five-door model of the Suzuki Swift in Hungary in 1992, with an initial production volume of 15 000 rising to 50 000 in 1995 and an eventual maximum of 100 000 units annually. Magyar Suzuki was established in April 1991 with $70 million of capital, which was increased by a further $90 million in December 1993. Twenty per cent of Suzuki's initial investment was in the form of forgone licence fees, and the *sogo shosha* C. Itoh contributed 11 per cent, taking the initial Japanese share of capital to 51 per cent. The December 1993 investment was necessitated by a combination of exchange rate difficulties and plans to begin production of a sedan model.

The Hungarian government promoted the joint venture by granting a series of preferences, including subsidised land, and exemptions from taxes on income and the import of machinery, and parts. Imported parts used in cars sold in Hungary are subject to a 5 per cent tax, while parts used in cars assembled by Suzuki for export will not be taxed. The Japanese investors were nevertheless keen to secure additional concessions, including barriers to imports, infrastructural improvements and the relaxation of environmental codes. The Hungarian government reached a compromise position on the quite comprehensive package of market protection measures proposed by the company president when visiting Hungary in 1993, promising to prohibit the import of used cars which are more than six years old.[5]

Co-operation with the local component supply industry will determine the scale of benefits which the project is expected to bring to the Hungarian economy. In the first year of the project Suzuki provided

Table 15.7 Magyar Suzuki local content

	1992	1993	1994
Imported from Suzuki Japan	65	45	35
From West European sources	5	5	10
Magyar Suzuki added-value	20	25	25
Local subcontractors	10	25	30

Source: Magyar Suzuki (1993).

the engine and gear-box assemblies, while 25 per cent of value-added derived from the inclusion of local components, and a similar amount was associated with assembly work performed in the Magyar Suzuki plant. This total is expected to rise to between 55 and 70 per cent by the late 1990s, with most of the anticipated rise due to the greater involvement of local subcontractors and component supply firms.

Suzuki initially targeted 50 Hungarian companies as potential sub-contractors, but was faced with two major problems in the economy: first, the ambitious programme to privatise state companies was making the legal status of companies uncertain; and second, the government's problem with its budget deficit made the provision of financial support difficult, even though most potential subcontractors were in need of funds for immediate investment in restructuring. Twenty supply firms were given contracts initially, rising to 35 in October 1993, and in some cases Suzuki and its affiliates invested in the local firm in the form of a joint venture, providing technology and helping to train the local workforce.

Problems have nevertheless been perceived in the early operational strategy of the plant, with the secrecy surrounding Suzuki's main feasibility study, and a lack of clarity associated with the projected capacity of the plant, causing concern. The general study submitted to the public authorities in Hungary failed to disclose estimates for important indicators such as profitability and the development of output. In particular, the projected maximum output of 50 000 units annually is half the level generally accepted as optimal, and may be the main reason behind continuing losses. Low volume in turn creates problems for local suppliers, especially when Suzuki's specifications are incompatible with production for export to West European markets.

Table 15.8 Magyar Suzuki production and sales (projected figures), 1992–5

	1992	1993	1994	1995
Production	1000	20 000	40 000	50 000
Sales in Hungary	1000	18 000	30 000	30 000
Exports	–	2 000	10 000	20 000

Source: Magyar Suzuki (1993).

LABOUR MANAGEMENT AND MARKETING

The Magyar Suzuki plant in Esztergom employs 1200, and the project is expected to generate 17 000–18 000 jobs in other companies. Suzuki chose to employ persons with little experience of vehicle production, just as most other Japanese motor manufacturers have chosen to do in the US and the UK. Males in their twenties without a Communist Party background, and without experience of engineering work, were preferred. The plant has no union, just a consultative works council, and managerial posts are shared between Japanese and Hungarians. Only Japanese managers at Magyar Suzuki are provided with a car, although both expatriate and Hungarian managers receive this benefit at Hungarian Opel. After a considerable period of initial training very few trainees left the company, although discontent with low wages was to become a serious problem in 1993.

With regard to marketing responsibilities, these are principally the concern of the Hungarian joint venture partners. Plans to export over 40 per cent of production after 1995 have led to the establishment of a sales office in Moscow, and exports to China, Russia and the Ukraine began in 1993, with 3000 cars exported to China by the beginning of 1995. The main export market is the European Union however, and Hungary's associate membership means that virtually tax-free imports of manufactured goods are accepted in the Union, providing *local content* exceeds 50 per cent. Magyar Suzuki exported its first few hundred cars to Italy and the Netherlands after April 1994.[6]

Market conditions in Hungary have changed considerably since the Magyar Suzuki project was originally devised. Rival joint venture projects have appeared, and several Western automobile firms have opened sales outlets in Hungary. The GM-Opel project was agreed at the same time as the Suzuki joint venture,[7] and the DM80 million invested in an assembly plant, together with the DM440 million invested in an engine plant, will result in 15 000 cars and 200 000 engines being produced annually in Hungary. This project began operations in July 1992,[8] just after the opening of a Ford components plant in Hungary, and was followed by a major Audi engine plant investment, intended to commence production in 1994. In recent years, also, the sales offices of 20 Western producers have opened in Hungary, further increasing the competitive pressures upon Magyar Suzuki's marketing activities.[9] In Hungary, Suzuki had acquired a market share of 25 per cent in 1993, compared with a figure of 20 per cent for Opel.

CONCLUSION

Hungary has received inward manufacturing investment from Western Europe, North America and Japan. The country has a central location within Europe, and is perceived to be politically stable with a relatively long (25-year) history of market liberalisation. Labour is very inexpensive when comparisons are made with Western Europe or Japan, and despite a Japanese preference for inexperienced workforces, the Hungarian workforce has many traditional manufacturing skills. Furthermore, transport costs are typically low.

Because of the oligopolistic nature of Central European markets, considerable market share can be acquired quickly through purchase or joint venture activity involving local producers, and a relative lack of competition, when compared with operating in Western Europe, can make the initial establishment of a manufacturing presence less uncertain and risky. The relatively small scale of Japanese productive involvement in Central Europe, and its preponderant focus upon one country, can be explained by an aversion to risk and uncertainty, combined with lack of local knowledge and a slow decision-making process. This has meant that West European and North American firms have been quicker to seize market opportunities in the developing market economies of Central and Eastern Europe.

It is likely, therefore, that the future performance of the Magyar Suzuki joint venture will be watched carefully by other potential Japanese investors, and its progress will provide the main indication of the pace and prospects of Japan's future economic links with Hungary and the region as a whole.

NOTES

1. This figure is based upon Hungarian data which register joint ventures with capital in excess of 1 million Hungarian forints (HUF) which is approximately 1 million yen. In the Japanese Ministry of Finance data the equivalent threshold is 30 million yen.
2. K. Morita, 'Daihatsu-FSO kesu no keizai bunseki' (Economic analysis of the Daihatsu-FSO case), *Otaru Shoka Daigaku: Shogaku Tokyu*, No. 10 (1989).
3. 'Magyar Suzuki Swiftek indulnak a FAK-ba' (Hungarian Suzuki Swift to the CIS), *Népszabadság* (1 March 1993).
4. 'Uj ember ül a volánnál' (New man at the wheel), *Figyelö* (3 May 1994).
5. 'A Suzuki' (The Suzuki), *Figyelö* (1 July 1993).
6. 'Aremelésre készül a Suzuki' (Suzuki wants to raise prices), *Népszabadság* (28 May 1994).
7. G. Bakos, 'Japanese Capital in Hungary: the Case of the Automotive Industry', in *In Search of a New Relationship between Japan and Europe* (Tokyo: JAES, 1991).
8. 'Az Opel motorja' (Opel's Engine), *Figyelö* (23 July 1992).
9. 'Verseny a magyar autópiacon' (Competition in the Hungarian Car Market), *Népszabadság* (15 July 1993).

Bibliography

Andersen Consulting, *The Lean Enterprise Benchmarking Project Report* (London: 1992).
—— *World-wide Manufacturing Competitiveness Study* (Boston: 1994).
—— *World-wide Manufacturing Competitiveness Study: Implications for UK Companies* (London: 1995).
Andersson, Thomas and Hans Karlander, 'Vad betyder utvecklingen i Ostasien?' (What does the development in East Asia mean?), *Aktuellt om Näringspolitik och Ekonomi* 3 (1994).
Andreosso, B. and D. Jacobson, 'Le double processus d'intégration spatiale et industrielle à la lumière du cas irlandais', *Revue du Marché Commun et de l'Union Européenne* (Paris: September 1991), No. 350, pp. 648–58.
Androuais, A. 'Les Investissements extérieurs directs japonais dans les pays de la C.E.E. – Vers de nouvelles formes d'implantation', in A. Androuais, ed., *L'Investissement Extérieur Direct* (Grenoble: Presses Universitaires de Grenoble, 1990).
Axelsson, Cecilia, 'Teceremoni och industribesök under statsministervisit i Japan' (Tea ceremony and industrial visits during the prime minister's visit to Japan), *TT:s nyhetstelegram*, 368 (13 March 1991).
—— 'Carlsson framme i Tokyo' (Carlsson arrives in Tokyo), *TT:s nyhetstelegram* 136 (16 March 1991).
Balasubramanyam, V.N. and D. Greenaway, 'Economic Integration and Foreign Direct Investment: Japanese Investment in the EC', *Journal of Common Market Studies*, 2 (1992).
Belderbos, R., *Strategic Trade Policy and Multinational Enterprises: Essays on Trade and Investment by Japanese Electronics Firms* (Amsterdam: Thesis Publishers, Tinbergen Institute Research Series No. 68, 1994).
de Bernis, G., 'Investissement extérieur direct et systèmes productifs en France et au Japon', in A. Androuais, ed., *L'Investissement extérieur direct* (Grenoble: Presses Universitaire de Grenoble, 1990).
Bianchi, P., 'Nivells de política i naturalesa de la competencia post-Fordista', *Revista Econòmica de Catalunya* 14 (1990), pp. 94–102.
Bildt, Carl, 'Tyst produktivitetsrevolution i ekonomin' (Silent productivity revolution in the economy), *Svenska Dagbladet* (15 May 1993).
—— 'Svensk ekonomi bör lära av Sydöstasien' (Swedish economy should learn from South East Asia), *Svenska Dagbladet* (3 April 1994).
Bisault, L., V. Destival and D. Goux, 'Emploi et chômage des non-qualifiés en France', *Economie et Statistique*, No. 273 (1994), pp. 17–27.
Blackbourne, A., 'Multinational Enterprise and Regional Development: A Comment', *Regional Studies* 12 (1978).
Bonavoglia, R. and M. Gresti, *Al servizio dell'industria. Il ruolo della finanza nello sviluppo economico del Giappone* (Bologna: Il Mulino, 1993).
Breathnach, P., 'Japanese Manufacturing Investment in the Republic of Ireland', *Area*, Vol. 29 (1989).

Burgman, Torsten, *Japanbilden i Sverige 1667–1984* (The Swedish image of Japan, 1667–1984) (Stockholm: Almqvist & Wiksell International, 1986), pp. 81–108.

Cantwell, J., ed., *Multinational Investment in Modern Europe – Strategic Interaction in the Integrated Community* (Aldershot: Edward Elgar, 1992).

Caves, R.E., *Multinational Enterprise and Economic Analysis* (Cambridge: Cambridge University Press, 1982).

Central Statistical Office, *Census of Industrial Production* (Dublin: Central Statistical Office, 1990).

—— *Census of Production*, Summary Tables PA1002 (London: Central Statistical Office, 1990).

—— *Economic Series* (Dublin: Central Statistical Office, February 1994).

Chambre Syndicale des Constructeurs d'Automobiles, *Répertoire Mondial des Activités d'Assemblage et de Production de Véhicules Automobiles* (Paris: CSCA, 1983 and 1985).

Cohen, R.B., 'The New Spatial Organisation of the European and American Automotive Industries', in Noulart and Wilson Salinas, eds, *Regional Analysis and the New International Division of Labour* (1983), pp. 135–43.

Collis, C. and P. Roberts, 'FDI in the West Midlands: An Analysis and Evaluation', *Local Economy*, 7.2 (1992), pp. 114–31.

Cominotti, R. and S. Mariotti, eds, *Italia multinazionale 1994. Le nuove frontiere dell'internazionalizzazione produttiva* (Milan: Etaslibri, 1994).

Coughlin, C.C., J.V. Terza and V. Arromdee, 'State Characteristics and the Location of Foreign Direct Investment within the United States', *Review of Economics and Statistics* (1991), pp. 675–83.

Darby, J., 'A New Environment for Public Policy: Japanese Manufacturing in Europe', *West European Politics*, Vol. 9, No. 2 (April 1986).

—— *The Political Economy of Japanese Manufacturing Investment in France and the UK (1970–86)*, Unpublished doctoral thesis (Florence: European University Institute, 1987).

DATAR, *Foreign Investment Flows in France for 1993* (Paris: Invest in France Network, 1994).

Dentsu PR Centre Ltd, *Report on Market Research Conducted for the Invest in Sweden Office among Japanese Companies*, Prepared for Invest in Sweden Office, Embassy of Sweden, Tokyo (26 August 1994).

Department of Finance and Personnel, *Northern Ireland Structural Funds Plan 1994–99* (Belfast: 1993).

Drudy, P.J., 'The Regional Impact of Overseas Industry', in A. Foley and D. McAleese, eds., *Overseas Industry in Ireland* (Dublin: Gill and Macmillan, 1991).

Dufey, G., 'Comment', in Mark Mason and Dennis Encarnation, eds., *Does Ownership Matter? Japanese Multinationals in Europe* (Oxford: Oxford University Press, 1994).

Dunning, J.H., *Multinational Enterprises and the Global Economy* (Wokingham: Addison-Wesley, 1992).

—— 'The Globalisation of Service Activities', in J.H. Dunning, ed., *The Globalisation of Business* (London: Routledge, 1993).

—— 'The Strategy of Japanese and US Manufacturing Investment in Europe', in Mark Mason and Dennis Encarnation, eds., *Does Ownership Matter?*

Japanese Multinationals in Europe (Oxford: Oxford University Press, 1994).

Economic Commission for Europe, *Annual Bulletin of Transport Statistics for Europe* (1994).

Edström, Bert, 'Inledning' (Introduction), in Bert Edström, ed., *Japans globala roll: Implikationer för Sverige* (Japan's global role: Implications for Sweden) (Stockholm: Carlssons, 1994).

Ekdahl, Hans, *Japans ekonomiska förbindelser med EG* (Japan's economic relations with the EC). Centre for Pacific Asia Studies at Stockholm University Occasional Paper 18 (September 1993).

Encarnation, D., 'Investment and Trade by American, European, and Japanese Multinationals across the Triad', in Mark Mason and Dennis Encarnation, eds., *Does Ownership Matter? Japanese Multinationals in Europe* (Oxford: Oxford University Press, 1994).

Eurostat, *Regions Statistical Yearbook*, Theme 1, Series A (Luxembourg 1994).

Fahlström, Jan Magnus, 'Recept för arbetsmarknaden: Sverige måste lära av Japan' (A recipe for the labour market: Sweden has to learn from Japan), *Dagens Nyheter* (30 June 1984).

Fujimoto, T., T. Nishiguchi and S. Sei, 'The Strategy and Structure of Japanese Automobile Manufacturing in Europe', in Mark Mason and Dennis Encarnation, eds., *Does Ownership Matter? Japanese Multinationals in Europe* (Oxford: Oxford University Press, 1994).

Gaimusho Kokusai keizai Dai 1-ka (Ministry of Foreign Affairs International Economics First Section), *Nichi–Sueden keizai kankei to Sueden keizai* (Japanese–Swedish relations and the Swedish economy). Keizai-shiryo 93C1-W03T (December 1994).

Gårdö, Lars, 'Utanför EG får vi nobben av Japan' (Outside of the EC, Sweden will be brushed off by Japan), *Dagens Industri* (27 January 1989).

Giavazzi, F. and L. Spaventa, 'Italy: The Real Effects of Inflation and Disinflation', *Economic Policy* (April 1983).

Gittelman, M. and E. Graham, 'The Performance and Structure of Japanese Affiliates in the European Community', in M. Mason and D. Encarnation, eds., *Does Ownership Matter?* (Oxford: Oxford University Press, 1994).

Glickman, N.J. and D.P. Woodward, 'The Location of Foreign Direct Investment in the United States: Patterns and Determinants', *International Regional Science Review* (1988), pp. 137–54.

Gravier, Jean François, *Paris et le désert français* (Paris: Le Portulan, 1947).

Gustafsson, Sten, 'Riskfyllt att stå utanför EG' (Dangerous to be outside the EC), *Dagens Nyheter* (22 February 1993).

Hamilton, D., 'Foreign Investment and Industrial Development in Northern Ireland', in P. Teague, ed., *The Economy of Northern Ireland* (London: Lawrence and Wishart, 1993).

Hatem, F. and J.D. Tordjman, *La France face à l'investissement international* (Paris: Economica, 1995).

Hawawini, G. and M. Schill, 'The Japanese Presence in the European Financial Services Sector', in M. Mason and D. Encarnation, eds., *Does Ownership Matter? Japanese Multinationals in Europe* (Oxford: Oxford University Press, 1994).

Hedberg, Håkan, *Den japanska utmaningen* (The Japanese challenge) (Stockholm: Bonniers, 1969).

Hill, S. and M. Munday, 'The UK Regional Distribution of Foreign Investment: Analysis and Determinants', *Regional Studies* (1992), pp. 535–44.

—— *The Regional Distribution of Foreign Manufacturing in the UK* (London: Macmillan, 1994).

—— 'A Tale of Two Regions', *The South West Economy Trends and Prospects* (Plymouth: SWERC, 1995), pp. 45–59.

Hill, S. and A. Roberts, 'Inward Investment and Regional Economic Development', Paper delivered at the 17th Annual ANZRSA Conference, New South Wales (December 1993).

Hood, N. and S. Young, *The Economics of Multinational Enterprise* (London: Longman, 1979).

Horiuchi, T. and H. Tomizawa, *Daihatsu to Piajjio no yonrinjidosha no jointo seisan keiyaku no jittai to gijutsuiten no genkai no bunseki* (Joint Automobile Production by Daihatsu and Piaggio: an Empirical Analysis of the Contract and the Transfer of Japanese Production Technology), *Keizai-Keiei Ronso* (September 1984).

Hounshell, D., *From the American System to Mass Production 1800–1932. The Development of Manufacturing Technology in the US* (Baltimore: Johns Hopkins University Press, 1975).

ICE, *Rapporto sul commercio estero* (Rome: Istituto nazionale per il commercio estero, 1994).

IDB, *Forward Strategy 1991–93* (Belfast: Industrial Development Board, December 1990).

Industrial Bank of Japan, *Monthly Report* (Tokyo: August 1994).

—— *Report on Currency Appreciation* (Tokyo: 1994).

INSEE, *Tableaux de l'Economie Française* (Paris: Institut National de la Statistique et des Etudes Economiques, 1994/5).

Intermatrix, *Market Opportunities for Electronic Component Manufacturers* (London: Department of Trade and Industry, 1991).

ISESAO, *Gli investimenti diretti giapponesi in Italia* (Milano: Istituto di Studi Economico-Sociali per l'Asia Orientale, 1993).

Itaki, M. and M. Waterson, *European Multinationals and 1992*, University of Reading Working Papers in International Investment and Business Studies B, 141 (1991).

Ivarsson, I., 'Small Foreign-Owned Affiliates in Sweden. An Empirical Survey of Export and Import Performance', *Choros* (Dept of Human and Economic Geography, Gothenburg University No. 5, 1994).

Jacobson, D., 'Theorising Irish Industrialisation: The Case of the Motor Industry', *Science and Society*, Vol. 53, No. 2 (Summer 1989).

—— and B. Andréosso, 'Ireland as a Location for Multinational Investment', in A. Foley and M. Mulreany, eds., *The Single European Market and the Irish Economy* (Dublin: Institute of Public Administration, 1990).

James, B.G., *Trojan Horse* (London: Mercury Books, 1989).

JETRO, *Kaigai Shijo Hakusho – Toshihen* (White Paper on Overseas Markets – Investment) (Tokyo: Japan External Trade Organisation, 1981 and 1988).

—— *Potential Investors from Japan* (Tokyo: Japan External Trade Organisation 1993).

—— *Nippon Business Facts and Figures* (Tokyo: 1994).

—— *Hakusho Toshi-hen: Sekai to Nihon no Kaigai Chokusetsu Toshi (White*

Paper on Direct Investment: Direct Investment of Japan and the World)
(JETRO: Tokyo, 1994).
—— *10th Survey of European Operations of Japanese Companies in the Manu-
facturing Sector* (Tokyo: Japan External Trade Organisation, October 1994).
Kimura, Y., 'Host Country and Industry Effects on Multinationals' Com-
petitiveness: The Case of Foreign Direct Investment in the Semiconductor
Industry in Japan', in Schon Beechler and Allan Bird, eds., *Research in
International Business and International Relations: Emerging Trends in
Japanese Management* (Greenwich, CT: JAI Press, 1994).
—— and T.A. Pugel, 'Keiretsu and Japanese Direct Investment in U.S.
Manufacturing', *Japan and the World Economy*, forthcoming.
Kirkland, R.I., 'The Big Japanese Push into Europe', *Fortune* (2 July 1990).
Kogut, B. and Sea Jin Chang, 'Technological Capabilities and Japanese Direct
Investment in the United States', *Review of Economics and Statistics* (1989).
—— and A. Singh, 'The Effects of National Culture on the Choice of Entry
Mode', *Journal of International Business Studies* Vol. 19 (1988).
Kojima, K., *Japanese Direct Foreign Investment* (Tokyo: C.E. Tuttle, 1978).
Kommerskollegium (National Board of Trade), *Handelspolitiska relationer mellan
EU, USA och Japan: Konsekvenser för Sverige som EU-medlem* (Trade policy
relations between the EU, the United States and Japan: Consequences for
Sweden as a member of the EU), Rapport 1994:3 (Stockholm, 1994).
Kravis, I.B. and R.E. Lipsey, 'The Location of Overseas Production and
Production for Export by U.S. Multinational Firms', *Journal of International
Economics* (1982), pp. 201–23.
Larsson, Gerd, 'Molin vill öppna yen-väg till Sverige' (Molin wants to open
a yen route to Sweden), *Dagens Industri* (19 March 1991).
Lövkvist, Christer, 'Volvo siktar högt i Japan: på väg mot 25 000 bilar' (Volvo
aims high in Japan: on its way to 25 000 cars), *Göteborgs-Posten* (21 May
1989).
Lundgren, Nils, *Ekonomin över gränserna* (Transborder economy), in *Utsikt
mot Europa* (Perspective on Europe) (Höganäs: Bokförlaget Bra Böcker,
1991), pp. 61–76.
McAleese, D. and A. Foley, 'The Role of Overseas Industry in Industrial
Development', in A. Foley and D. McAleese, eds., *Overseas Industry in
Ireland* (Dublin: Gill and Macmillan, 1991).
McDermott, P.J., 'Overseas Investment and the Industrial Geography of the
UK', *Area* 9 (1977), pp. 200–7.
Mayuya, R. and D. Jacobson, 'Japanese Direct Investment in Ireland', *Irish
Business and Administrative Research* Vol. 12 (1991).
Mazier, J. 'Intégration européenne, investissements directs étrangers et régimes
de croissance', *Japon in Extenso* (Poitiers: June–Sept. 1994), No. 32/33,
pp. 25–45.
Ministry of Finance, *Direct Overseas Investment Registered During Fiscal
1982* (Tokyo: MoF, May 1983).
—— *Report on Direct Foreign Investment* (Tokyo: MoF, 1991).
—— *Yukashoken Hokokusho Soran – Daihatsu Kogyo Kabushikikaisha* (Report
on Securities – Daihatsu Industries Ltd) (Tokyo: MoF, June 1994).
MITI, *Survey on Globalisation of the Japanese Economy* (Tokyo: Ministry of
International Trade and Industry, 1991).

—— *Dai 22 kai wagakuni kigyo no kaigai-jigyo katsudo* (22nd Survey on Overseas Business Activities of Japanese Companies) (Tokyo: Ministry of International Trade and Industry, 1993).

Molteni, Corrado, 'Japanese Joint Ventures in Italy. A Second Best Strategy?,' in Nigel Campbell and Fred Burton, eds., *Japanese Multinationals* (London: Routledge, 1994).

Morris, J., 'Japanese Inward Investment and the Importation of Sub-Contracting Complexes', *Area*, 21 (1989), pp. 269–77.

——, M. Munday and B. Wilkinson, *Working for the Japanese* (London: Athlone, 1993).

Munday, M., 'The Financial Consequences of Linkages with Japanese Manufacturers', *Management Accounting*, 68.7 (1990), pp. 42–3.

—— 'The Regional Consequences of the Japanese Second Wave', *Local Economy*, 10.1 (1995), pp. 4–20.

—— et al., 'Factories or Warehouses? A Welsh Perspective on Japanese Transplant Manufacturing', *Regional Studies*, 29.1 (1995), pp. 1–17.

Murata, R., 'Political Relations between the United States and Western Europe: Their Implications for Japan', *International Affairs*, No. 1 (1987/8).

Nagamoto, Y., *Japanese Investments Abroad: Past, Present and Future* (Louvain: Japanese Presence in Europe, 1990).

Nardozzi, G., ed., *Il ruolo della banca centrale nella recente evoluzione dell'economia italiana* (Milan: Angeli, 1993).

National Economic and Social Council (NESC), *A Review of Industrial Policy* (*Telesis Report*) Report No. 64 (1982).

Nihon Zaigai Kigyo Kyokai (Association of Japanese Companies Overseas), *Itaria, Berugii, Lukusenburugu no Toshi Kankyo – Kaigai Toshi Kankyo Chosadan Hokokusho* (Investment Environment of Italy, Belgium and Luxembourg – Report of the Overseas Investment Environment Survey Mission) (Tokyo, June 1988).

Nolan, S., 'Economic Growth: Theory and Analysis', in J. O'Hagan, ed., *The Economy of Ireland* (Dublin: Irish Management Institute, 1987).

Northern Ireland Economic Council (NIEC), *Inward Investment in Northern Ireland* (Belfast: November 1992), Report No. 99.

O'Hearn, D., 'Global Competition, Europe and Irish Peripherality', *Economic and Social Review*, Vol. 24, No. 2 (January 1993), p. 179.

Ozawa, T., *Multinationalism, Japanese Style* (Princeton: Princeton University Press, 1979).

—— 'Japanese Multinationals and 1992', in B. Burgenmeier and J.L. Mucchielli, eds., *Multinationals and Europe 1992 – Strategies for the future* (London: Routledge, 1991).

Pallares-Barbera, M., *The Structural and Spatial Adjustments of the Automobile Industry in Spain: 1975–1990*, PhD (Boston University, 1993).

Peck, F. and I. Stone, 'Japanese Inward Investment in the Northeast of England: Reassessing "Japanisation"', *Environment and Planning C*, Vol. 11 (1993).

Poitier, C., 'Les Unités de production asiatiques en Europe: Quel contenu local de la production?' in F. Hatem and J.D. Tordjman, *La France face à l'investissement international* (Paris: Economica, 1995).

Porter, M.E., *The Competitive Advantage of Nations* (New York: Basic Books, 1990).

Pugel, T.A., E. Kragas and Y. Kimura, 'Further Evidence on Japanese Direct Investment in U.S. Manufacturing', *Review of Economics and Statistics* (forthcoming).

Ruane, F. and A. McGibney, 'The Performance of Overseas Industry 1973–89', in A. Foley and D. McAleese, eds., *Overseas Industry in Ireland* (Dublin: Gill and Macmillan, 1991).

Sekiguchi, S., 'Japanese Direct Foreign Investment', in L. Tsoukalis and M. White, eds., *Japan and Western Europe* (London: Frances Pinter, 1982), pp. 166–83.

Shimura, Y., *IC Sangyo no Himitsu* (The Secret of the IC Industry) (Tokyo: Shobunsha, 1981).

Statistiska Centralbyrån (National Statistics Office of Sweden), *Utlandsägda företag 1993* (Foreign owned enterprises 1993), *Statistiska meddelanden*, F 18 SM 9301 (Stockholm: 1994).

—— (National Statistics Office of Sweden), *Anställda utomlands i svenska industri- och tjänstekoncerner 1990–1993* (Employees abroad in Swedish-owned manufacturing and service groups 1990–93), *Statistiska meddelanden* F 20 SM 9501 (Stockholm 1995).

Strandell, Anne-Christine, *Kan japanska investeringar öka i Sverige?* (Can Japanese investments increase in Sweden?), SIND 1991:7 (Stockholm: Statens industriverk, 1991).

Strange, Roger, *Japanese Manufacturing Investment in Europe* (London: Routledge, 1993).

Sveriges Ambassad (Embassy of Sweden, Tokyo), *Förbindelserna Sverige–Japan* (Swedish–Japanese relations), 62 A 1990-12-18. 1991-02-26, Nr 29.

Sweden–Japan Foundation, *Relations between Sweden and Japan 1994* (Stockholm: Sweden–Japan Foundation, 1994).

Tajoli, B., 'Il modello di specializzazione internazionale dell'Italia', *Congiuntura IRS* (September 1994).

Tandeau, B., *Marché unique et stratégies de localisation des entreprises industrielles étrangères* (Communication au Colloque International sur le thème *Les groupes industriels et financiers et l'intégration européenne*, LEREP, Toulouse, 28–30 September 1989).

Thiran, J-M. and H. Yamawaki, *Regional and Country Determinants of Loca tional Decisions: Japanese Multinationals in European Manufacturing IRES Discussion Paper 9517* (Louvain: Département des Sciences économiques U.C.L., 1995).

Thomsen, S. and S. Woolcock, *Direct Investment and European Integration* (London: Frances Pinter/RIIA, 1993).

Toyo Keizai, ed., *Kaigai Shinshutsu Kigyo Soran* (Directory of Japanese Multinational Corporations) (Tokyo: Toyo Keizai Shimposha, 1994).

Toyoda, E., *Toyota: Fifty Years in Motion* (Tokyo: Kodansha International, 1987).

Tsoukalis, L., *The New European Economy* (Oxford: Oxford University Press, 1993).

Tsurumi, Y., *The Japanese are Coming* (Cambridge, MA: Ballinger, 1976).

Turok, I., 'Inward Investment and Local Linkages: How Deeply Embedded is Silicon Glen?' *Regional Studies*, 27.5 (1993), pp. 401–18.

UNCTAD, *World Investment Report 1994 – Transnational Corporations, Employment and the Workplace* (New York: United Nations, 1994).

UNCTC, *Transnational Corporations in World Development: Trends and Prospects* (New York: United Nations, 1988).

Utrikesdepartementet Handelsavdelningen Enhet 5 (Ministry for Foreign Affairs Trade Section Unit 5), *Något om de svensk–japanska ekonomiska förbindelserna m.m.* (A short presentation of Swedish–Japanese economic relations, etc.), Promemoria 1991-10–11.

Veugelers, R., 'Locational Determinants and Ranking of Host Countries: an Empirical Assessment', *Kyklos* (1991), pp. 363–82.

Wells, P. and M. Rawlinson, 'New Procurement Regimes and the Spatial Distribution of Suppliers: the Case of Ford in Europe', *Area*, 24.4 (1992), pp. 380–90.

Welsh Affairs Committee, *Inward Investment into Wales and its Interaction with Regional and EEC Policies* (London: HMSO, 1988).

Wickham, J., 'Dependence and State Structure: Foreign Firms and Industrial Policy in the Republic of Ireland', in O. Höll, ed., *Small States in Europe and Dependence* (Vienna: Bramuller, 1983).

Wilkinson, B., J. Morris and M. Munday, 'Japan in Wales: A new IR?' *Industrial Relations Journal*, 24.4 (1993), pp. 273–83.

Williams, K., C. Haslam, J. Williams, A. Adcroft and S. Johal, *Factories v. Warehouses: Japanese Foreign Direct Investment in the UK and America*, University of East London Occasional Paper No. 6 (1992).

——, C. Haslam, S. Johal and J. Williams, *Cars: Analysis, History, Cases* (Oxford: Berg, 1994).

Womack, J., D. Jones and D. Roos, *The Machine that Changed the World* (New York: Rawson Associates, 1990).

Yamawaki, H., *Japanese Multinationals in U.S. and European Manufacturing Industries: Entry, Strategy and Patterns*, paper presented at the *Japanese Direct Investment in an Unifying Europe: Impacts on Japan and the European Community* Conference (Fontainebleau, June 1992).

—— 'Location Decisions of Japanese Multinational Firms in European Manufacturing Industries', in K. Hughes, ed., *European Competitiveness* (Cambridge: Cambridge University Press, 1993), pp. 11–28.

—— 'Entry Patterns of Japanese Multinationals in US and European Manufacturing', in Mark Mason and Dennis Encarnation, eds., *Does Ownership Matter? Japanese Multinationals in Europe* (Oxford: Oxford University Press, 1994).

Yamazawa, I., 'Japan', in S. Borner and H. Grubel, eds., *The European Community after 1992. Perspectives from the Outside* (London: Macmillan, 1992).

Young, S., 'Scotland v. Wales in the Inward Investment Game', *Fraser of Allander Institute Quarterly Economic Commentary*, 14.3 (1989), pp. 59–63.

Zaidan Hojin Yano Tsuneta Kinenkai, ed., *Suji de miru Nihon no 100 nen* (100 years of Japan seen in figures), 3rd revised and enlarged edition (Tokyo: Kokuseisha, 1991).

Index

Sanyo Denki   138, 144, 169
SDK   125
Seiko   138, 145, 169
Sekiguchi, S.   126
semiconductor industry   7, 27–8,
   32, 34, 62
Sharp   56–7, 170
Shimano   138
Siemens   19, 26
Single European Act   45
Single European Market   25
   single market for cars   95
skill levels   60–1, 102, 113, 186–7,
   252
Social Chapter   84
Sogo Shosha   169, 172, 239, 244,
   246, 249
Sony   6, 52, 56–7, 59, 126, 138–9,
   145, 169, 177, 195
Sord   88–90, 101
Southern Europe   1, 5, 42
Star Micronics   58
Sumitomo Corporation   99, 138, 169
Sumitomo Rubber   116, 124
Suntory   115, 118
Suzuki   4, 28–30, 34, 170, 174,
   234, 238, 240, 244–52

Takata   96–7
Takeda   138, 144
Takeshita, N.   235
Tandeau, B.   122
tariff jumping   25, 34, 112–13

tax rates   50, 98, 197
Teijin   138
Telesis Report   88, 106
textile industry   49, 95, 153
TGV (Train à Grande Vitesse)   127
Toho   88–90, 101
Tomen   169
Toray   136
Toshiba   9, 195
Toyo Keizai   37
Toyoda Machine   116
Toyota   26, 28, 58, 78
Trabant   248
trade disputes, Japan–EC/EU   81,
   90, 93, 152, 205
transfer pricing   76
Troubles (Northern Ireland)   95
tyre industry   7

Ugglas, M.   197
Unitica   138, 144
US Bureau of Commerce   76, 81

Volkswagen   19, 25

Wartburg   248
Welsh Affairs Committee   54
Welsh Office   54

Yamaha   120, 138, 177
Yamanouchi   93
Yamazawa, I.   158
YKK (Yoshida Kogyo Kaisha)   136